The Wisdom of Life

and

Counsels and Maxims

By Arthur Schopenhauer

Translated by T. Bailey Saunders

Adansonia
Press

Published in 2018

Logo art adapted from work by Bernard Gagnon

ISBN-13: 978-1-387-94197-1

The Wisdom of Life was published in 1851

Counsels and Maxims was first published in 1851

Contents

The Wisdom of Life

Introduction

In these pages I shall speak of The Wisdom of Life in the common meaning of the term, as the art, namely, of ordering our lives so as to obtain the greatest possible amount of pleasure and success; an art the theory of which may be called Eudaemonology, for it teaches us how to lead a happy existence. Such an existence might perhaps be defined as one which, looked at from a purely objective point of view, or, rather, after cool and mature reflection—for the question necessarily involves subjective considerations,—would be decidedly preferable to non-existence; implying that we should cling to it for its own sake, and not merely from the fear of death; and further, that we should never like it to come to an end.

Now whether human life corresponds, or could possibly correspond, to this conception of existence, is a question to which, as is well-known, my philosophical system returns a negative answer. On the eudaemonistic hypothesis, however, the question must be answered in the affirmative; and I have shown, in the second volume of my chief work (ch. 49), that this hypothesis is based upon a fundamental mistake. Accordingly, in elaborating the scheme of a happy existence, I have had to make a complete surrender of the higher metaphysical and ethical standpoint to which my own theories lead; and everything I shall say here will to some extent rest upon a compromise; in so far, that is, as I take the common standpoint of every day, and embrace the error which is at the bottom of it. My remarks, therefore, will possess only a qualified value, for the very word eudaemonology is a euphemism. Further, I make no claims to completeness; partly because the subject is inexhaustible, and partly because I should otherwise have to say over again what has been already said by others.

The only book composed, as far as I remember, with a like purpose to that which animates this collection of aphorisms, is Cardan's De utilitate ex adversis capienda, which is well worth reading, and may be used to supplement the present work. Aristotle, it is true, has a few words on eudaemonology in the fifth chapter of the first book of his Rhetoric; but what he says does not come to very much. As compilation is not my business, I have made no use of these predecessors; more especially because in the process of compiling, individuality of view is lost, and individuality of view is the kernel of works of this kind. In general, indeed, the wise in all ages have always said the same thing, and the fools, who at all times form the immense majority, have in their way too acted alike, and done just the opposite; and so it will continue. For, as Voltaire says, we shall leave this world as foolish and as wicked as we found it on our arrival.

Chapter I - Division of The Subject

Aristotle[1] divides the blessings of life into three classes—those which come to us from without, those of the soul, and those of the body. Keeping nothing of this division but the number, I observe that the fundamental differences in human lot may be reduced to three distinct classes:

(1)   What a man is: that is to say, personality, in the widest sense of the word; under which are included health, strength, beauty, temperament, moral character, intelligence, and education.

(2)   What a man has: that is, property and possessions of every kind.

(3)   How a man stands in the estimation of others: by which is to be understood, as everybody knows, what a man is in the eyes of his fellowmen, or, more strictly, the light in which they regard him. This is shown by their opinion of him; and their opinion is in its turn manifested by the honor in which he is held, and by his rank and reputation.

The differences which come under the first head are those which Nature herself has set between man and man; and from this fact alone we may at once infer that they influence the happiness or unhappiness of mankind in a much more vital and radical way than those contained under the two following heads, which are merely the effect of human arrangements. Compared with genuine personal advantages, such as a great mind or a great heart, all the privileges of rank or birth, even of royal birth, are but as kings on the stage, to kings in real life. The same thing was said long ago by Metrodorus, the earliest disciple of Epicurus, who wrote as the title of one of his chapters, The happiness we receive from ourselves is greater than that which we obtain from our surroundings[2] And it is an obvious fact, which cannot be called in question, that the principal element in a man's well-being,—indeed, in the whole tenor of his existence,—is what he is made of, his inner constitution. For this is the immediate source of that inward satisfaction or dissatisfaction resulting from the sum total of his sensations, desires and thoughts; whilst his surroundings, on the other hand, exert only a mediate or indirect influence upon him. This is why the same external events or circumstances affect no two people alike; even with perfectly similar surroundings every one lives in a world of his own. For a man has immediate apprehension only of his own ideas, feelings and volitions; the outer world can influence him only in so far as it brings these to life. The world in which a man lives shapes itself chiefly by the way in which he looks at it, and so it proves different to different men; to one it is barren, dull, and superficial; to another rich, interesting, and full of meaning. On hearing of the
interesting events which have happened in the course of a man's experience, many people will wish that similar things had happened in their lives too, completely forgetting that they should be envious rather of the mental
aptitude which lent those events the significance they possess when he describes them; to a man of genius they were interesting adventures; but to the dull perceptions of an ordinary individual they would have been stale, everyday occurrences.

This is in the highest degree the case with many of Goethe's and Byron's poems, which are obviously founded upon actual facts; where it is open to a foolish reader to envy the poet because so many delightful things happened to him, instead of envying that mighty power of phantasy which was capable of turning a fairly common experience into something so great and beautiful.

In the same way, a person of melancholy temperament will make a scene in a tragedy out of what appears to the sanguine man only in the light of an interesting conflict, and to a phlegmatic soul as something without any meaning;—all of which rests upon the fact that every event, in order to be realized and appreciated, requires the co-operation of two factors, namely, a subject and an object, although these are as closely and necessarily connected as oxygen and hydrogen in water. When therefore the objective or external factor in an experience is actually the same, but the subjective or personal appreciation of it varies, the event is just as much a different one in the eyes of different persons as if the objective factors had not been alike; for to a blunt intelligence the fairest and best object in the world presents only a poor reality, and is therefore only poorly appreciated,—like a fine landscape in dull weather, or in the reflection of a bad camera obscura. In plain language, every man is pent up within the limits of his own consciousness, and cannot directly get beyond those limits any more than he can get beyond his own skin; so external aid is not of much use to him. On the stage, one man is a prince, another a minister, a third a servant or a soldier or a general, and so on,—mere external differences: the inner reality, the kernel of all these appearances is the same—a poor player, with all the anxieties of his lot. In life it is just the same. Differences of rank and wealth give every man his part to play, but this by no means implies a difference of inward happiness and pleasure; here, too, there is the same being in all—a poor mortal, with his hardships and troubles. Though these may, indeed, in every case proceed from dissimilar causes, they are in their essential nature much the same in all their forms, with degrees of intensity which vary, no doubt, but in no wise correspond to the part a man has to play, to the presence or absence of position and wealth. Since everything which exists or happens for a man exists only in his consciousness and happens for it alone, the most essential thing for a man is the constitution of this consciousness, which is in most cases far more important than the circumstances which go to form its contents. All the pride and pleasure of the world, mirrored in the dull consciousness of a fool, are poor indeed compared with the imagination of Cervantes writing his Don Quixote in a miserable prison. The objective half of life and reality is in the hand of fate, and accordingly takes various forms in different cases: the subjective half is ourself, and in essentials is always remains the same.

Hence the life of every man is stamped with the same character throughout, however much his external circumstances may alter; it is like a series of variations on a single theme. No one can get beyond his own individuality. An animal, under whatever circumstances it is placed, remains within the narrow limits to which nature has irrevocably consigned it; so that our endeavors to make a pet happy must always keep within the compass of its nature, and be restricted to what it can feel. So it is with man; the measure of the happiness he can attain is determined beforehand by his individuality. More especially is this the case with the mental powers, which fix once for all his capacity for the higher kinds of pleasure. If these powers are small, no efforts from without, nothing that his fellowmen or that fortune can do for him, will suffice to raise him above the ordinary degree of human happiness and pleasure, half animal though it be; his only resources are his sensual appetite,—a cozy and cheerful family life at the most,—low company and vulgar pastime; even education, on the whole, can avail little, if anything, for the enlargement of his horizon. For the highest, most varied and lasting pleasures are those of the mind, however much our youth may deceive us on this point; and the pleasures of the mind turn chiefly on the powers of the mind. It is clear, then, that our happiness depends in a great degree upon what we are, upon our individuality, whilst lot or destiny is generally taken to mean only what we have, or our reputation. Our lot, in this sense, may improve; but we do not ask much of it if we are inwardly rich: on the other hand, a fool remains a fool, a dull blockhead, to his last hour, even though he were surrounded by houris in paradise. This is why Goethe, in the West-östliclien Divan, says that every man, whether he occupies a low position in life, or emerges as its victor, testifies to personality as the greatest factor in happiness:—

Volk und Knecht und Uberwinder
Sie gestehen, zu jeder Zeit,
Höchtes Glück der Erdenkinder
Sei nur die Persönlichkeit.

Everything confirms the fact that the subjective element in life is incomparably more important for our happiness and pleasure than the objective, from such sayings as Hunger is the best sauce, and Youth and Age cannot live together, up to the life of the Genius and the Saint. Health outweighs all other blessings so much that one may really say that a healthy beggar is happier than an ailing king. A quiet and cheerful temperament, happy in the enjoyment of a perfectly sound physique, an intellect clear, lively, penetrating and seeing things as they are, a moderate and gentle will, and therefore a good conscience—these are privileges which no rank or wealth can make up for or replace. For what a man is in himself, what accompanies him when he is alone, what no one can give or take away, is obviously more essential to him than everything he has in the way of possessions, or even what he may be in the eyes of the world. An intellectual man in complete solitude has excellent entertainment in his own thoughts and fancies, while no amount of diversity or social pleasure, theatres, excursions and amusements, can ward off boredom from a dullard. A good, temperate, gentle character can be happy in needy circumstances, whilst a covetous, envious and malicious man, even if he be the richest in the world, goes miserable. Nay more; to one who has the constant delight of a special individuality, with a high degree of intellect, most of the pleasures which are run after by mankind are simply superfluous; they are even a trouble and a burden. And so Horace says of himself, that, however many are deprived of the fancy-goods of life, there is one at least who can live without them:—

Gemmas, marmor, ebur, Tyrrhena sigilla, tabellas, Argentum, vestes, Gaetulo murice tinctas Sunt qui non habeant, est qui non curat habere;

and when Socrates saw various articles of luxury spread out for sale, he exclaimed: How much there is in the world I do not want.

So the first and most essential element in our life's happiness is what we are,—our personality, if for no other reason than that it is a constant factor coming into play under all circumstances: besides, unlike the blessings which are described under the other two heads, it is not the sport of destiny and cannot be wrested from us;—and, so far, it is endowed with an absolute value in contrast to the merely relative worth of the other two. The consequence of this is that it is much more difficult than people commonly suppose to get a hold on a man from without. But here the all-powerful agent, Time, comes in and claims its rights, and before its influence physical and mental advantages gradually waste away. Moral character alone remains inaccessible to it. In view of the destructive effect of time, it seems, indeed, as if the blessings named under the other two heads, of which time cannot directly rob us, were superior to those of the first. Another advantage might be claimed for them, namely, that being in their very nature objective and external, they are attainable, and every one is presented with the possibility, at least, of coming into possession of them; whilst what is subjective is not open to us to acquire, but making its entry by a kind of divine right, it remains for life, immutable, inalienable, an inexorable doom. Let me quote those lines in which Goethe describes how an unalterable destiny is assigned to every man at the hour of his birth, so that he can develop only in the lines laid down for him, as it were, by the conjunctions of the stars: and how the Sybil and the prophets declare that himself a man can never escape, nor any power of time avail to change the path on which his life is cast:—

Wie an dem Tag, der dich der Welt verliehen,
Die Sonne stand zum Grusse der Planeten,
Bist alsobald und fort und fort gediehen,
Nach dem Gesetz, wonach du angetreten.
So musst du sein, dir kannst du nicht entfliehen,
So tagten schon Sybillen und Propheten;
Und keine Zeit, und keine Macht zerstückelt
Geprägte Form, die lebend sich entwickelt.

The only thing that stands in our power to achieve, is to make the most advantageous use possible of the personal qualities we possess, and accordingly to follow such pursuits only as will call them into play, to strive after the kind of perfection of which they admit and to avoid every other; consequently, to choose the position, occupation and manner of life which are most suitable for their development.

Imagine a man endowed with herculean strength who is compelled by circumstances to follow a sedentary occupation, some minute exquisite work of the hands, for example, or to engage in study and mental labor demanding quite other powers, and just those which he has not got,—compelled, that is, to leave unused the powers in which he is pre-eminently strong; a man placed like this will never feel happy all his life through. Even more miserable will be the lot of the man with intellectual powers of a very high order, who has to leave them undeveloped and unemployed, in the pursuit of a calling which does not require them, some bodily labor, perhaps, for which his strength is insufficient. Still, in a case of this kind, it should be our care, especially in youth, to avoid the precipice of presumption, and not ascribe to ourselves a superfluity of power which is not there.

Since the blessings described under the first head decidedly outweigh those contained under the other two, it is manifestly a wiser course to aim at the maintenance of our health and the cultivation of our faculties, than at the amassing of wealth; but this must not be mistaken as meaning that we should neglect to acquire an adequate supply of the necessaries of life. Wealth, in the strict sense of the word, that is, great superfluity, can do little for our happiness; and many rich people feel unhappy just because they are without any true mental culture or knowledge, and consequently have no objective interests which would qualify them for intellectual occupations. For beyond the satisfaction of some real and natural necessities, all that the possession of wealth can achieve has a very small influence upon our happiness, in the proper sense of the word; indeed, wealth rather disturbs it, because the preservation of property entails a great many unavoidable anxieties. And still men are a thousand times more intent on becoming rich than on acquiring culture, though it is quite certain that what a man is contributes much more to his happiness than what he has. So you may see many a man, as industrious as an ant, ceaselessly occupied from morning to night in the endeavor to increase his heap of gold. Beyond the narrow horizon of means to this end, he knows nothing; his mind is a blank, and consequently unsusceptible to any other influence. The highest pleasures, those of the intellect, are to him inaccessible, and he tries in vain to replace them by the fleeting pleasures of sense in which he indulges, lasting but a brief hour and at tremendous cost. And if he is lucky, his struggles result in his having a really great pile of gold, which he leaves to his heir, either to make it still larger, or to squander it in extravagance. A life like this, though pursued with a sense of earnestness and an air of importance, is just as silly as many another which has a fool's cap for its symbol.

What a man has in himself is, then, the chief element in his happiness. Because this is, as a rule, so very little, most of those who are placed beyond the struggle with penury feel at bottom quite as unhappy as those who are still engaged in it. Their minds are vacant, their imagination dull, their spirits poor, and so they are driven to the company of those like them—for *similis simili gaudet*—where they make common pursuit of pastime and entertainment, consisting for the most part in sensual pleasure, amusement of every kind, and finally, in excess and libertinism. A young man of rich family enters upon life with a large patrimony, and often runs through it in an incredibly short space of time, in vicious extravagance; and why? Simply because, here too, the mind is empty and void, and so the man is bored with existence. He was sent forth into the world outwardly rich but inwardly poor, and his vain endeavor was to make his external wealth compensate for his inner poverty, by trying to obtain everything from without, like an old man who seeks to strengthen himself as King David or Maréchal de Rex tried to do. And so in the end one who is inwardly poor comes to be also poor outwardly.

I need not insist upon the importance of the other two kinds of blessings which make up the happiness of human life; now-a-days the value of possessing them is too well known to require advertisement. The third class, it is true, may seem, compared with the second, of a very ethereal character, as it consists only of other people's opinions. Still every one has to strive for reputation, that is to say, a good name. Rank, on the other hand, should be aspired to only by those who serve the state, and fame by very few indeed. In any case, reputation is looked upon as a priceless treasure, and fame as the most precious of all the blessings a man can attain,—the Golden Fleece, as it were, of the elect: whilst only fools will prefer rank to property. The second and third classes, moreover, are reciprocally cause and effect; so far, that is, as Petronius' maxim, *habes habeberis*, is true; and conversely, the favor of others, in all its forms, often puts us in the way of getting what we want.

[1: *Eth. Nichom., I. 8.*]   [2: *Cf. Clemens Alex. Strom. II., 21.*]

10

Chapter II - Personality, Or What A Man Is

We have already seen, in general, that what a man is contributes much more to his happiness than what he has, or how he is regarded by others. What a man is, and so what he has in his own person, is always the chief thing to consider; for his individuality accompanies him always and everywhere, and gives its color to all his experiences. In every kind of enjoyment, for instance, the pleasure depends principally upon the man himself. Every one admits this in regard to physical, and how much truer it is of intellectual, pleasure. When we use that English expression, "to enjoy one's self," we are employing a very striking and appropriate phrase; for observe— one says, not "he enjoys Paris," but "he enjoys himself in Paris." To a man possessed of an ill-conditioned individuality, all pleasure is like delicate wine in a mouth made bitter with gall. Therefore, in the blessings as well as in the ills of life, less depends upon what befalls us than upon the way in which it is met, that is, upon the kind and degree of our general susceptibility. What a man is and has in himself,—in a word personality, with all it entails, is the only immediate and direct factor in his happiness and welfare. All else is mediate and indirect, and its influence can be neutralized and frustrated; but the influence of personality never. This is why the envy which personal qualities excite is the most implacable of all,—as it is also the most carefully dissembled.

Further, the constitution of our consciousness is the ever present and lasting element in all we do or suffer; our individuality is persistently at work, more or less, at every moment of our life: all other influences are temporal, incidental, fleeting, and subject to every kind of chance and change. This is why Aristotle says: It is not wealth but character that lasts.[1]

[Greek: —hae gar phusis bebion ou ta chraemata]

And just for the same reason we can more easily bear a misfortune which comes to us entirely from without, than one which we have drawn upon ourselves; for fortune may always change, but not character. Therefore, subjective blessings,—a noble nature, a capable head, a joyful temperament, bright spirits, a well-constituted, perfectly sound physique, in a word, *mens sana in corpore sano*, are the first and most important elements in happiness; so that we should be more intent on promoting and preserving such qualities than on the possession of external wealth and external honor.

And of all these, the one which makes us the most directly happy is a genial flow of good spirits; for this excellent quality is its own immediate reward. The man who is cheerful and merry has always a good reason for being so,—the fact, namely, that he is so. There is nothing which, like this quality, can so completely replace the loss of every other blessing. If you know anyone who is young, handsome, rich and esteemed, and you want to know, further, if he is happy, ask, Is he cheerful and genial?—and if he is, what does it matter whether he is young or old, straight or humpbacked, poor or rich?—he is happy. In my early days I once opened an old book and found these words: If you laugh a great deal, you are happy; if you cry a great deal, you are unhappy;—a very simple remark, no doubt;

11

but just because it is so simple I have never been able to forget it, even though it is in the last degree a truism. So if cheerfulness knocks at our door, we should throw it wide open, for it never comes inopportunely; instead of that, we often make scruples about letting it in. We want to be quite sure that we have every reason to be contented; then we are afraid that cheerfulness of spirits may interfere with serious reflections or weighty cares. Cheerfulness is a direct and immediate gain,—the very coin, as it were, of happiness, and not, like all else, merely a cheque upon the bank; for it alone makes us immediately happy in the present moment, and that is the highest blessing for beings like us, whose existence is but an infinitesimal moment between two eternities. To secure and promote this feeling of cheerfulness should be the supreme aim of all our endeavors after happiness.

Now it is certain that nothing contributes so little to cheerfulness as riches, or so much, as health. Is it not in the lower classes, the so-called working classes, more especially those of them who live in the country, that we see cheerful and contented faces? and is it not amongst the rich, the upper classes, that we find faces full of ill-humor and vexation? Consequently we should try as much as possible to maintain a high degree of health; for cheerfulness is the very flower of it. I need hardly say what one must do to be healthy—avoid every kind of excess, all violent and unpleasant emotion, all mental overstrain, take daily exercise in the open air, cold baths and such like hygienic measures. For without a proper amount of daily exercise no one can remain healthy; all the processes of life demand exercise for the due performance of their functions, exercise not only of the parts more immediately concerned, but also of the whole body. For, as Aristotle rightly says, Life is movement; it is its very essence. Ceaseless and rapid motion goes on in every part of the organism. The heart, with its complicated double systole and diastole, beats strongly and untiringly; with twenty-eight beats it has to drive the whole of the blood through arteries, veins and capillaries; the lungs pump like a steam-engine, without intermission; the intestines are always in peristaltic action; the glands are all constantly absorbing and secreting; even the brain has a double motion of its own, with every beat of the pulse and every breath we draw. When people can get no exercise at all, as is the case with the countless numbers who are condemned to a sedentary life, there is a glaring and fatal disproportion between outward inactivity and inner tumult. For this ceaseless internal motion requires some external counterpart, and the want of it produces effects like those of emotion which we are obliged to suppress. Even trees must be shaken by the wind, if they are to thrive. The rule which finds its application here may be most briefly expressed in Latin: omnis motus, quo celerior, eo magis motus.

How much our happiness depends upon our spirits, and these again upon our state of health, may be seen by comparing the influence which the same external circumstances or events have upon us when we are well and strong with the effects which they have when we are depressed and troubled with ill-health. It is not what things are objectively and in themselves, but what they are for us, in our way of looking at them, that makes us happy or the reverse. As Epictetus says, Men are not influenced by things, but by their thoughts about things. And, in general, nine-tenths of our happiness depends upon health alone. With health, everything is a source of pleasure; without it, nothing else, whatever it may be, is enjoyable; even the other personal blessings,—a great mind, a happy temperament—are degraded and dwarfed for want of it. So it is really with good reason that, when two people meet, the first thing they do is to inquire after each other's health, and to express the hope

12

that it is good; for good health is by far the most important element in human happiness. It follows from all this that the greatest of follies is to sacrifice health for any other kind of happiness, whatever it may be, for gain, advancement, learning or fame, let alone, then, for fleeting sensual pleasures. Everything else should rather be postponed to it.

But however much health may contribute to that flow of good spirits which is so essential to our happiness, good spirits do not entirely depend upon health; for a man may be perfectly sound in his physique and still possess a melancholy temperament and be generally given up to sad thoughts. The ultimate cause of this is undoubtedly to be found in innate, and therefore unalterable, physical constitution, especially in the more or less normal relation of a man's sensitiveness to his muscular and vital energy. Abnormal sensitiveness produces inequality of spirits, a predominating melancholy, with periodical fits of unrestrained liveliness. A genius is one whose nervous power or sensitiveness is largely in excess; as Aristotle[2] has very correctly observed, Men distinguished in philosophy, politics, poetry or art appear to be all of a melancholy temperament. This is doubtless the passage which Cicero has in his mind when he says, as he often does, Aristoteles ait omnes ingeniosos melancholicos esse.[3] Shakespeare has very neatly expressed this radical and innate diversity of temperament in those lines in The Merchant of Venice:

Nature has framed strange fellows in her time;
Some that will evermore peep through their eyes,
And laugh, like parrots at a bag-piper;
And others of such vinegar aspect,
That they'll not show their teeth in way of smile,
Though Nestor swear the jest be laughable.

This is the difference which Plato draws between [Greek: eukolos] and *[Greek: dyskolos]*—the man of easy, and the man of difficult disposition—in proof of which he refers to the varying degrees of susceptibility which different people show to pleasurable and painful impressions; so that one man will laugh at what makes another despair. As a rule, the stronger the susceptibility to unpleasant impressions, the weaker is the susceptibility to pleasant ones, and vice versa. If it is equally possible for an event to turn out well or ill, the [Greek: dyskolos] will be annoyed or grieved if the issue is unfavorable, and will not rejoice, should it be happy. On the other hand, the [Greek: eukolos] will neither worry nor fret over an unfavorable issue, but rejoice if it turns out well. If the one is successful in nine out of ten undertakings, he will not be pleased, but rather annoyed that one has miscarried; whilst the other, if only a single one succeeds, will manage to find consolation in the fact and remain cheerful. But here is another instance of the truth, that hardly any evil is entirely without its compensation; for the misfortunes and sufferings which the [Greek: auskoloi], that is, people of gloomy and anxious character, have to overcome, are, on the whole, more imaginary and therefore less real than those which befall the gay and careless; for a man who paints everything black, who constantly fears the worst and takes measures accordingly, will not be disappointed so often in this world, as one who always looks upon the bright side of things. And when a morbid affection of the nerves, or a derangement of the digestive organs, plays into the hands of an innate tendency to gloom, this tendency may reach such a height that permanent discomfort produces a weariness of life. So arises an inclination to suicide, which even the most trivial unpleasantness may actually bring about; nay, when the tendency attains its worst form, it may be occasioned by nothing in particular, but a man may resolve to put an end to his existence, simply because he is permanently unhappy, and then coolly and firmly carry out his determination; as may be seen by the way in which the sufferer, when placed under supervision, as he usually is, eagerly waits to seize the first unguarded moment, when, without a shudder, without a struggle or recoil, he may use the now natural and welcome means of effecting his release.[4] Even the healthiest, perhaps even the most cheerful man, may resolve upon death under certain circumstances; when, for instance, his sufferings, or his fears of some inevitable misfortune, reach such a pitch as to outweigh the terrors of death. The only difference lies in the degree of suffering necessary to bring about the fatal act, a degree which will be high in the case of a cheerful, and low in that of a gloomy man. The greater the melancholy, the lower need the degree be; in the end, it may even sink to zero. But if a man is cheerful, and his spirits are supported by good health, it requires a high degree of suffering to make him lay hands upon himself. There are countless steps in the scale between the two extremes of suicide, the suicide which springs merely from a morbid intensification of innate gloom, and the suicide of the healthy and cheerful man, who has entirely objective grounds for putting an end to his existence.

Beauty is partly an affair of health. It may be reckoned as a personal advantage; though it does not, properly speaking, contribute directly to our happiness. It does so indirectly, by impressing other people; and it is no unimportant advantage, even in man. Beauty is an open letter of recommendation, predisposing the heart to favor the person who presents it. As is well said in these lines of Homer, the gift of beauty is not lightly to be thrown away, that glorious gift which none can bestow save the gods alone—

[Greek: *outoi hapoblaet erti theon erikuoea dora, ossa ken autoi dosin, ekon douk an tis eloito*].[5]

The most general survey shows us that the two foes of human happiness are pain and boredom. We may go further, and say that in the degree in which we are fortunate enough to get away from the one, we approach the other. Life presents, in fact, a more or less violent oscillation between the two. The reason of this is that each of these two poles stands in a double antagonism to the other, external or objective, and inner or subjective. Needy surroundings and poverty produce pain; while, if a man is more than well off, he is bored. Accordingly, while the lower classes are engaged in a ceaseless struggle with need, in other words, with pain, the upper carry on a constant and often desperate battle with boredom.[6] The inner or subjective antagonism arises from the fact that, in the individual, susceptibility to pain varies inversely with susceptibility to boredom, because susceptibility is directly proportionate to mental power. Let me explain. A dull mind is, as a rule, associated with dull sensibilities, nerves which no stimulus can affect, a temperament, in short, which does not feel pain or anxiety very much, however great or terrible it may be. Now, intellectual dullness is at the bottom of that vacuity of soul which is stamped on so many faces, a state of mind which betrays itself by a constant and lively attention to all the trivial circumstances in the external world. This is the true source of boredom—a continual panting after excitement, in order to have a pretext for giving the mind and spirits something to occupy them. The kind of things people choose for this purpose shows

that they are not very particular, as witness the miserable pastimes they have recourse to, and their ideas of social pleasure and conversation: or again, the number
of people who gossip on the doorstep or gape out of the window. It is mainly because
of this inner vacuity of soul that people go in quest of society, diversion, amusement,
luxury of every sort, which lead many to extravagance and misery. Nothing is so good
a protection against such misery as inward wealth, the wealth of the mind, because
the greater it grows, the less room it leaves for boredom. The inexhaustible activity
of thought! Finding ever new material to work upon in the multifarious phenomena
of self and nature, and able and ready to form new combinations of them,—there you
have something that invigorates the mind, and apart from moments of relaxation,
sets it far above the reach of boredom.

But, on the other hand, this high degree of intelligence is rooted in a high degree of
susceptibility, greater strength of will, greater passionateness; and from the union of
these qualities comes an increased capacity for emotion, an enhanced sensibility to
all mental and even bodily pain, greater impatience of obstacles, greater resentment
of interruption;—all of which tendencies are augmented by the power of the imagination, the vivid character of the whole range of thought, including what is disagreeable. This applies, in various degrees, to every step in the long scale of mental power,
from the veriest dunce to the greatest genius that ever lived. Therefore the nearer
anyone is, either from a subjective or from an objective point of view, to one of those
sources of suffering in human life, the farther he is from the other. And so a man's
natural bent will lead him to make his objective world conform to his subjective as
much as possible; that is to say, he will take the greatest measures against that form
of suffering to which he is most liable. The wise man will, above all, strive after freedom from pain and annoyance, quiet and leisure, consequently a tranquil, modest
life, with as few encounters as may be; and so, after a little experience of his so-called
fellowmen, he will elect to live in retirement, or even, if he is a man of great intellect,
in solitude. For the more a man has in himself, the less he will want from other people,—the less, indeed, other people can be to him. This is why a high degree of intellect tends to make a man unsocial. True, if quality of intellect could be made up for by
quantity, it might be worth while to live even in the great world; but unfortunately, a
hundred fools together will not make one wise man.

But the individual who stands at the other end of the scale is no sooner free from
the pangs of need than he endeavors to get pastime and society at any cost, taking up
with the first person he meets, and avoiding nothing so much as himself. For in solitude, where every one is thrown upon his own resources, what a man has in himself
comes to light; the fool in fine raiment groans under the burden of his miserable personality, a burden which he can never throw off, whilst the man of talent peoples the
waste places with his animating thoughts. Seneca declares that folly is its own burden,—omnis stultitia laborat fastidio sui,—a very true saying, with which may be
compared the words of Jesus, the son of Sirach, The life of a fool is worse than
death[7]. And, as a rule, it will be found that a man is sociable just in the degree in
which he is intellectually poor and generally vulgar. For one's choice in this world
does not go much beyond solitude on one side and vulgarity on the other. It is said
that the most sociable of all people are the negroes; and they are at the bottom of the
scale in intellect. I remember reading once in a French paper[8] that the blacks in
North America, whether free or enslaved, are fond of shutting themselves up in large

numbers in the smallest space, because they cannot have too much of one another's snub-nosed company.

The brain may be regarded as a kind of parasite of the organism, a pensioner, as it were, who dwells with the body: and leisure, that is, the time one has for the free enjoyment of one's consciousness or individuality, is the fruit or produce of the rest of existence, which is in general only labor and effort. But what does most people's leisure yield?—boredom and dullness; except, of course, when it is occupied with sensual pleasure or folly. How little such leisure is worth may be seen in the way in which it is spent: and, as Ariosto observes, how miserable are the idle hours of ignorant men!—ozio lungo d'uomini ignoranti. Ordinary people think merely how they shall spend their time; a man of any talent tries to use it. The reason why people of limited intellect are apt to be bored is that their intellect is absolutely nothing more than the means by which the motive power of the will is put into force: and whenever there is nothing particular to set the will in motion, it rests, and their intellect takes a holiday, because, equally with the will, it requires something external to bring it into play. The result is an awful stagnation of whatever power a man has—in a word, boredom. To counteract this miserable feeling, men run to trivialities which please for the moment they are taken up, hoping thus to engage the will in order to rouse it to action, and so set the intellect in motion; for it is the latter which has to give effect to these motives of the will. Compared with real and natural motives, these are but as paper money to coin; for their value is only arbitrary—card games and the like, which have been invented for this very purpose. And if there is nothing else to be done, a man will twirl his thumbs or beat the devil's tattoo; or a cigar may be a welcome substitute for exercising his brains. Hence, in all countries the chief occupation of society is card-playing,[9] and it is the gauge of its value, and an outward sign that it is bankrupt in thought. Because people have no thoughts to deal in, they deal cards, and try and win one another's money. Idiots! But I do not wish to be unjust; so let me remark that it may certainly be said in defence of card-playing that it is a preparation for the world and for business life, because one learns thereby how to make a clever use of fortuitous but unalterable circumstances (cards, in this case), and to get as much out of them as one can: and to do this a man must learn a little dissimulation, and how to put a good face upon a bad business. But, on the other hand, it is exactly for this reason that card-playing is so demoralizing, since the whole object of it is to employ every kind of trick and machination in order to win what belongs to another. And a habit of this sort, learnt at the card-table, strikes root and pushes its way into practical life; and in the affairs of every day a man gradually comes to regard meum and tuum in much the same light as cards, and to consider that he may use to the utmost whatever advantages he possesses, so long as he does not come within the arm of the law. Examples of what I mean are of daily occurrence in mercantile life. Since, then, leisure is the flower, or rather the fruit, of existence, as it puts a man into possession of himself, those are happy indeed who possess something real in themselves. But what do you get from most people's leisure?—only a good-for-nothing fellow, who is terribly bored and a burden to himself. Let us, therefore, rejoice, dear brethren, for we are not children of the bondwoman, but of the free.

Further, as no land is so well off as that which requires few imports, or none at all, so the happiest man is one who has enough in his own inner wealth, and requires little or nothing from outside for his maintenance, for imports are expensive things, reveal dependence, entail danger, occasion trouble, and when all is said and done, are a poor substitute for home produce. No man ought to expect much from others, or, in general, from the external world. What one human being can be to another is not a very great deal: in the end every one stands alone, and the important thing is who it is that stands alone. Here, then, is another application of the general truth which Goethe recognizes in Dichtung und Wahrheit (Bk. III.), that in everything a man has ultimately to appeal to himself; or, as Goldsmith puts it in The Traveller:

Still to ourselves in every place consign'd Our own felicity we make or find.

Himself is the source of the best and most a man can be or achieve. The more this is so—the more a man finds his sources of pleasure in himself—the happier he will be. Therefore, it is with great truth that Aristotle[10] says, To be happy means to be self-sufficient. For all other sources of happiness are in their nature most uncertain, precarious, fleeting, the sport of chance; and so even under the most favorable circumstances they can easily be exhausted; nay, this is unavoidable, because they are not always within reach. And in old age these sources of happiness must necessarily dry up:—love leaves us then, and wit, desire to travel, delight in horses, aptitude for social intercourse; friends and relations, too, are taken from us by death. Then more than ever, it depends upon what a man has in himself; for this will stick to him longest; and at any period of life it is the only genuine and lasting source of happiness. There is not much to be got anywhere in the world. It is filled with misery and pain; and if a man escapes these, boredom lies in wait for him at every corner. Nay more; it is evil which generally has the upper hand, and folly makes the most noise. Fate is cruel, and mankind is pitiable. In such a world as this, a man who is rich in himself is like a bright, warm, happy room at Christmastide, while without are the frost and snow of a December night. Therefore, without doubt, the happiest destiny on earth is to have the rare gift of a rich individuality, and, more especially to be possessed of a good endowment of intellect; this is the happiest destiny, though it may not be, after all, a very brilliant one.

There was a great wisdom in that remark which Queen Christina of Sweden made, in her nineteenth year, about Descartes, who had then lived for twenty years in the deepest solitude in Holland, and, apart from report, was known to her only by a single essay: M. Descartes, she said, is the happiest of men, and his condition seems to me much to be envied.[11] Of course, as was the case with Descartes, external circumstances must be favorable enough to allow a man to be master of his life and happiness; or, as we read in Ecclesiastes[12]—Wisdom is good together with an inheritance, and profitable unto them that see the sun. The man to whom nature and fate have granted the blessing of wisdom, will be most anxious and careful to keep open the fountains of happiness which he has in himself; and for this, independence and leisure are necessary. To obtain them, he will be willing to moderate his desires and harbor his resources, all the more because he is not, like others, restricted to the external world for his pleasures. So he will not be misled by expectations of office, or money, or the favor and applause of his fellowmen, into surrendering himself in order to conform to low desires and vulgar tastes; nay, in such a case he will follow the advice that Horace gives in his epistle to Maecenas.[13]

Nec somnum plebis laudo, satur altilium, nec Otia divitiis Arabum liberrima muto.

It is a great piece of folly to sacrifice the inner for the outer man, to give the whole or the greater part of one's quiet, leisure and independence for splendor, rank, pomp, titles and honor. This is what Goethe did. My good luck drew me quite in the other direction.

The truth which I am insisting upon here, the truth, namely, that the chief source of human happiness is internal, is confirmed by that most accurate observation of Aristotle in the Nichomachean Ethics[14] that every pleasure presupposes some sort of activity, the application of some sort of power, without which it cannot exist. The doctrine of Aristotle's, that a man's happiness consists in the free exercise of his highest faculties, is also enunciated by Stobaeus in his exposition of the Peripatetic philosophy[15]: happiness, he says, means vigorous and successful activity in all your undertakings; and he explains that by vigor [Greek: aretae] he means mastery in any thing, whatever it be. Now, the original purpose of those forces with which nature has endowed man is to enable him to struggle against the difficulties which beset him on all sides. But if this struggle comes to an end, his unemployed forces become a burden to him; and he has to set to work and play with them,—to use them, I mean, for no purpose at all, beyond avoiding the other source of human suffering, boredom, to which he is at once exposed. It is the upper classes, people of wealth, who are the greatest victims of boredom. Lucretius long ago described their miserable state, and the truth of his description may be still recognized to-day, in the life of every great capital—where the rich man is seldom in his own halls, because it bores him to be there, and still he returns thither, because he is no better off outside;—or else he is away in post-haste to his house in the country, as if it were on fire; and he is no sooner arrived there, than he is bored again, and seeks to forget everything in sleep, or else hurries back to town once more.

Exit saepe foras magnis ex aedibus ille,
Esse domi quem pertaesum est, subitoque reventat,
Quippe foris nihilo melius qui sentiat esse.
Currit, agens mannos, ad villam precipitanter,
Auxilium tectis quasi ferre ardentibus instans:
Oscitat extemplo, tetigit quum limina villae;
Aut abit in somnum gravis, atque oblivia quaerit;
Aut etiam properans urbem petit atque revisit.[16]

In their youth, such people must have had a superfluity of muscular and vital energy,—powers which, unlike those of the mind, cannot maintain their full degree of vigor very long; and in later years they either have no mental powers at all, or cannot develop any for want of employment which would bring them into play; so that they are in a wretched plight. Will, however, they still possess, for this is the only power that is inexhaustible; and they try to stimulate their will by passionate excitement, such as games of chance for high stakes—undoubtedly a most degrading form of vice. And one may say generally that if a man finds himself with nothing to do, he is sure to choose some amusement suited to the kind of power in which he excels,—bowls, it may be, or chess; hunting or painting; horse-racing or music; cards, or poetry, heraldry, philosophy, or some other dilettante interest. We might classify these interests methodically, by reducing them to expressions of the three fundamental powers, the factors, that is to say, which go to make up the physiological constitution of man; and further, by considering these powers by themselves, and apart from any of the definite aims which they may subserve, and simply as affording three sources of possible pleasure, out of which every man will choose what suits him, according as he excels in one direction or another.

First of all come the pleasures of vital energy, of food, drink, digestion, rest and sleep; and there are parts of the world where it can be said that these are characteristic and national pleasures. Secondly, there are the pleasures of muscular energy, such as walking, running, wrestling, dancing, fencing, riding and similar athletic pursuits, which sometimes take the form of sport, and sometimes of a military life and real warfare. Thirdly, there are the pleasures of sensibility, such as observation, thought, feeling, or a taste for poetry or culture, music, learning, reading, meditation, invention, philosophy and the like. As regards the value, relative worth and duration of each of these kinds of pleasure, a great deal might be said, which, however, I leave the reader to supply. But every one will see that the nobler the power which is brought into play, the greater will be the pleasure which it gives; for pleasure always involves the use of one's own powers, and happiness consists in a frequent repetition of pleasure. No one will deny that in this respect the pleasures of sensibility occupy a higher place than either of the other two fundamental kinds; which exist in an equal, nay, in a greater degree in brutes; it is this preponderating amount of sensibility which distinguishes man from other animals. Now, our mental powers are forms of sensibility, and therefore a preponderating amount of it makes us capable of that kind of pleasure which has to do with mind, so-called intellectual pleasure; and the more sensibility predominates, the greater the pleasure will be.[17]

The normal, ordinary man takes a vivid interest in anything only in so far as it excites his will, that is to say, is a matter of personal interest to him. But constant excitement of the will is never an unmixed good, to say the least; in other words, it involves pain. Card-playing, that universal occupation of "good society" everywhere, is a device for providing this kind of excitement, and that, too, by means of interests so small as to produce slight and momentary, instead of real and permanent, pain. Card-playing is, in fact, a mere tickling of the will.[18]

On the other hand, a man of powerful intellect is capable of taking a vivid interest in things in the way of mere knowledge, with no admixture of will; nay, such an interest is a necessity to him. It places him in a sphere where pain is an alien,—a diviner air, where the gods live serene.

[Greek: phusis bebion ou ta chraematatheoi reia xoontes][19]

Look on these two pictures—the life of the masses, one long, dull record of struggle and effort entirely devoted to the petty interests of personal welfare, to misery in all its forms, a life beset by intolerable boredom as soon as ever those aims are satisfied and the man is thrown back upon himself, whence he can be roused again to some sort of movement only by the wild fire of passion. On the other side you have a man endowed with a high degree of mental power, leading an existence rich in thought and full of life and meaning, occupied by worthy and interesting objects as soon as ever he is free to give himself to them, bearing in himself a source of the noblest pleasure. What external promptings he wants come from the works of nature, and from the contemplation of human affairs and the achievements of the great of all ages and countries, which are thoroughly appreciated by a man of this type alone, as being the only one who can quite understand and feel with them. And so it is for him alone that those great ones have really lived; it is to him that they make their appeal; the rest are but casual hearers who only half understand either them or their follow-

19

ers. Of course, this characteristic of the intellectual man implies that he has one more need than the others, the need of reading, observing, studying, meditating, practising, the need, in short, of undisturbed leisure. For, as Voltaire has very rightly said, there are no real pleasures without real needs; and the need of them is why to such a man pleasures are accessible which are denied to others,—the varied beauties of nature and art and literature. To heap these pleasures round people who do not want them and cannot appreciate them, is like expecting gray hairs to fall in love. A man who is privileged in this respect leads two lives, a personal and an intellectual life; and the latter gradually comes to be looked upon as the true one, and the former as merely a means to it. Other people make this shallow, empty and troubled existence an end in itself. To the life of the intellect such a man will give the preference over all his other occupations: by the constant growth of insight and knowledge, this intellectual life, like a slowly-forming work of art, will acquire a consistency, a permanent intensity, a unity which becomes ever more and more complete; compared with which, a life devoted to the attainment of personal comfort, a life that may broaden indeed, but can never be deepened, makes but a poor show: and yet, as I have said, people make this baser sort of existence an end in itself.

The ordinary life of every day, so far as it is not moved by passion, is tedious and insipid; and if it is so moved, it soon becomes painful. Those alone are happy whom nature has favored with some superfluity of intellect, something beyond what is just necessary to carry out the behests of their will; for it enables them to lead an intellectual life as well, a life unattended by pain and full of vivid interests. Mere leisure, that is to say, intellect unoccupied in the service of the will, is not of itself sufficient: there must be a real superfluity of power, set free from the service of the will and devoted to that of the intellect; for, as Seneca says, otium sine litteris mors est et vivi hominis sepultura—illiterate leisure is a form of death, a living tomb. Varying with the amount of the superfluity, there will be countless developments in this second life, the life of the mind; it may be the mere collection and labelling of insects, birds, minerals, coins, or the highest achievements of poetry and philosophy. The life of the mind is not only a protection against boredom; it also wards off the pernicious effects of boredom; it keeps us from bad company, from the many dangers, misfortunes, losses and extravagances which the man who places his happiness entirely in the objective world is sure to encounter, My philosophy, for instance, has never brought me in a six-pence; but it has spared me many an expense.

The ordinary man places his life's happiness in things external to him, in property, rank, wife and children, friends, society, and the like, so that when he loses them or finds them disappointing, the foundation of his happiness is destroyed. In other words, his centre of gravity is not in himself; it is constantly changing its place, with every wish and whim. If he is a man of means, one day it will be his house in the country, another buying horses, or entertaining friends, or traveling,—a life, in short, of general luxury, the reason being that he seeks his pleasure in things outside him. Like one whose health and strength are gone, he tries to regain by the use of jellies and drugs, instead of by developing his own vital power, the true source of what he has lost. Before proceeding to the opposite, let us compare with this common type the man who comes midway between the two, endowed, it may be, not exactly with distinguished powers of mind, but with somewhat more than the ordinary amount of intellect. He will take a dilettante interest in art, or devote his attention to some branch of science—botany, for example, or physics, astronomy, history, and find a

20

great deal of pleasure in such studies, and amuse himself with them when external forces of happiness are exhausted or fail to satisfy him any more. Of a man like this it may be said that his centre of gravity is partly in himself. But a dilettante interest in art is a very different thing from creative activity; and an amateur pursuit of science is apt to be superficial and not to penetrate to the heart of the matter. A man cannot entirely identify himself with such pursuits, or have his whole existence so completely filled and permeated with them that he loses all interest in everything else. It is only the highest intellectual power, what we call genius, that attains to this degree of intensity, making all time and existence its theme, and striving to express its peculiar conception of the world, whether it contemplates life as the subject of poetry or of philosophy. Hence, undisturbed occupation with himself, his own thoughts and works, is a matter of urgent necessity to such a man; solitude is welcome, leisure is the highest good, and everything else is unnecessary, nay, even burdensome.

This is the only type of man of whom it can be said that his centre of gravity is entirely in himself; which explains why it is that people of this sort—and they are very rare—no matter how excellent their character may be, do not show that warm and unlimited interest in friends, family, and the community in general, of which others are so often capable; for if they have only themselves they are not inconsolable for the loss of everything else. This gives an isolation to their character, which is all the more effective since other people never really quite satisfy them, as being, on the whole, of a different nature: nay more, since this difference is constantly forcing itself upon their notice they get accustomed to move about amongst mankind as alien beings, and in thinking of humanity in general, to say they instead of we.

So the conclusion we come to is that the man whom nature has endowed with intellectual wealth is the happiest; so true it is that the subjective concerns us more than the objective; for whatever the latter may be, it can work only indirectly, secondly, and through the medium of the former—a truth finely expressed by Lucian:—

[Greek: Aeloutos ho taes psychaes ploutus monos estin alaethaes Talla dechei ataen pleiona ton kteanon—][20]

the wealth of the soul is the only true wealth, for with all other riches comes a bane even greater than they. The man of inner wealth wants nothing from outside but the negative gift of undisturbed leisure, to develop and mature his intellectual faculties, that is, to enjoy his wealth; in short, he wants permission to be himself, his whole life long, every day and every hour. If he is destined to impress the character of his mind upon a whole race, he has only one measure of happiness or unhappiness—to succeed or fail in perfecting his powers and completing his work. All else is of small consequence. Accordingly, the greatest minds of all ages have set the highest value upon undisturbed leisure, as worth exactly as much as the man himself. Happiness appears to consist in leisure, says Aristotle;[21] and Diogenes Laertius reports that Socrates praised leisure as the fairest of all possessions. So, in the Nichomachean Ethics, Aristotle concludes that a life devoted to philosophy is the happiest; or, as he says in the Politics,[22] the free exercise of any power, whatever it may be, is happiness. This again, tallies with what Goethe says in Wilhelm Meister: The man who is born with a talent which he is meant to use, finds his greatest happiness in using it.

But to be in possession of undisturbed leisure, is far from being the common lot; nay, it is something alien to human nature, for the ordinary man's destiny is to spend life in procuring what is necessary for the subsistence of himself and his family; he is a son of struggle and need, not a free intelligence. So people as a rule soon get tired of

21

undisturbed leisure, and it becomes burdensome if there are no fictitious and forced aims to occupy it, play, pastime and hobbies of every kind. For this very reason it is full of possible danger, and *difficilis in otio quies* is a true saying,—it is difficult to keep quiet if you have nothing to do. On the other hand, a measure of intellect far surpassing the ordinary, is as unnatural as it is abnormal. But if it exists, and the man endowed with it is to be happy, he will want precisely that undisturbed leisure which the others find burdensome or pernicious; for without it he is a Pegasus in harness, and consequently unhappy. If these two unnatural circumstances, external, and internal, undisturbed leisure and great intellect, happen to coincide in the same person, it is a great piece of fortune; and if the fate is so far favorable, a man can lead the higher life, the life protected from the two opposite sources of human suffering, pain and boredom, from the painful struggle for existence, and the incapacity for enduring leisure (which is free existence itself)—evils which may be escaped only by being mutually neutralized.

But there is something to be said in opposition to this view. Great intellectual gifts mean an activity pre-eminently nervous in its character, and consequently a very high degree of susceptibility to pain in every form. Further, such gifts imply an intense temperament, larger and more vivid ideas, which, as the inseparable accompaniment of great intellectual power, entail on its possessor a corresponding intensity of the emotions, making them incomparably more violent than those to which the ordinary man is a prey. Now, there are more things in the world productive of pain than of pleasure. Again, a large endowment of intellect tends to estrange the man who has it from other people and their doings; for the more a man has in himself, the less he will be able to find in them; and the hundred things in which they take delight, he will think shallow and insipid. Here, then, perhaps, is another instance of that law of compensation which makes itself felt everywhere. How often one hears it said, and said, too, with some plausibility, that the narrow-minded man is at bottom the happiest, even though his fortune is unenviable. I shall make no attempt to forestall the reader's own judgment on this point; more especially as Sophocles himself has given utterance to two diametrically opposite opinions:—

[Greek: Pollo to phronein eudaimonias proton uparchei.][23]

he says in one place—wisdom is the greatest part of happiness; and again, in another passage, he declares that the life of the thoughtless is the most pleasant of all—

[Greek: En ta phronein gar maeden aedistos bios.][24]

The philosophers of the Old Testament find themselves in a like contradiction. The life of a fool is worse than death[25]

and—

In much wisdom is much grief; and he that increaseth knowledge increaseth sorrow.[26]

I may remark, however, that a man who has no mental needs, because his intellect is of the narrow and normal amount, is, in the strict sense of the word, what is called a philistine—an expression at first peculiar to the German language, a kind of slang term at the Universities, afterwards used, by analogy, in a higher sense, though still in its original meaning, as denoting one who is not a Son of the Muses. A philistine is and remains [Greek: amousos anaer]. I should prefer to take a higher point of view, and apply the term philistine to people who are always seriously occupied with realities which are no realities; but as such a definition would be a transcendental one, and therefore not generally intelligible, it would hardly be in place in the present

22

treatise, which aims at being popular. The other definition can be more easily eluci-
dated, indicating, as it does, satisfactorily enough, the essential nature of all those
qualities which distinguish the philistine. He is defined to be a man without mental
needs. From this is follows, firstly, in relation to himself, that he has no intellectual
pleasures; for, as was remarked before, there are no real pleasures without real
needs. The philistine's life is animated by no desire to gain knowledge and insight for
their own sake, or to experience that true aeesthetic pleasure which is so nearly akin
to them. If pleasures of this kind are fashionable, and the philistine finds himself
compelled to pay attention to them, he will force himself to do so, but he will take as
little interest in them as possible. His only real pleasures are of a sensual kind, and he
thinks that these indemnify him for the loss of the others. To him oysters and cham-
pagne are the height of existence; the aim of his life is to procure what will contribute
to his bodily welfare, and he is indeed in a happy way if this causes him some trouble.
If the luxuries of life are heaped upon him, he will inevitably be bored, and against
boredom he has a great many fancied remedies, balls, theatres, parties, cards, gambling, horses, women, drinking, traveling and so on; all of which can not protect a
man from being bored, for where there are no intellectual needs, no intellectual
pleasures are possible. The peculiar characteristic of the philistine is a dull, dry kind
of gravity, akin to that of animals. Nothing really pleases, or excites, or interests him,
for sensual pleasure is quickly exhausted, and the society of philistines soon becomes
burdensome, and one may even get tired of playing cards. True, the pleasures of vanity are left, pleasures which he enjoys in his own way, either by feeling himself superior in point of wealth, or rank, or influence and power to other people, who thereupon pay him honor; or, at any rate, by going about with those who have a superfluity of these blessings, sunning himself in the reflection of their splendor—what the
English call a snob.

From the essential nature of the philistine it follows, secondly, in regard to others,
that, as he possesses no intellectual, but only physical need, he will seek the society
of those who can satisfy the latter, but not the former. The last thing he will expect
from his friends is the possession of any sort of intellectual capacity; nay, if he chances to meet with it, it will rouse his antipathy and even hatred; simply because in addition to an unpleasant sense of inferiority, he experiences, in his heart, a dull kind of
envy, which has to be carefully concealed even from himself. Nevertheless, it sometimes grows into a secret feeling of rancor. But for all that, it will never occur to him
to make his own ideas of worth or value conform to the standard of such qualities; he
will continue to give the preference to rank and riches, power and influence, which in
his eyes seem to be the only genuine advantages in the world; and his wish will be to
excel in them himself. All this is the consequence of his being a man without intellectual needs. The great affliction of all philistines is that they have no interest in ideas,
and that, to escape being bored, they are in constant need of realities. But realities
are either unsatisfactory or dangerous; when they lose their interest, they become
fatiguing. But the ideal world is illimitable and calm, something afar From the sphere
of our sorrow.

NOTE.—In these remarks on the personal qualities which go to make happiness, I
have been mainly concerned with the physical and intellectual nature of man. For an
account of the direct and immediate influence of morality upon happiness, let me
refer to my prize essay on The Foundation of Morals (Sec. 22.)

[Note 1: Eth. Eud., vii. 2. 37:]

[2: Probl. xxx., ep. 1]

[3: Tusc. i., 33.]

[4: For a detailed description of this condition of mind Cf Esquirol, Des maladies mentales.]

[5: Iliad 3, 65.]

[6: And the extremes meet; for the lowest state of civilization, a nomad or wandering life, finds its counterpart in the highest, where everyone is at times a tourist. The earlier stage was a case of necessity; the latter is a remedy for boredom.]

[7: Ecclesiasticus, xxii. 11.]

[8: Le Commerce, Oct. 19th, 1837.]

[9: Translator's Note.—Card-playing to this extent is now, no doubt, a thing of the past, at any rate amongst the nations of northern Europe. The present fashion is rather in favor of a dilettante interest in art or literature.]

[10: Eth. Eud, vii 2]

[11: Vie de Descartes, par Baillet. Liv. vii., ch. 10.]

[12: vii. 12.]

[13: Lib. 1., ep. 7.]

[14: i. 7 and vii. 13, 14.]

[15: Ecl. eth. ii., ch 7.]

[16: III 1073.]

[17: Nature exhibits a continual progress, starting from the mechanical and chemical activity of the inorganic world, proceeding to the vegetable, with its dull enjoyment of self, from that to the animal world, where intelligence and consciousness begin, at first very weak, and only after many intermediate stages attaining its last great development in man, whose intellect is Nature's crowning point, the goal of all her efforts, the most perfect and difficult of all her works. And even within the range of the human intellect, there are a great many observable differences of degree, and it is very seldom that intellect reaches its highest point, intelligence properly so-called, which in this narrow and strict sense of the word, is Nature's most consummate product, and so the rarest and most precious thing of which the world can boast. The highest product of Nature is the clearest degree of consciousness, in which the world mirrors itself more plainly and completely than anywhere else. A man endowed with this form of intelligence is in possession of what is noblest and best on earth; and accordingly, he has a source of pleasure in comparison with which all others are small. From his surroundings he asks nothing but leisure for the free enjoyment of what he has got, time, as it were, to polish his diamond. All other pleasures that are not of the intellect are of a lower kind; for they are, one and all, movements of will—desires, hopes, fears and ambitions, no matter to what directed: they are always satisfied at the cost of pain, and in the case of ambition, generally with more or less of illusion. With intellectual pleasure, on the other hand, truth becomes clearer and clearer. In the realm of intelligence pain has no power. Knowledge is all in all. Further, intellectual pleasures are accessible entirely and only through the medium of the intelligence, and are limited by its capacity. For all the wit there is in the world is useless to him who has none. Still this advantage is accompanied by a substantial disadvantage; for the whole of Nature shows that with the growth of intelligence comes increased capacity for pain, and it is only with the highest degree of intelligence that suffering reaches its supreme point.]

[18: Vulgarity is, at bottom, the kind of consciousness in which the will completely predominates over the intellect, where the latter does nothing more than perform the service of its master, the will. Therefore, when the will makes no demands, supplies no motives, strong or weak, the intellect entirely loses its power, and the result is complete vacancy of mind. Now will without intellect is the most vulgar and common thing in the world, possessed by every blockhead, who, in the gratification of his passions, shows the stuff of which he is made. This is the condition of mind called vulgarity, in which the only active elements are the organs of sense, and that small amount of intellect which is necessary for apprehending the data of sense. Accordingly, the vulgar man is constantly open to all sorts of impressions, and immediately perceives all the little trifling things that go on in his environment: the lightest whisper, the most trivial circumstance, is sufficient to rouse his attention; he is just like an animal. Such a man's mental condition reveals itself in his face, in his whole exterior; and hence that vulgar, repulsive appearance, which is all the more offensive, if, as is usually the case, his will—the only factor in his consciousness—is a base, selfish and altogether bad one.]

[19: Odyssey IV., 805.]

[20: Epigrammata, 12.]

[21: Eth. Nichom. x. 7.]
[22: iv. 11.]
[23: Antigone, 1347-8.]

[24: Ajax, 554.]
[25: Ecclesiasticus, xxii. 11.]
[26: Ecclesiastes, i. 18.]

Chapter III - Property, Or What A Man Has

Epicurus divides the needs of mankind into three classes, and the division made by this great professor of happiness is a true and a fine one. First come natural and necessary needs, such as, when not satisfied, produce pain,—food and clothing, victus et amictus, needs which can easily be satisfied. Secondly, there are those needs which, though natural, are not necessary, such as the gratification of certain of the senses. I may add, however, that in the report given by Diogenes Laertius, Epicurus does not mention which of the senses he means; so that on this point my account of his doctrine is somewhat more definite and exact than the original. These are needs rather more difficult to satisfy. The third class consists of needs which are neither natural nor necessary, the need of luxury and prodigality, show and splendor, which never come to an end, and are very hard to satisfy.[1]

It is difficult, if not impossible, to define the limits which reason should impose on the desire for wealth; for there is no absolute or definite amount of wealth which will satisfy a man. The amount is always relative, that is to say, just so much as will maintain the proportion between what he wants and what he gets; for to measure a man's happiness only by what he gets, and not also by what he expects to get, is as futile as to try and express a fraction which shall have a numerator but no denominator. A man never feels the loss of things which it never occurs to him to ask for; he is just as happy without them; whilst another, who may have a hundred times as much, feels miserable because he has not got the one thing he wants. In fact, here too, every man has an horizon of his own, and he will expect as much as he thinks it is possible for him to get. If an object within his horizon looks as though he could confidently reckon on getting it, he is happy; but if difficulties come in the way, he is miserable. What lies beyond his horizon has no effect at all upon him. So it is that the vast possessions of the rich do not agitate the poor, and conversely, that a wealthy man is not consoled by all his wealth for the failure of his hopes. Riches, one may say, are like sea-water; the more you drink the thirstier you become; and the same is true of fame. The loss of wealth and prosperity leaves a man, as soon as the first pangs of grief are over, in very much the same habitual temper as before; and the reason of this is, that as soon as fate diminishes the amount of his possessions, he himself immediately reduces the amount of his claims. But when misfortune comes upon us, to reduce the amount of our claims is just what is most painful; once that we have done so, the pain becomes less and less, and is felt no more; like an old wound which has healed. Conversely, when a piece of good fortune befalls us, our claims mount higher and higher, as there is nothing to regulate them; it is in this feeling of expansion that the delight of it lies. But it lasts no longer than the process itself, and when the expansion is complete, the delight ceases; we have become accustomed to the increase in our claims, and consequently indifferent to the amount of wealth which satisfies them. There is a passage in the Odyssey[2] illustrating this truth, of which I may quote the last two lines:

[Greek: Toios gar noos estin epichthonion anthropon Oion eth aemar agei pataer andron te theou te]

the thoughts of man that dwells on the earth are as the day granted him by the father of gods and men. Discontent springs from a constant endeavor to increase the amount of our claims, when we are powerless to increase the amount which will satisfy them.

When we consider how full of needs the human race is, how its whole existence is based upon them, it is not a matter for surprise that wealth is held in more sincere esteem, nay, in greater honor, than anything else in the world; nor ought we to wonder that gain is made the only good of life, and everything that does not lead to it pushed aside or thrown overboard—philosophy, for instance, by those who profess it. People are often reproached for wishing for money above all things, and for loving it more than anything else; but it is natural and even inevitable for people to love that which, like an unwearied Proteus, is always ready to turn itself into whatever object their wandering wishes or manifold desires may for the moment fix upon. Everything else can satisfy only one wish, one need: food is good only if you are hungry; wine, if you are able to enjoy it; drugs, if you are sick; fur for the winter; love for youth, and so on. These are all only relatively good, [Greek: agatha pros ti]. Money alone is absolutely good, because it is not only a concrete satisfaction of one need in particular; it is an abstract satisfaction of all.

If a man has an independent fortune, he should regard it as a bulwark against the many evils and misfortunes which he may encounter; he should not look upon it as giving him leave to get what pleasure he can out of the world, or as rendering it incumbent upon him to spend it in this way. People who are not born with a fortune, but end by making a large one through the exercise of whatever talents they possess, almost always come to think that their talents are their capital, and that the money they have gained is merely the interest upon it; they do not lay by a part of their earnings to form a permanent capital, but spend their money much as they have earned it. Accordingly, they often fall into poverty; their earnings decreased, or come to an end altogether, either because their talent is exhausted by becoming antiquated,—as, for instance, very often happens in the case of fine art; or else it was valid only under a special conjunction of circumstances which has now passed away. There is nothing to prevent those who live on the common labor of their hands from treating their earnings in that way if they like; because their kind of skill is not likely to disappear, or, if it does, it can be replaced by that of their fellow-workmen; moreover, the kind of work they do is always in demand; so that what the proverb says is quite true, a useful trade is a mine of gold. But with artists and professionals of every kind the case is quite different, and that is the reason why they are well paid. They ought to build up a capital out of their earnings; but they recklessly look upon them as merely interest, and end in ruin. On the other hand, people who inherit money know, at least, how to distinguish between capital and interest, and most of them try to make their capital secure and not encroach upon it; nay, if they can, they put by at least an eighth of their interests in order to meet future contingencies. So most of them maintain their position. These few remarks about capital and interest are not applicable to commercial life, for merchants look upon money only as a means of further gain, just as a workman regards his tools; so even if their capital has been entirely the result of their own efforts, they try to preserve and increase it by using it. Accordingly, wealth is nowhere so much at home as in the merchant class.

It will generally be found that those who know what it is to have been in need and destitution are very much less afraid of it, and consequently more inclined to extravagance, than those who know poverty only by hearsay. People who have been born and bred in good circumstances are as a rule much more careful about the future, more economical, in fact, than those who, by a piece of good luck, have suddenly passed from poverty to wealth. This looks as if poverty were not really such a very wretched thing as it appears from a distance. The true reason, however, is rather the fact that the man who has been born into a position of wealth comes to look upon it as something without which he could no more live than he could live without air; he guards it as he does his very life; and so he is generally a lover of order, prudent and economical. But the man who has been born into a poor position looks upon it as the natural one, and if by any chance he comes in for a fortune, he regards it as a superfluity, something to be enjoyed or wasted, because, if it comes to an end, he can get on just as well as before, with one anxiety the less; or, as Shakespeare says in Henry VI.,[3]

.... the adage must be verified That beggars mounted run their horse to death.

But it should be said that people of this kind have a firm and excessive trust, partly in fate, partly in the peculiar means which have already raised them out of need and poverty,—a trust not only of the head, but of the heart also; and so they do not, like the man born rich, look upon the shallows of poverty as bottomless, but console themselves with the thought that once they have touched ground again, they can take another upward flight. It is this trait in human character which explains the fact that women who were poor before their marriage often make greater claims, and are more extravagant, than those who have brought their husbands a rich dowry; because, as a rule, rich girls bring with them, not only a fortune, but also more eagerness, nay, more of the inherited instinct, to preserve it, than poor girls do. If anyone doubts the truth of this, and thinks that it is just the opposite, he will find authority for his view in Ariosto's first Satire; but, on the other hand, Dr. Johnson agrees with my opinion. A woman of fortune, he says, being used to the handling of money, spends it judiciously; but a woman who gets the command of money for the first time upon her marriage, has such a gusto in spending it, that she throws it away with great profusion.[4] And in any case let me advise anyone who marries a poor girl not to leave her the capital but only the interest, and to take especial care that she has not the management of the children's fortune.

I do not by any means think that I am touching upon a subject which is not worth my while to mention when I recommend people to be careful to preserve what they have earned or inherited. For to start life with just as much as will make one independent, that is, allow one to live comfortably without having to work—even if one has only just enough for oneself, not to speak of a family—is an advantage which cannot be over-estimated; for it means exemption and immunity from that chronic disease of penury, which fastens on the life of man like a plague; it is emancipation from that forced labor which is the natural lot of every mortal. Only under a favorable fate like this can a man be said to be born free, to be, in the proper sense of the word, sui juris, master of his own time and powers, and able to say every morning, This day is my own. And just for the same reason the difference between the man who has a hundred a year and the man who has a thousand, is infinitely smaller than the difference between the former and a man who has nothing at all. But inherited wealth reaches its utmost value when it falls to the individual endowed with mental powers of a high order, who is resolved to pursue a line of life not compatible with the making of money; for he is then doubly endowed by fate and can live for his genius; and he will pay his debt to mankind a hundred times, by achieving what no other could achieve, by producing some work which contributes to the general good, and redounds to the honor of humanity at large. Another, again, may use his wealth to further philanthropic schemes, and make himself well-deserving of his fellowmen. But a man who does none of these things, who does not even try to do them, who never attempts to learn the rudiments of any branch of knowledge so that he may at least do what he can towards promoting it—such a one, born as he is into riches, is a mere idler and thief of time, a contemptible fellow. He will not even be happy, because, in his case, exemption from need delivers him up to the other extreme of human suffering, boredom, which is such martyrdom to him, that he would have been better off if poverty had given him something to do. And as he is bored he is apt to be extravagant, and so lose the advantage of which he showed himself unworthy. Countless numbers of people find themselves in want, simply because, when they had money, they spent it only to get momentary relief from the feeling of boredom which oppressed them.

It is quite another matter if one's object is success in political life, where favor, friends and connections are all-important, in order to mount by their aid step by step on the ladder of promotion, and perhaps gain the topmost rung. In this kind of life, it is much better to be cast upon the world without a penny; and if the aspirant is not of noble family, but is a man of some talent, it will redound to his advantage to be an absolute pauper. For what every one most aims at in ordinary contact with his fellows is to prove them inferior to himself; and how much more is this the case in politics. Now, it is only an absolute pauper who has such a thorough conviction of his own complete, profound and positive inferiority from every point of view, of his own utter insignificance and worthlessness, that he can take his place quietly in the political machine.[5] He is the only one who can keep on bowing low enough, and even go right down upon his face if necessary; he alone can submit to everything and laugh at it; he alone knows the entire worthlessness of merit; he alone uses his loudest voice and his boldest type whenever he has to speak or write of those who are placed over his head, or occupy any position of influence; and if they do a little scribbling, he is ready to applaud it as a masterwork. He alone understands how to beg, and so betimes, when he is hardly out of his boyhood, he becomes a high priest of that hidden mystery which Goethe brings to light.

Uber's Niederträchtige
Niemand sich beklage:
Denn es ist das Machtige
Was man dir auch sage:

it is no use to complain of low aims; for, whatever people may say, they rule the world.

On the other hand, the man who is born with enough to live upon is generally of a somewhat independent turn of mind; he is accustomed to keep his head up; he has not learned all the arts of the beggar; perhaps he even presumes a little upon the possession of talents which, as he ought to know, can never compete with cringing mediocrity; in the long run he comes to recognize the inferiority of those who are placed over his head, and when they try to put insults upon him, he becomes refractory and shy. This is not the way to get on in the world. Nay, such a man may at least incline to the opinion freely expressed by Voltaire: We have only two days to live; it is not worth our while to spend them in cringing to contemptible rascals. But alas! let me observe by the way, that contemptible rascal is an attribute which may be predicated of an abominable number of people. What Juvenal says—it is difficult to rise if your poverty is greater than your talent—

    Haud facile emergunt quorum virtutibus obstat Res angusta domi—

is more applicable to a career of art and literature than to a political and social ambition.

    Wife and children I have not reckoned amongst a man's possessions: he is rather in their possession. It would be easier to include friends under that head; but a man's friends belong to him not a whit more than he belongs to them.

[Note 1: Cf. Diogenes Laertius, Bk. x., ch. xxvii., pp. 127 and 149; also Cicero de finibus, i., 13.]
[2: xviii., 130-7.]
[3: Part III., Act 1., Sc. 4.]
[4: Boswell's Life of Johnson: ann: 1776, aetat: 67.]
[5: Translator's Note.—Schopenhauer is probably here making one of his most virulent attacks upon Hegel; in this case on account of what he thought to be the philosopher's abject servility to the government of his day. Though the Hegelian system has been the fruitful mother of many liberal ideas, there can be no doubt that Hegel's influence, in his own lifetime, was an effective support of Prussian bureaucracy.]

Chapter IV - Position, or a Man's Place in the Estimation of Others

Section 1. - Reputation

By a peculiar weakness of human nature, people generally think too much about the opinion which others form of them; although the slightest reflection will show that this opinion, whatever it may be, is not in itself essential to happiness. Therefore it is hard to understand why everybody feels so very pleased when he sees that other people have a good opinion of him, or say anything flattering to his vanity. If you stroke a cat, it will purr; and, as inevitably, if you praise a man, a sweet expression of delight will appear on his face; and even though the praise is a palpable lie, it will be welcome, if the matter is one on which he prides himself. If only other people will applaud him, a man may console himself for downright misfortune or for the pittance he gets from the two sources of human happiness already discussed: and conversely, it is astonishing how infallibly a man will be annoyed, and in some cases deeply pained, by any wrong done to his feeling of self-importance, whatever be the nature, degree, or circumstances of the injury, or by any depreciation, slight, or disregard.

    If the feeling of honor rests upon this peculiarity of human nature, it may have a very salutary effect upon the welfare of a great many people, as a substitute for morality; but upon their happiness, more especially upon that peace of mind and independence which are so essential to happiness, its effect will be disturbing and prejudicial rather than salutary. Therefore it is advisable, from our point of view, to set limits to this weakness, and duly to consider and rightly to estimate the relative value of advantages, and thus temper, as far as possible, this great susceptibility to other people's opinion, whether the opinion be one flattering to our vanity, or whether it causes us pain; for in either case it is the same feeling which is touched. Otherwise, a man is the slave of what other people are pleased to think,—and how little it requires to disconcert or soothe the mind that is greedy of praise:

Sic leve, sic parvum est, animum quod laudis avarum Subruit ac reficit.[1]

Therefore it will very much conduce to our happiness if we duly compare the value of what a man is in and for himself with what he is in the eyes of others. Under the former conies everything that fills up the span of our existence and makes it what it is, in short, all the advantages already considered and summed up under the heads of personality and property; and the sphere in which all this takes place is the man's own consciousness. On the other hand, the sphere of what we are for other people is their consciousness, not ours; it is the kind of figure we make in their eyes, together with the thoughts which this arouses.[2] But this is something which has no direct and immediate existence for us, but can affect us only mediately and indirectly, so far, that is, as other people's behavior towards us is directed by it; and even then it ought to affect us only in so far as it can move us to modify what we are in and for ourselves. Apart from this, what goes on in other people's consciousness is, as such, a matter of indifference to us; and in time we get really indifferent to it, when we come to see how superficial and futile are most people's thoughts, how narrow their ideas, how mean their sentiments, how perverse their opinions, and how much of error there is in most of them; when we learn by experience with what depreciation a man will speak of his fellow, when he is not obliged to fear him, or thinks that what he says will not come to his ears. And if ever we have had an opportunity of seeing how the greatest of men will meet with nothing but slight from half-a-dozen blockheads, we shall understand that to lay great value upon what other people say is to pay them too much honor.

At all events, a man is in a very bad way, who finds no source of happiness in the first two classes of blessings already treated of, but has to seek it in the third, in other words, not in what he is in himself, but in what he is in the opinion of others. For, after all, the foundation of our whole nature, and, therefore, of our happiness, is our physique, and the most essential factor in happiness is health, and, next in importance after health, the ability to maintain ourselves in independence and freedom from care. There can be no competition or compensation between these essential factors on the one side, and honor, pomp, rank and reputation on the other, however much value we may set upon the latter. No one would hesitate to sacrifice the latter for the former, if it were necessary. We should add very much to our happiness by a timely recognition of the simple truth that every man's chief and real existence is in his own skin, and not in other people's opinions; and, consequently, that the actual conditions of our personal life,—health, temperament, capacity, income, wife, children, friends, home, are a hundred times more important for our happiness than what other people are pleased to think of us: otherwise we shall be miserable. And if people insist that honor is dearer than life itself, what they really mean is that existence and well-being are as nothing compared with other people's opinions. Of course, this may be only an exaggerated way of stating the prosaic truth that reputation, that is, the opinion others have of us, is indispensable if we are to make any progress in the world; but I shall come back to that presently. When we see that almost everything men devote their lives to attain, sparing no effort and enc ountering a thousand toils and dangers in the process, has, in the end, no further object than to raise themselves in the estimation of others; when we see that not only offices, titles, decorations, but also wealth, nay, even knowledge[3] and art, are striven for only to obtain, as the ultimate goal of all effort, greater respect from one's fellowmen,—is not this a lamentable proof of the extent to which human folly can go? To set much too high a value on other people's opinion is a common error everywhere; an error, it may be, rooted in human nature itself, or the result of civilization, and social arrangements generally; but, whatever its source, it exercises a very immoderate influence on all we do, and is very prejudicial to our happiness. We can trace it from a timorous and slavish regard for what other people will say, up to the feeling which made Virginius plunge the dagger into his daughter's heart, or induces many a man to sacrifice quiet, riches, health and even life itself, for posthumous glory. Undoubtedly this feeling is a very convenient instrument in the hands of those who have the control or direction of their fellowmen; and accordingly we find that in every scheme for training up humanity in the way it should go, the maintenance and strengthening of the feeling of honor occupies an important place. But it is quite a different matter in its effect on human happiness, of which it is here our object to treat; and we should rather be careful to dissuade people from setting too much store by what others think of them. Daily experience shows us, however, that this is just the mistake people persist in making; most men set the utmost value precisely on what other people think, and are more concerned about it than about what goes on in their own consciousness, which is the thing most immediately and directly present to them. They reverse the natural order,—regarding the opinions of others as real existence and their own consciousness as something shadowy; making the derivative and secondary into the principal, and considering the picture they present to the world of more importance than their own selves. By thus trying to get a direct and immediate result out of what has no really direct or immediate existence, they fall into the kind of folly which is called vanity—the appropriate term for that which has no solid or instrinsic value. Like a miser, such people forget the end in their eagerness to obtain the means.

The truth is that the value we set upon the opinion of others, and our constant endeavor in respect of it, are each quite out of proportion to any result we may reasonably hope to attain; so that this attention to other people's attitude may be regarded as a kind of universal mania which every one inherits. In all we do, almost the first thing we think about is, what will people say; and nearly half the troubles and bothers of life may be traced to our anxiety on this score; it is the anxiety which is at the bottom of all that feeling of self-importance, which is so often mortified because it is so very morbidly sensitive. It is solicitude about what others will say that underlies all our vanity and pretension, yes, and all our show and swagger too. Without it, there would not be a tenth part of the luxury which exists. Pride in every form, point d'honneur and punctilio, however varied their kind or sphere, are at bottom nothing but this—anxiety about what others will say—and what sacrifices it costs! One can see it even in a child; and though it exists at every period of life, it is strongest in age; because, when the capacity for sensual pleasure fails, vanity and pride have only avarice to share their dominion. Frenchmen, perhaps, afford the best example of this feeling, and amongst them it is a regular epidemic, appearing sometimes in the most absurd ambition, or in a ridiculous kind of national vanity and the most shameless boasting. However, they frustrate their own gains, for other people make fun of them and call them la grande nation.

By way of specially illustrating this perverse and exuberant respect for other people's opinion, let me take passage from the Times of March 31st, 1846, giving a detailed account of the execution of one Thomas Wix, an apprentice who, from motives of vengeance, had murdered his master. Here we have very unusual circumstances and an extraordinary character, though one very suitable for our purpose; and these combine to give a striking picture of this folly, which is so deeply rooted in human nature, and allow us to form an accurate notion of the extent to which it will go. On the morning of the execution, says the report, the rev. ordinary was early in attendance upon him, but Wix, beyond a quiet demeanor, betrayed no interest in his ministrations, appearing to feel anxious only to acquit himself "bravely" before the spectators of his ignomininous end.... In the procession Wix fell into his proper place with alacrity, and, as he entered the Chapel-yard, remarked, sufficiently loud to be heard by several persons near him, "Now, then, as Dr. Dodd said, I shall soon know the grand secret." On reaching the scaffold, the miserable wretch mounted the drop without the slightest assistance, and when he got to the centre, he bowed to the spectators twice, a proceeding which called forth a tremendous cheer from the degraded crowd beneath.

This is an admirable example of the way in which a man, with death in the most dreadful form before his very eyes, and eternity beyond it, will care for nothing but the impression he makes upon a crowd of gapers, and the opinion he leaves behind him in their heads. There was much the same kind of thing in the case of Lecompte, who was executed at Frankfurt, also in 1846, for an attempt on the king's life. At the trial he was very much annoyed that he was not allowed to appear, in decent attire, before the Upper House; and on the day of the execution it was a special grief to him that he was not permitted to shave. It is not only in recent times that this kind of thing has been known to happen. Mateo Aleman tells us, in the Introduction to his celebrated romance, Juzman de Alfarache, that many infatuated criminals, instead of devoting their last hours to the welfare of their souls, as they ought to have done, neglect this duty for the purpose of preparing and committing to memory a speech to be made from the scaffold.

I take these extreme cases as being the best illustrations to what I mean; for they give us a magnified reflection of our own nature. The anxieties of all of us, our worries, vexations, bothers, troubles, uneasy apprehensions and strenuous efforts are due, in perhaps the large majority of instances, to what other people will say; and we are just as foolish in this respect as those miserable criminals. Envy and hatred are very often traceable to a similar source.

Now, it is obvious that happiness, which consists for the most part in peace of mind and contentment, would be served by nothing so much as by reducing this impulse of human nature within reasonable limits,—which would perhaps make it one fiftieth part of what it is now. By doing so, we should get rid of a thorn in the flesh which is always causing us pain. But it is a very difficult task, because the impulse in question is a natural and innate perversity of human nature. Tacitus says, The lust of fame is the last that a wise man shakes off[4] The only way of putting an end to this universal folly is to see clearly that it is a folly; and this may be done by recognizing the fact that most of the opinions in men's heads are apt to be false, perverse, erroneous and absurd, and so in themselves unworthy of attention; further, that other people's opinions can have very little real and positive influence upon us in most of the circumstances and affairs of life. Again, this opinion is generally of such an unfavorable character that it would worry a man to death to hear everything that was said of him, or the tone in which he was spoken of. And finally, among other things, we should be clear about the fact that honor itself has no really direct, but only an indirect, value. If people were generally converted from this universal folly, the result would be such an addition to our piece of mind and cheerfulness as at present seems inconceivable; people would present a firmer and more confident front to the world, and generally behave with less embarrassment and restraint. It is observable that a retired mode of life has an exceedingly beneficial influence on our peace of mind, and this is mainly because we thus escape having to live constantly in the sight of others, and pay everlasting regard to their casual opinions; in a word, we are able to return upon ourselves. At the same time a good deal of positive misfortune might be avoided, which we are now drawn into by striving after shadows, or, to speak more correctly, by indulging a mischievous piece of folly; and we should consequently have more attention to give to solid realities and enjoy them with less interruption that at present. But [Greek: chalepa ga kala]—what is worth doing is hard to do.

Section 2.- Pride

The folly of our nature which we are discussing puts forth three shoots, ambition, vanity and pride. The difference between the last two is this: pride is an established conviction of one's own paramount worth in some particular respect; while vanity is the desire of rousing such a conviction in others, and it is generally accompanied by the secret hope of ultimately coming to the same conviction oneself. Pride works from within; it is the direct appreciation of oneself. Vanity is the desire to arrive at this

appreciation indirectly, from without. So we find that vain people are talkative, proud, and taciturn. But the vain person ought to be aware that the good opinion of others, which he strives for, may be obtained much more easily and certainly by persistent silence than by speech, even though he has very good things to say. Anyone who wishes to affect pride is not therefore a proud man; but he will soon have to drop this, as every other, assumed character.

It is only a firm, unshakeable conviction of pre-eminent worth and special value which makes a man proud in the true sense of the word,—a conviction which may, no doubt, be a mistaken one or rest on advantages which are of an adventitious and conventional character: still pride is not the less pride for all that, so long as it be present in real earnest. And since pride is thus rooted in conviction, it resembles every other form of knowledge in not being within our own arbitrament. Pride's worst foe,—I mean its greatest obstacle,—is vanity, which courts the applause of the world in order to gain the necessary foundation for a high opinion of one's own worth, whilst pride is based upon a pre-existing conviction of it.

It is quite true that pride is something which is generally found fault with, and cried down; but usually, I imagine, by those who have nothing upon which they can pride themselves. In view of the impudence and foolhardiness of most people, anyone who possesses any kind of superiority or merit will do well to keep his eyes fixed on it, if he does not want it to be entirely forgotten; for if a man is good-natured enough to ignore his own privileges, and hob-nob with the generality of other people, as if he were quite on their level, they will be sure to treat him, frankly and candidly, as one of themselves. This is a piece of advice I would specially offer to those whose superiority is of the highest kind—real superiority, I mean, of a purely personal nature—which cannot, like orders and titles, appeal to the eye or ear at every moment; as, otherwise, they will find that familiarity breeds contempt, or, as the Romans used to say, sus Minervam. Joke with a slave, and he'll soon show his heels, is an excellent Arabian proverb; nor ought we to despise what Horace says,

Sume superbiam Quaesitam meritis.

usurp the fame you have deserved. No doubt, when modesty was made a virtue, it was a very advantageous thing for the fools; for everybody is expected to speak of himself as if he were one. This is leveling down indeed; for it comes to look as if there were nothing but fools in the world.

The cheapest sort of pride is national pride; for if a man is proud of his own nation, it argues that he has no qualities of his own of which he can be proud; otherwise he would not have recourse to those which he shares with so many millions of his fellowmen. The man who is endowed with important personal qualities will be only too ready to see clearly in what respects his own nation falls short, since their failings will be constantly before his eyes. But every miserable fool who has nothing at all of which he can be proud adopts, as a last resource, pride in the nation to which he belongs; he is ready and glad to defend all its faults and follies tooth and nail, thus reimbursing himself for his own inferiority. For example, if you speak of the stupid and degrading bigotry of the English nation with the contempt it deserves, you will hardly find one Englishman in fifty to agree with you; but if there should be one, he will generally happen to be an intelligent man.

The Germans have no national pride, which shows how honest they are, as everybody knows! and how dishonest are those who, by a piece of ridiculous affectation, pretend that they are proud of their country—the Deutsche Bruder and the demagogues who flatter the mob in order to mislead it. I have heard it said that gunpowder was invented by a German. I doubt it. Lichtenberg asks, Why is it that a man who is not a German does not care about pretending that he is one; and that if he makes any pretence at all, it is to be a Frenchman or an Englishman?[5]

However that may be, individuality is a far more important thing than nationality, and in any given man deserves a thousand-fold more consideration. And since you cannot speak of national character without referring to large masses of people, it is impossible to be loud in your praises and at the same time honest. National character is only another name for the particular form which the littleness, perversity and baseness of mankind take in every country. If we become disgusted with one, we praise another, until we get disgusted with this too. Every nation mocks at other nations, and all are right.

The contents of this chapter, which treats, as I have said, of what we represent in the world, or what we are in the eyes of others, may be further distributed under three heads: honor rank and fame.

Section 3. - Rank

Let us take rank first, as it may be dismissed in a few words, although it plays an important part in the eyes of the masses and of the philistines, and is a most useful wheel in the machinery of the State.

It has a purely conventional value. Strictly speaking, it is a sham; its method is to exact an artificial respect, and, as a matter of fact, the whole thing is a mere farce.

Orders, it may be said, are bills of exchange drawn on public opinion, and the measure of their value is the credit of the drawer. Of course, as a substitute for pensions, they save the State a good deal of money; and, besides, they serve a very useful purpose, if they are distributed with discrimination and

judgment. For people in general have eyes and ears, it is true; but not much else, very little judgment indeed, or even memory. There are many services of the State quite beyond the range of their understanding; others, again, are appreciated and made much of for a time, and then soon forgotten. It seems to me, therefore, very proper, that a cross or a star should proclaim to the mass of people always and everywhere, This man is not like you; he has done something. But orders lose their value when they are distributed unjustly, or without due selection, or in too great numbers: a prince should be as careful in conferring them as a man of business is in signing a bill. It is a pleonasm to inscribe on any order for distinguished service; for every order ought to be for distinguished service. That stands to reason.

Section 4. - Honor

Honor is a much larger question than rank, and more difficult to discuss. Let us begin by trying to define it.

If I were to say Honor is external conscience, and conscience is inward honor, no doubt a good many people would assent; but there would be more show than reality about such a definition, and it would hardly go to the root of the matter. I prefer to say, Honor is, on its objective side, other people's opinion of what we are worth; on its subjective side, it is the respect we pay to this opinion. From the latter point of view, to be a man of honor is to exercise what is often a very wholesome, but by no means a purely moral, influence.

The feelings of honor and shame exist in every man who is not utterly depraved, and honor is everywhere recognized as something particularly valuable. The reason of this is as follows. By and in himself a man can accomplish very little; he is like Robinson Crusoe on a desert island. It is only in society that a man's powers can be called into full activity. He very soon finds this out when his consciousness begins to develop, and there arises in him the desire to be looked upon as a useful member of society, as one, that is, who is capable of playing his part as a man—pro parte virili—thereby acquiring a right to the benefits of social life. Now, to be a useful member of society, one must do two things: firstly, what everyone is expected to do everywhere; and, secondly, what one's own particular position in the world demands and requires.

But a man soon discovers that everything depends upon his being useful, not in his own opinion, but in the opinion of others; and so he tries his best to make that favorable impression upon the world, to which he attaches such a high value. Hence, this

35

primitive and innate characteristic of human nature, which is called the feeling of honor, or, under another aspect, the feeling of shame—verecundia. It is this which brings a blush to his cheeks at the thought of having suddenly to fall in the estimation of others, even when he knows that he is innocent, nay, even if his remissness extends to no absolute obligation, but only to one which he has taken upon himself of his own free will. Conversely, nothing in life gives a man so much courage as the attainment or renewal of the conviction that other people regard him with favor; because it means that everyone joins to give him help and protection, which is an infinitely stronger bulwark against the ills of life than anything he can do himself.

The variety of relations in which a man can stand to other people so as to obtain their confidence, that is, their good opinion, gives rise to a distinction between several kinds of honor, resting chiefly on the different bearings that meum may take to tuum; or, again, on the performance of various pledges; or finally, on the relation of the sexes. Hence, there are three main kinds of honor, each of which takes various forms—civic honor, official honor, and sexual honor.

Civic honor has the widest sphere of all. It consists in the assumption that we shall pay unconditional respect to the rights of others, and, therefore, never use any unjust or unlawful means of getting what we want. It is the condition of all peaceable intercourse between man and man; and it is destroyed by anything that openly and manifestly militates against this peaceable intercourse, anything, accordingly, which entails punishment at the hands of the law, always supposing that the punishment is a just one.

The ultimate foundation of honor is the conviction that moral character is unalterable: a single bad action implies that future actions of the same kind will, under similar circumstances, also be bad. This is well expressed by the English use of the word character as meaning credit, reputation, honor. Hence honor, once lost, can never be recovered; unless the loss rested on some mistake, such as may occur if a man is slandered or his actions viewed in a false light. So the law provides remedies against slander, libel, and even insult; for insult though it amounts to no more than mere abuse, is a kind of summary slander with a suppression of the reasons. What I mean may be well put in the Greek phrase—not quoted from any author—[Greek: estin hae loidoria diabolae]. It is true that if a man abuses another, he is simply showing that he has no real or true causes of complaint against him; as, otherwise, he would bring these forward as the premises, and rely upon his hearers to draw the conclusion themselves: instead of which, he gives the conclusion and leaves out the premises, trusting that people will suppose that he has done so only for the sake of being brief.

Civic honor draws its existence and name from the middle classes; but it applies equally to all, not excepting the highest. No man can disregard it, and it is a very serious thing, of which every one should be careful not to make light. The man who breaks confidence has for ever forfeited confidence, whatever he may do, and whoever he may be; and the bitter consequences of the loss of confidence can never be averted.

There is a sense in which honor may be said to have a negative character in opposition to the positive character of fame. For honor is not the opinion people have of particular qualities which a man may happen to possess exclusively: it is rather the opinion they have of the qualities which a man may be expected to exhibit, and to which he should not prove false. Honor, therefore, means that a man is not exceptional; fame, that he is. Fame is something which must be won; honor, only some-

36

thing which must not be lost. The absence of fame is obscurity, which is only a nega-tive; but loss of honor is shame, which is a positive quality. This negative character of honor must not be confused with anything passive; for honor is above all things ac-tive in its working. It is the only quality which proceeds directly from the man who exhibits it; it is concerned entirely with what he does and leaves undone, and has nothing to do with the actions of others or the obstacles they place in his way. It is something entirely in our own power—[Greek: ton ephaemon]. This distinction, as we shall see presently, marks off true honor from the sham honor of chivalry.

Slander is the only weapon by which honor can be attacked from without; and the only way to repel the attack is to confute the slander with the proper amount of pub-licity, and a due unmasking of him who utters it.

The reason why respect is paid to age is that old people have necessarily shown in the course of their lives whether or not they have been able to maintain their honor unblemished; while that of young people has not been put to the proof, though they are credited with the possession of it. For neither length of years,—equalled, as it is, and even excelled, in the case of the lower animals,—nor, again, experience, which is only a closer knowledge of the world's ways, can be any sufficient reason for the re-spect which the young are everywhere required to show towards the old: for if it were merely a matter of years, the weakness which attends on age would call rather for consideration than for respect. It is, however, a remarkable fact that white hair always commands reverence—a reverence really innate and instinctive. Wrinkles—a much surer sign of old age—command no reverence at all; you never hear any one speak of venerable wrinkles; but venerable white hair is a common expression.

Honor has only an indirect value. For, as I explained at the beginning of this chap-ter, what other people think of us, if it affects us at all, can affect us only in so far as it governs their behavior towards us, and only just so long as we live with, or have to do with, them. But it is to society alone that we owe that safety which we and our possessions enjoy in a state of civilization; in all we do we need the help of others, and they, in their turn, must have confidence in us before they can have anything to do with us. Accordingly, their opinion of us is, indirectly, a matter of great im-portance; though I cannot see how it can have a direct or immediate value. This is an opinion also held by Cicero. I quite agree, he writes, with what Chrysippus and Diog-enes used to say, that a good reputation is not worth raising a finger to obtain, if it were not that it is so useful.[6] This truth has been insisted upon at great length by Helvetius in his chief work De l'Esprit,[7] the conclusion of which is that we love es-teem not for its own sake, but solely for the advantages which it brings. And as the means can never be more than the end, that saying, of which so much is made, Honor is dearer than life itself, is, as I have remarked, a very exaggerated statement. So much then, for civic honor.

Official honor is the general opinion of other people that a man who fills any office really has the necessary qualities for the proper discharge of all the duties which ap-pertain to it. The greater and more important the duties a man has to discharge in the State, and the higher and more influential the office which he fills, the stronger must be the opinion which people have of the moral and intellectual qualities which render him fit for his post. Therefore, the higher his position, the greater must be the degree of honor paid to him, expressed, as it is, in titles, orders and the generally subservient behavior of others towards him. As a rule, a man's official rank implies the particular degree of honor which ought to be paid to him, however much this degree may be modified by the capacity of the masses to form any notion of its importance. Still, as a matter of fact, greater honor is paid to a man who fulfills special duties than to the common citizen, whose honor mainly consists in keeping clear of dishonor.

Official honor demands, further, that the man who occupies an office must maintain respect for it, for the sake both of his colleagues and of those who will come after him. This respect an official can maintain by a proper observance of his duties, and by repelling any attack that may be made upon the office itself or upon its occupant: he must not, for instance, pass over unheeded any statement to the effect that the duties of the office are not properly discharged, or that the office itself does not conduce to the public welfare. He must prove the unwarrantable nature of such attacks by enforcing the legal penalty for them.

Subordinate to the honor of official personages comes that of those who serve the State in any other capacity, as doctors, lawyers, teachers, anyone, in short, who, by graduating in any subject, or by any other public declaration that he is qualified to exercise some special skill, claims to practice it; in a word, the honor of all those who take any public pledges whatever. Under this head comes military honor, in the true sense of the word, the opinion that people who have bound themselves to defend their country really possess the requisite qualities which will enable them to do so, especially courage, personal bravery and strength, and that they are perfectly ready to defend their country to the death, and never and under any circumstances desert the flag to which they have once sworn allegiance. I have here taken official honor in a wider sense than that in which it is generally used, namely, the respect due by citizens to an office itself.

In treating of sexual honor and the principles on which it rests, a little more attention and analysis are necessary; and what I shall say will support my contention that all honor really rests upon a utilitarian basis. There are two natural divisions of the subject—the honor of women and the honor of men, in either side issuing in a well-understood esprit de corps. The former is by far the more important of the two, because the most essential feature in woman's life is her relation to man.

Female honor is the general opinion in regard to a girl that she is pure, and in regard to a wife that she is faithful. The importance of this opinion rests upon the following considerations. Women depend upon men in all the relations of life; men upon women, it might be said, in one only. So an arrangement is made for mutual interdependence—man undertaking responsibility for all woman's needs and also for the children that spring from their union—an arrangement on which is based the welfare of the whole female race. To carry out this plan, women have to band together with a show of esprit de corps, and present one undivided front to their common enemy, man,—who possesses all the good things of the earth, in virtue of his superior physical and intellectual power,—in order to lay siege to and conquer him, and so get possession of him and a share of those good things. To this end the honor of all women depends upon the enforcement of the rule that no woman should give herself to a man except in marriage, in order that every man may be forced, as it were, to surrender and ally himself with a woman; by this arrangement provision is made for the whole of the female race. This is a result, however, which can be obtained only by a strict observance of the rule; and, accordingly, women everywhere show true esprit de corps in carefully insisting upon its maintenance. Any girl who commits a breach of the rule betrays the whole female race, because its welfare would be destroyed if

38

every woman were to do likewise; so she is cast out with shame as one who has lost her honor. No woman will have anything more to do with her; she is avoided like the plague. The same doom is awarded to a woman who breaks the marriage tie; for in so doing she is false to the terms upon which the man capitulated; and as her conduct is such as to frighten other men from making a similar surrender, it imperils the welfare of all her sisters. Nay, more; this deception and coarse breach of troth is a crime punishable by the loss, not only of personal, but also of civic honor. This is why we minimize the shame of a girl, but not of a wife; because, in the former case, marriage can restore honor, while in the latter, no atonement can be made for the breach of contract.

Once this esprit de corps is acknowledged to be the foundation of female honor, and is seen to be a wholesome, nay, a necessary arrangement, as at bottom a matter of prudence and interest, its extreme importance for the welfare of women will be recognized. But it does not possess anything more than a relative value. It is no absolute end, lying beyond all other aims of existence and valued above life itself. In this view, there will be nothing to applaud in the forced and extravagant conduct of a Lucretia or a Virginius—conduct which can easily degenerate into tragic farce, and produce a terrible feeling of revulsion. The conclusion of Emilia Galotti, for instance, makes one leave the theatre completely ill at ease; and, on the other hand, all the rules of female honor cannot prevent a certain sympathy with Clara in Egmont. To carry this principle of female honor too far is to forget the end in thinking of the means—and this is just what people often do; for such exaggeration suggests that the value of sexual honor is absolute; while the truth is that it is more relative than any other kind. One might go so far as to say that its value is purely conventional, when one sees from Thomasius how in all ages and countries, up to the time of the Reformation, irregularities were permitted and recognized by law, with no derogation to female honor,—not to speak of the temple of Mylitta at Babylon.[8]

There are also of course certain circumstances in civil life which make external forms of marriage impossible, especially in Catholic countries, where there is no such thing as divorce. Ruling princes everywhere, would, in my opinion, do much better, from a moral point of view, to dispense with forms altogether rather than contract a morganatic marriage, the descendants of which might raise claims to the throne if the legitimate stock happened to die out; so that there is a possibility, though, perhaps, a remote one, that a morganatic marriage might produce a civil war. And, besides, such a marriage, concluded in defiance of all outward ceremony, is a concession made to women and priests—two classes of persons to whom one should be most careful to give as little tether as possible. It is further to be remarked that every man in a country can marry the woman of his choice, except one poor individual, namely, the prince. His hand belongs to his country, and can be given in marriage only for reasons of State, that is, for the good of the country. Still, for all that, he is a man; and, as a man, he likes to follow whither his heart leads. It is an unjust, ungrateful and priggish thing to forbid, or to desire to forbid, a prince from following his inclinations in this matter; of course, as long as the lady has no influence upon the Government of the country. From her point of view she occupies an exceptional position, and does not come under the ordinary rules of sexual honor; for she has merely given herself to a man who loves her, and whom she loves but cannot marry. And in general, the fact that the principle of female honor has no origin in nature, is shown by the many bloody sacrifices which have been offered to it,—the murder of children and the mother's suicide. No doubt a girl who contravenes the code commits a breach of faith against her whole sex; but this faith is one which is only secretly taken for granted, and not sworn to. And since, in most cases, her own prospects suffer most immediately, her folly is infinitely greater than her crime.

The corresponding virtue in men is a product of the one I have been discussing. It is their esprit de corps, which demands that, once a man has made that surrender of himself in marriage which is so advantageous to his conqueror, he shall take care that the terms of the treaty are maintained; both in order that the agreement itself may lose none of its force by the permission of any laxity in its observance, and that men, having given up everything, may, at least, be assured of their bargain, namely, exclusive possession. Accordingly, it is part of a man's honor to resent a breach of the marriage tie on the part of his wife, and to punish it, at the very least by separating from her. If he condones the offence, his fellowmen cry shame upon him; but the shame in this case is not nearly so foul as that of the woman who has lost her honor; the stain is by no means of so deep a dye—levioris notae macula;—because a man's relation to woman is subordinate to many other and more important affairs in his life. The two great dramatic poets of modern times have each taken man's honor as the theme of two plays; Shakespeare in Othello and The Winter's Tale, and Calderon in El medico de su honra, (The Physician of his Honor), and A secreto agravio secreta venganza, (for Secret Insult Secret Vengeance). It should be said, however, that honor demands the punishment of the wife only; to punish her paramour too, is a work of supererogation. This confirms the view I have taken, that a man's honor originates in esprit de corps.

The kind of honor which I have been discussing hitherto has always existed in its various forms and principles amongst all nations and at all times; although the history of female honor shows that its principles have undergone certain local modifications at different periods. But there is another species of honor which differs from this entirely, a species of honor of which the Greeks and Romans had no conception, and up to this day it is perfectly unknown amongst Chinese, Hindoos or Mohammedans. It is a kind of honor which arose only in the Middle Age, and is indigenous only to Christian Europe, nay, only to an extremely small portion of the population, that is to say, the higher classes of society and those who ape them. It is knightly honor, or point d'honneur. Its principles are quite different from those which underlie the kind of honor I have been treating until now, and in some respects are even opposed to them. The sort I am referring to produces the cavalier; while the other kind creates the man of honor. As this is so, I shall proceed to give an explanation of its principles, as a kind of code or mirror of knightly courtesy.

(1.) To begin with, honor of this sort consists, not in other people's opinion of what we are worth, but wholly and entirely in whether they express it or not, no matter whether they really have any opinion at all, let alone whether they know of reasons for having one. Other people may entertain the worst opinion of us in consequence of what we do, and may despise us as much as they like; so long as no one dares to give expression to his opinion, our honor remains untarnished. So if our actions and qualities compel the highest respect from other people, and they have no option but to give this respect,—as soon as anyone, no matter how wicked or foolish he may be, utters something depreciatory of us, our honor is offended, nay, gone for ever, unless we can manage to restore it. A superfluous proof of what I say, namely, that knightly honor depends, not upon what people think, but upon what they say, is furnished by

40

the fact that insults can be withdrawn, or, if necessary, form the subject of an apology, which makes them as though they had never been uttered. Whether the opinion which underlays the expression has also been rectified, and why the expression should ever have been used, are questions which are perfectly unimportant: so long as the statement is withdrawn, all is well. The truth is that conduct of this kind aims, not at earning respect, but at extorting it.

(2.) In the second place, this sort of honor rests, not on what a man does, but on what he suffers, the obstacles he encounters; differing from the honor which prevails in all else, in consisting, not in what he says or does himself, but in what another man says or does. His honor is thus at the mercy of every man who can talk it away on the tip of his tongue; and if he attacks it, in a moment it is gone for ever,—unless the man who is attacked manages to wrest it back again by a process which I shall mention presently, a process which involves danger to his life, health, freedom, property and peace of mind. A man's whole conduct may be in accordance with the most righteous and noble principles, his spirit may be the purest that ever breathed, his intellect of the very highest order; and yet his honor may disappear the moment that anyone is pleased to insult him, anyone at all who has not offended against this code of honor himself, let him be the most worthless rascal or the most stupid beast, an idler, gambler, debtor, a man, in short, of no account at all. It is usually this sort of fellow who likes to insult people; for, as Seneca[10] rightly remarks, ut quisque contemtissimus et ludibrio est, ita solutissimae est, the more contemptible and ridiculous a man is,— the readier he is with his tongue. His insults are most likely to be directed against the very kind of man I have described, because people of different tastes can never be friends, and the sight of pre-eminent merit is apt to raise the secret ire of a ne'er-do-well. What Goethe says in the Westöstlicher Divan is quite true, that it is useless to complain against your enemies; for they can never become your friends, if your whole being is a standing reproach to them:—

Was klagst du über Feinde?
Sollten Solche je warden Freunde
Denen das Wesen, wie du bist,
Im stillen ein ewiger Vorwurf ist?

It is obvious that people of this worthless description have good cause to be thankful to the principle of honor, because it puts them on a level with people who in every other respect stand far above them. If a fellow likes to insult any one, attribute to him, for example, some bad quality, this is taken prima facie as a well-founded opinion, true in fact; a decree, as it were, with all the force of law; nay, if it is not at once wiped out in blood, it is a judgment which holds good and valid to all time. In other words, the man who is insulted remains—in the eyes of all honorable people—what the man who uttered the insult—even though he were the greatest wretch on earth—was pleased to call him; for he has put up with the insult—the technical term, I believe. Accordingly, all honorable people will have nothing more to do with him, and treat him like a leper, and, it may be, refuse to go into any company where he may be found, and so on.

This wise proceeding may, I think, be traced back to the fact that in the Middle Age, up to the fifteenth century, it was not the accuser in any criminal process who had to prove the guilt of the accused, but the accused who had to prove his innocence.[11]

41

This he could do by swearing he was not guilty; and his backers—consacramentales—had to come and swear that in their opinion he was incapable of perjury. If he could find no one to help him in this way, or the accuser took objection to his backers, recourse was had to trial by the Judgment of God, which generally meant a duel. For the accused was now in disgrace,[12] and had to clear himself. Here, then, is the origin of the notion of disgrace, and of that whole system which prevails now-a-days amongst honorable people—only that the oath is omitted. This is also the explanation of that deep feeling of indignation which honorable people are called upon to show if they are given the lie; it is a reproach which they say must be wiped out in blood. It seldom comes to this pass, however, though lies are of common occurrence; but in England, more than elsewhere, it is a superstition which has taken very deep root. As a matter of order, a man who threatens to kill another for telling a lie should never have told one himself. The fact is, that the criminal trial of the Middle Age also admitted of a shorter form. In reply to the charge, the accused answered: That is a lie; whereupon it was left to be decided by the Judgment of God. Hence, the code of knightly honor prescribes that, when the lie is given, an appeal to arms follows as a matter of course. So much, then, for the theory of insult.

But there is something even worse than insult, something so dreadful that I must beg pardon of all honorable people for so much as mentioning it in this code of knightly honor; for I know they will shiver, and their hair will stand on end, at the very thought of it—the summum malum, the greatest evil on earth, worse than death and damnation. A man may give another—horrible dictu!—a slap or a blow. This is such an awful thing, and so utterly fatal to all honor, that, while any other species of insult may be healed by blood-letting, this can be cured only by the coup-de-grace.

(3.) In the third place, this kind of honor has absolutely nothing to do with what a man may be in and for himself; or, again, with the question whether his moral character can ever become better or worse, and all such pedantic inquiries. If your honor happens to be attacked, or to all appearances gone, it can very soon be restored in its entirety if you are only quick enough in having recourse to the one universal remedy—a duel. But if the aggressor does not belong to the classes which recognize the code of knightly honor, or has himself once offended against it, there is a safer way of meeting any attack upon your honor, whether it consists in blows, or merely in words. If you are armed, you can strike down your opponent on the spot, or perhaps an hour later. This will restore your honor.

But if you wish to avoid such an extreme step, from fear of any unpleasant consequences arising therefrom, or from uncertainty as to whether the aggressor is subject to the laws of knightly honor or not, there is another means of making your position good, namely, the Avantage. This consists in returning rudeness with still greater rudeness; and if insults are no use, you can try a blow, which forms a sort of climax in the redemption of your honor; for instance, a box on the ear may be cured by a blow with a stick, and a blow with a stick by a thrashing with a horsewhip; and, as the approved remedy for this last, some people recommend you to spit at your opponent.[13] If all these means are of no avail, you must not shrink from drawing blood. And the reason for these methods of wiping out insult is, in this code, as follows:

(4.) To receive an insult is disgraceful; to give one, honorable. Let me take an example. My opponent has truth, right and reason on his side. Very well. I insult him. Thereupon right and honor leave him and come to me, and, for the time being, he has lost them—until he gets them back, not by the exercise of right or reason, but by shooting and sticking me. Accordingly, rudeness is a quality which, in point of honor, is a substitute for any other and outweighs them all. The rudest is always right. What more do you want? However stupid, bad or wicked a man may have been, if he is only rude into the bargain, he condones and legitimizes all his faults. If in any discussion or conversation, another man shows more knowledge, greater love of truth, a sounder judgment, better understanding than we, or generally exhibits intellectual qualities which cast ours into the shade, we can at once annul his superiority and our own shallowness, and in our turn be superior to him, by being insulting and offensive. For rudeness is better than any argument; it totally eclipses intellect. If our opponent does not care for our mode of attack, and will not answer still more rudely, so as to plunge us into the ignoble rivalry of the Avantage, we are the victors and honor is on our side. Truth, knowledge, understanding, intellect, wit, must beat a retreat and leave the field to this almighty insolence.

Honorable people immediately make a show of mounting their war-horse, if anyone utters an opinion adverse to theirs, or shows more intelligence than they can muster; and if in any controversy they are at a loss for a reply, they look about for some weapon of rudeness, which will serve as well and come readier to hand; so they retire masters of the position. It must now be obvious that people are quite right in applauding this principle of honor as having ennobled the tone of society. This principle springs from another, which forms the heart and soul of the entire code.

(5.) Fifthly, the code implies that the highest court to which a man can appeal in any differences he may have with another on a point of honor is the court of physical force, that is, of brutality. Every piece of rudeness is, strictly speaking, an appeal to brutality; for it is a declaration that intellectual strength and moral insight are incompetent to decide, and that the battle must be fought out by physical force—a struggle which, in the case of man, whom Franklin defines as a tool-making animal, is decided by the weapons peculiar to the species; and the decision is irrevocable. This is the well-known principle of right of might—irony, of course, like the wit of a fool, a parallel phrase. The honor of a knight may be called the glory of might.

(6.) Lastly, if, as we saw above, civic honor is very scrupulous in the matter of meum and tuum, paying great respect to obligations and a promise once made, the code we are here discussing displays, on the other hand, the noblest liberality. There is only one word which may not be broken, the word of honor—upon my honor, as people say—the presumption being, of course, that every other form of promise may be broken. Nay, if the worst comes to the worst, it is easy to break even one's word of honor, and still remain honorable—again by adopting that universal remedy, the duel, and fighting with those who maintain that we pledged our word. Further, there is one debt, and one alone, that under no circumstances must be left unpaid—a gambling debt, which has accordingly been called a debt of honor. In all other kinds of debt you may cheat Jews and Christians as much as you like; and your knightly honor remains without a stain.

The unprejudiced reader will see at once that such a strange, savage and ridiculous code of honor as this has no foundation in human nature, nor any warrant in a healthy view of human affairs. The extremely narrow sphere of its operation serves only to intensify the feeling, which is exclusively confined to Europe since the Middle Age, and then only to the upper classes, officers and soldiers, and people who imitate them. Neither Greeks nor Romans knew anything of this code of honor or of its principles; nor the highly civilized nations of Asia, ancient or modern. Amongst them no

43

other kind of honor is recognized but that which I discussed first, in virtue of which a man is what he shows himself to be by his actions, not what any wagging tongue is pleased to say of him. They thought that what a man said or did might perhaps affect his own honor, but not any other man's. To them, a blow was but a blow—and any horse or donkey could give a harder one—a blow which under certain circumstances might make a man angry and demand immediate vengeance; but it had nothing to do with honor. No one kept account of blows or insulting words, or of the satisfaction which was demanded or omitted to be demanded. Yet in personal bravery and contempt of death, the ancients were certainly not inferior to the nations of Christian Europe. The Greeks and Romans were thorough heroes, if you like; but they knew nothing about point d'honneur. If they had any idea of a duel, it was totally unconnected with the life of the nobles; it was merely the exhibition of mercenary gladiators, slaves devoted to slaughter, condemned criminals, who, alternately with wild beasts, were set to butcher one another to make a Roman holiday. When Christianity was introduced, gladiatorial shows were done away with, and their place taken, in Christian times, by the duel, which was a way of settling difficulties by the Judgment of God.

If the gladiatorial fight was a cruel sacrifice to the prevailing desire for great spectacles, dueling is a cruel sacrifice to existing prejudices—a sacrifice, not of criminals, slaves and prisoners, but of the noble and the free.[14]

There are a great many traits in the character of the ancients which show that they were entirely free from these prejudices. When, for instance, Marius was summoned to a duel by a Teutonic chief, he returned answer to the effect that, if the chief were tired of his life, he might go and hang himself; at the same time he offered him a veteran gladiator for a round or two. Plutarch relates in his life of Themistocles that Eurybiades, who was in command of the fleet, once raised his stick to strike him; whereupon Themistocles, instead of drawing his sword, simply said: Strike, but hear me. How sorry the reader must be, if he is an honorable man, to find that we have no information that the Athenian officers refused in a body to serve any longer under Themistocles, if he acted like that! There is a modern French writer who declares that if anyone considers Demosthenes a man of honor, his ignorance will excite a smile of pity; and that Cicero was not a man of honor either![15] In a certain passage in Plato's Laws[16] the philosopher speaks at length of [Greek: aikia] or assault, showing us clearly enough that the ancients had no notion of any feeling of honor in connection with such matters. Socrates' frequent discussions were often followed by his being severely handled, and he bore it all mildly. Once, for instance, when somebody kicked him, the patience with which he took the insult surprised one of his friends. Do you think, said Socrates, that if an ass happened to kick me, I should resent it?[17] On another occasion, when he was asked, Has not that fellow abused and insulted you? No, was his answer, what he says is not addressed to me[18] Stobaeus has preserved a long passage from Musonius, from which we can see how the ancients treated insults. They knew no other form of satisfaction than that which the law provided, and wise people despised even this. If a Greek received a box on the ear, he could get satisfaction by the aid of the law; as is evident from Plato's Gorgias, where Socrates' opinion may be found. The same thing may be seen in the account given by Gellius of one Lucius Veratius, who had the audacity to give some Roman citizens whom he met on the road a box on the ear, without any provocation whatever; but to avoid any ulterior consequences, he told a slave to bring a bag of small money, and on the spot paid the trivial legal penalty to the men whom he had astonished by his conduct.

Crates, the celebrated Cynic philosopher, got such a box on the ear from Nicodromus, the musician, that his face swelled up and became black and blue; whereupon he put a label on his forehead, with the inscription, Nicodromus fecit, which brought much disgrace to the fluteplayer who had committed such a piece of brutality upon the man whom all Athens honored as a household god.[19] And in a letter to Melesippus, Diogenes of Sinope tells us that he got a beating from the drunken sons of the Athenians; but he adds that it was a matter of no importance.[20] And Seneca devotes the last few chapters of his De Constantia to a lengthy discussion on insult—contumelia; in order to show that a wise man will take no notice of it. In Chapter XIV, he says, What shall a wise man do, if he is given a blow? What Cato did, when some one struck him on the mouth;—not fire up or avenge the insult, or even return the blow, but simply ignore it.

Yes, you say, but these men were philosophers.—And you are fools, eh? Precisely.

It is clear that the whole code of knightly honor was utterly unknown to the ancients; for the simple reason that they always took a natural and unprejudiced view of human affairs, and did not allow themselves to be influenced by any such vicious and abominable folly. A blow in the face was to them a blow and nothing more, a trivial physical injury; whereas the moderns make a catastrophe out of it, a theme for a tragedy; as, for instance, in the Cid of Corneille, or in a recent German comedy of middle-class life, called The Power of Circumstance, which should have been entitled The Power of Prejudice. If a member of the National Assembly at Paris got a blow on the ear, it would resound from one end of Europe to the other. The examples which I have given of the way in which such an occurrence would have been treated in classic times may not suit the ideas of honorable people; so let me recommend to their notice, as a kind of antidote, the story of Monsieur Desglands in Diderot's masterpiece, Jacques le fataliste. It is an excellent specimen of modern knightly honor, which, no doubt, they will find enjoyable and edifying.[21]

From what I have said it must be quite evident that the principle of knightly honor has no essential and spontaneous origin in human nature. It is an artificial product, and its source is not hard to find. Its existence obviously dates from the time when people used their fists more than their heads, when priestcraft had enchained the human intellect, the much bepraised Middle Age, with its system of chivalry. That was the time when people let the Almighty not only care for them but judge for them too; when difficult cases were decided by an ordeal, a Judgment of God; which, with few exceptions, meant a duel, not only where nobles were concerned, but in the case of ordinary citizens as well. There is a neat illustration of this in Shakespeare's Henry VI.[1] Every judicial sentence was subject to an appeal to arms—a court, as it were, of higher instance, namely, the Judgment of God: and this really meant that physical strength and activity, that is, our animal nature, usurped the place of reason on the judgment seat, deciding in matters of right and wrong, not by what a man had done, but by the force with which he was opposed, the same system, in fact, as prevails today under the principles of knightly honor. If any one doubts that such is really the origin of our modern duel, let him read an excellent work by J.B. Millingen, The History of Dueling.[2] Nay, you may still find amongst the supporters of the system,—who, by the way are not usually the most educated or thoughtful of men,—some who look upon the result of a duel as really constituting a divine judgment in the matter in dispute; no doubt in consequence of the traditional feeling on the subject.

But leaving aside the question of origin, it must now be clear to us that the main tendency of the principle is to use physical menace for the purpose of extorting an appearance of respect which is deemed too difficult or superfluous to acquire in reality; a proceeding which comes to much the same thing as if you were to prove the warmth of your room by holding your hand on the thermometer and so make it rise. In fact, the kernel of the matter is this: whereas civic honor aims at peaceable intercourse, and consists in the opinion of other people that we deserve full confidence, because we pay unconditional respect to their rights; knightly honor, on the other hand, lays down that we are to be feared, as being determined at all costs to maintain our own.

As not much reliance can be placed upon human integrity, the principle that it is more essential to arouse fear than to invite confidence would not, perhaps, be a false one, if we were living in a state of nature, where every man would have to protect himself and directly maintain his own rights. But in civilized life, where the State undertakes the protection of our person and property, the principle is no longer applicable: it stands, like the castles and watch-towers of the age when might was right, a useless and forlorn object, amidst well-tilled fields and frequented roads, or even railways.

Accordingly, the application of knightly honor, which still recognizes this principle, is confined to those small cases of personal assault which meet with but slight punishment at the hands of the law, or even none at all, for de minimis non,—mere trivial wrongs, committed sometimes only in jest. The consequence of this limited application of the principle is that it has forced itself into an exaggerated respect for the value of the person,—a respect utterly alien to the nature, constitution or destiny of man—which it has elated into a species of sanctity: and as it considers that the State has imposed a very insufficient penalty on the commission of such trivial injuries, it takes upon itself to punish them by attacking the aggressor in life or limb. The whole thing manifestly rests upon an excessive degree of arrogant pride, which, completely forgetting what man really is, claims that he shall be absolutely free from all attack or even censure. Those who determine to carry out this principle by main force, and announce, as their rule of action, whoever insults or strikes me shall die! ought for their pains to be banished the country.[22]

As a palliative to this rash arrogance, people are in the habit of giving way on everything. If two intrepid persons meet, and neither will give way, the slightest difference may cause a shower of abuse, then fisticuffs, and, finally, a fatal blow: so that it would really be a more decorous proceeding to omit the intermediate steps and appeal to arms at once. An appeal to arms has its own special formalities; and these have developed into a rigid and precise system of laws and regulations, together forming the most solemn farce there is—a regular temple of honor dedicated to folly! For if two intrepid persons dispute over some trivial matter, (more important affairs are dealt with by law), one of them, the cleverer of the two, will of course yield; and they will agree to differ. That this is so is proved by the fact that common people,—or, rather, the numerous classes of the community who do not acknowledge the principle of knightly honor, let any dispute run its natural course. Amongst these classes homicide is a hundredfold rarer than amongst those—and they amount, perhaps, in all, to hardly one in a thousand,—who pay homage to the principle: and even blows are of no very frequent occurrence.

Then it has been said that the manners and tone of good society are ultimately based upon this principle of honor, which, with its system of duels, is made out to be a bulwark against the assaults of savagery and rudeness. But Athens, Corinth and Rome could assuredly boast of good, nay, excellent society, and manners and tone of a high order, without any support from the bogey of knightly honor. It is true that women did not occupy that prominent place in ancient society which they hold now, when conversation has taken on a frivolous and trifling character, to the exclusion of that weighty discourse which distinguished the ancients.

This change has certainly contributed a great deal to bring about the tendency, which is observable in good society now-a-days, to prefer personal courage to the possession of any other quality. The fact is that personal courage is really a very subordinate virtue,—merely the distinguishing mark of a subaltern,—a virtue, indeed, in which we are surpassed by the lower animals; or else you would not hear people say, as brave as a lion. Far from being the pillar of society, knightly honor affords a sure asylum, in general for dishonesty and wickedness, and also for small incivilities, want of consideration and unmannerliness. Rude behavior is often passed over in silence because no one cares to risk his neck in correcting it.

After what I have said, it will not appear strange that the dueling system is carried to the highest pitch of sanguinary zeal precisely in that nation whose political and financial records show that they are not too honorable. What that nation is like in its private and domestic life, is a question which may be best put to those who are experienced in the matter. Their urbanity and social culture have long been conspicuous by their absence.

There is no truth, then, in such pretexts. It can be urged with more justice that as, when you snarl at a dog, he snarls in return, and when you pet him, he fawns; so it lies in the nature of men to return hostility by hostility, and to be embittered and irritated at any signs of depreciatory treatment or hatred: and, as Cicero says, there is something so penetrating in the shaft of envy that even men of wisdom and worth find its wound a painful one; and nowhere in the world, except, perhaps, in a few religious sects, is an insult or a blow taken with equanimity. And yet a natural view of either would in no case demand anything more than a requital proportionate to the offence, and would never go to the length of assigning death as the proper penalty for anyone who accuses another of lying or stupidity or cowardice. The old German theory of blood for a blow is a revolting superstition of the age of chivalry. And in any case the return or requital of an insult is dictated by anger, and not by any such obligation of honor and duty as the advocates of chivalry seek to attach to it. The fact is that, the greater the truth, the greater the slander; and it is clear that the slightest hint of some real delinquency will give much greater offence than a most terrible accusation which is perfectly baseless: so that a man who is quite sure that he has done nothing to deserve a reproach may treat it with contempt, and will be safe in doing so. The theory of honor demands that he shall show a susceptibility which he does not possess, and take bloody vengeance for insults which he cannot feel. A man must himself have but a poor opinion of his own worth who hastens to prevent the utterance of an unfavorable opinion by giving his enemy a black eye.

True appreciation of his own value will make a man really indifferent to insult; but if he cannot help resenting it, a little shrewdness and culture will enable him to save appearances and dissemble his anger. If he could only get rid of this superstition about honor—the idea, I mean, that it disappears when you are insulted, and can be restored by returning the insult; if we could only stop people from thinking that wrong, brutality and insolence can be legalized by expressing readiness to give satisfaction, that is, to fight in defence of it, we should all soon come to the general opinion that insult and depreciation are like a battle in which the loser wins; and that, as Vincenzo Monti says, abuse resembles a church-procession, because it always returns to the point from which it set out. If we could only get people to look upon insult in this light, we should no longer have to say something rude in order to prove that we are in the right. Now, unfortunately, if we want to take a serious view of any question, we have first of all to consider whether it will not give offence in some way or other to the dullard, who generally shows alarm and resentment at the merest sign of intelligence; and it may easily happen that the head which contains the intelligent view has to be pitted against the noodle which is empty of everything but narrowness and stupidity. If all this were done away with, intellectual superiority could take the leading place in society which is its due—a place now occupied, though people do not like to confess it, by excellence of physique, mere fighting pluck, in fact; and the natural effect of such a change would be that the best kind of people would have one reason the less for withdrawing from society. This would pave the way for the introduction of real courtesy and genuinely good society, such as undoubtedly existed in Athens, Corinth and Rome. If anyone wants to see a good example of what I mean, I should like him to read Xenophon's Banquet.

The last argument in defence of knightly honor no doubt is, that, but for its existence, the world—awful thought!—would be a regular bear-garden. To which I may briefly reply that nine hundred and ninety-nine people out of a thousand who do not recognize the code, have often given and received a blow without any fatal consequences: whereas amongst the adherents of the code a blow usually means death to one of the parties. But let me examine this argument more closely.

I have often tried to find some tenable, or at any rate, plausible basis—other than a merely conventional one—some positive reasons, that is to say, for the rooted conviction which a portion of mankind entertains, that a blow is a very dreadful thing; but I have looked for it in vain, either in the animal or in the rational side of human nature. A blow is, and always will be, a trivial physical injury which one man can do to another; proving, thereby, nothing more than his superiority in strength or skill, or that his enemy was off his guard. Analysis will carry us no further. The same knight who regards a blow from the human hand as the greatest of evils, if he gets a ten times harder blow from his horse, will give you the assurance, as he limps away in suppressed pain, that it is a matter of no consequence whatever. So I have come to think that it is the human hand which is at the bottom of the mischief. And yet in a battle the knight may get cuts and thrusts from the same hand, and still assure you that his wounds are not worth mentioning. Now, I hear that a blow from the flat of a sword is not by any means so bad as a blow from a stick; and that, a short time ago, cadets were liable to be punished by the one but not the other, and that the very greatest honor of all is the accolade. This is all the psychological or moral basis that I can find; and so there is nothing left me but to pronounce the whole thing an antiquated superstition that has taken deep root, and one more of the many examples which show the force of tradition. My view is confirmed by the well-known fact that in China a beating with a bamboo is a very frequent punishment for the common people, and even for officials of every class; which shows that human nature, even in a highly civilized state, does not run in the same groove here and in China.

On the contrary, an unprejudiced view of human nature shows that it is just as natural for a man to beat as it is for savage animals to bite and rend in pieces, or for horned beasts to butt or push. Man may be said to be the animal that beats. Hence it is revolting to our sense of the fitness of things to hear, as we sometimes do, that one man bitten another; on the other hand, it is a natural and everyday occurrence for him to get blows or give them. It is intelligible enough that, as we become educated, we are glad to dispense with blows by a system of mutual restraint. But it is a cruel thing to compel a nation or a single class to regard a blow as an awful misfortune which must have death and murder for its consequences. There are too many genuine evils in the world to allow of our increasing them by imaginary misfortunes, which brings real ones in their train: and yet this is the precise effect of the superstition, which thus proves itself at once stupid and malign.

It does not seem to me wise of governments and legislative bodies to promote any such folly by attempting to do away with flogging as a punishment in civil or military life. Their idea is that they are acting in the interests of humanity; but, in point of fact, they are doing just the opposite; for the abolition of flogging will serve only to strengthen this inhuman and abominable superstition, to which so many sacrifices have already been made. For all offences, except the worst, a beating is the obvious, and therefore the natural penalty; and a man who will not listen to reason will yield to blows. It seems to me right and proper to administer corporal punishment to the man who possesses nothing and therefore cannot be fined, or cannot be put in prison because his master's interests would suffer by the loss of his service. There are really no arguments against it: only mere talk about the dignity of man—talk which proceeds, not from any clear notions on the subject, but from the pernicious superstition I have been describing. That it is a superstition which lies at the bottom of the whole business is proved by an almost laughable example. Not long ago, in the military discipline of many countries, the cat was replaced by the stick. In either case the object was to produce physical pain; but the latter method involved no disgrace, and was not derogatory to honor.

By promoting this superstition, the State is playing into the hands of the principle of knightly honor, and therefore of the duel; while at the same time it is trying, or at any rate it pretends it is trying, to abolish the duel by legislative enactment. As a natural consequence we find that this fragment of the theory that might is right, which has come down to us from the most savage days of the Middle Age, has still in this nineteenth century a good deal of life left in it—more shame to us! It is high time for the principle to be driven out bag and baggage. Now-a-days no one is allowed to set dogs or cocks to fight each other,—at any rate, in England it is a penal offence,—but men are plunged into deadly strife, against their will, by the operation of this ridiculous, superstitious and absurd principle, which imposes upon us the obligation, as its narrow-minded supporters and advocates declare, of fighting with one another like gladiators, for any little trifle. Let me recommend our purists to adopt the expression baiting[23] instead of duel, which probably comes to us, not from the Latin duellum, but from the Spanish duelo,—meaning suffering, nuisance, annoyance.

In any case, we may well laugh at the pedantic excess to which this foolish system has been carried. It is really revolting that this principle, with its absurd code, can form a power within the State—imperium in imperio—a power too easily put in motion, which, recognizing no right but might, tyrannizes over the classes which come within its range, by keeping up a sort of inquisition, before which any one may be haled on the most flimsy pretext, and there and then be tried on an issue of life and death between himself and his opponent. This is the lurking place from which every rascal, if he only belongs to the classes in question, may menace and even exterminate the noblest and best of men, who, as such, must of course be an object of hatred to him. Our system of justice and police-protection has made it impossible in these days for any scoundrel in the street to attack us with—Your money or your life! An end should be put to the burden which weighs upon the higher classes—the burden, I mean, of having to be ready every moment to expose life and limb to the mercy of anyone who takes it into his rascally head to be coarse, rude, foolish or malicious. It is perfectly atrocious that a pair of silly, passionate boys should be wounded, maimed or even killed, simply because they have had a few words.

The strength of this tyrannical power within the State, and the force of the superstition, may be measured by the fact that people who are prevented from restoring their knightly honor by the superior or inferior rank of their aggressor, or anything else that puts the persons on a different level, often come to a tragic-comic end by committing suicide in sheer despair. You may generally know a thing to be false and ridiculous by finding that, if it is carried to its logical conclusion, it results in a contradiction; and here, too, we have a very glaring absurdity. For an officer is forbidden to take part in a duel; but if he is challenged and declines to come out, he is punished by being dismissed the service.

As I am on the matter, let me be more frank still. The important distinction, which is often insisted upon, between killing your enemy in a fair fight with equal weapons, and lying in ambush for him, is entirely a corollary of the fact that the power within the State, of which I have spoken, recognizes no other right than might, that is, the right of the stronger, and appeals to a Judgment of God as the basis of the whole code. For to kill a man in a fair fight, is to prove that you are superior to him in strength or skill; and to justify the deed, you must assume that the right of the stronger is really a right.

But the truth is that, if my opponent is unable to defend himself, it gives me the possibility, but not by any means the right, of killing him. The right, the moral justification, must depend entirely upon the motives which I have for taking his life. Even supposing that I have sufficient motive for taking a man's life, there is no reason why I should make his death depend upon whether I can shoot or fence better than he. In such a case, it is immaterial in what way I kill him, whether I attack him from the front or the rear. From a moral point of view, the right of the stronger is no more convincing than the right of the more skillful; and it is skill which is employed if you murder a a man treacherously. Might and skill are in this case equally right; in a duel, for instance, both the one and the other come into play; for a feint is only another name for treachery. If I consider myself morally justified in taking a man's life, it is stupid of me to try first of all whether he can shoot or fence better than I; as, if he can, he will not only have wronged me, but have taken my life into the bargain.

It is Rousseau's opinion that the proper way to avenge an insult is, not to fight a duel with your aggressor, but to assassinate him,—an opinion, however, which he is cautious enough only to barely indicate in a mysterious note to one of the books of his Emile. This shows the philosopher so completely under the influence of the mediaeval superstition of knightly honor that he considers it justifiable to murder a man who accuses you of lying: whilst he must have known that every man, and himself especially, has deserved to have the lie given him times without number.

The prejudice which justifies the killing of your adversary, so long as it is done in an open contest and with equal weapons, obviously looks upon might as really right, and a duel as the interference of God. The Italian who, in a fit of rage, falls upon his aggressor wherever he finds him, and despatches him without any ceremony, acts, at any rate, consistently and naturally: he may be cleverer, but he is not worse, than the duelist. If you say, I am justified in killing my adversary in a duel, because he is at the moment doing his best to kill me; I can reply that it is your challenge which has placed him under the necessity of defending himself; and that by mutually putting it on the ground of self-defence, the combatants are seeking a plausible pretext for committing murder. I should rather justify the deed by the legal maxim Volenti non fit injuria; because the parties mutually agree to set their life upon the issue.

This argument may, however, be rebutted by showing that the injured party is not injured volens; because it is this tyrannical principle of knightly honor, with its absurd code, which forcibly drags one at least of the combatants before a bloody inquisition.

I have been rather prolix on the subject of knightly honor, but I had good reason for being so, because the Augean stable of moral and intellectual enormity in this world can be cleaned out only with the besom of philosophy. There are two things which more than all else serve to make the social arrangements of modern life compare unfavorably with those of antiquity, by giving our age a gloomy, dark and sinister aspect, from which antiquity, fresh, natural and, as it were, in the morning of life, is completely free; I mean modern honor and modern disease,—par nobile fratrum!—which have combined to poison all the relations of life, whether public or private. The second of this noble pair extends its influence much farther than at first appears to be the case, as being not merely a physical, but also a moral disease. From the time that poisoned arrows have been found in Cupid's quiver, an estranging, hostile, nay, devilish element has entered into the relations of men and women, like a sinister thread of fear and mistrust in the warp and woof of their intercourse; indirectly shaking the foundations of human fellowship, and so more or less affecting the whole tenor of existence. But it would be beside my present purpose to pursue the subject further.

An influence analogous to this, though working on other lines, is exerted by the principle of knightly honor,—that solemn farce, unknown to the ancient world, which makes modern society stiff, gloomy and timid, forcing us to keep the strictest watch on every word that falls. Nor is this all. The principle is a universal Minotaur; and the goodly company of the sons of noble houses which it demands in yearly tribute, comes, not from one country alone, as of old, but from every land in Europe. It is high time to make a regular attack upon this foolish system; and this is what I am trying to do now. Would that these two monsters of the modern world might disappear before the end of the century!

Let us hope that medicine may be able to find some means of preventing the one, and that, by clearing our ideals, philosophy may put an end to the other: for it is only by clearing our ideas that the evil can be eradicated. Governments have tried to do so by legislation, and failed.

Still, if they are really concerned to stop the dueling system; and if the small success that has attended their efforts is really due only to their inability to cope with the evil, I do not mind proposing a law the success of which I am prepared to guarantee. It will involve no sanguinary measures, and can be put into operation without recourse either to the scaffold or the gallows, or to imprisonment for life. It is a small homeopathic pilule, with no serious after effects. If any man send or accept a challenge, let the corporal take him before the guard house, and there give him, in broad daylight, twelve strokes with a stick a la Chinoise; a non-commissioned officer or a private to receive six. If a duel has actually taken place, the usual criminal proceedings should be instituted.

A person with knightly notions might, perhaps, object that, if such a punishment were carried out, a man of honor would possibly shoot himself; to which I should answer that it is better for a fool like that to shoot himself rather than other people. However, I know very well that governments are not really in earnest about putting down dueling. Civil officials, and much more so, officers in the army, (except those in the highest positions), are paid most inadequately for the services they perform; and the deficiency is made up by honor, which is represented by titles and orders, and, in general, by the system of rank and distinction. The duel is, so to speak, a very serviceable extra-horse for people of rank: so they are trained in the knowledge of it at the universities. The accidents which happen to those who use it make up in blood for the deficiency of the pay.

Just to complete the discussion, let me here mention the subject of national honor. It is the honor of a nation as a unit in the aggregate of nations. And as there is no court to appeal to but the court of force; and as every nation must be prepared to defend its own interests, the honor of a nation consists in establishing the opinion, not only that it may be trusted (its credit), but also that it is to be feared. An attack upon its rights must never be allowed to pass unheeded. It is a combination of civic and knightly honor.

Section 5. - Fame

Under the heading of place in the estimation of the world we have put Fame; and this we must now proceed to consider.

Fame and honor are twins; and twins, too, like Castor and Pollux, of whom the one was mortal and the other was not. Fame is the undying brother of ephemeral honor. I speak, of course, of the highest kind of fame, that is, of fame in the true and genuine sense of the word; for, to be sure, there are many sorts of fame, some of which last but a day. Honor is concerned merely with such qualities as everyone may be expected to show under similar circumstances; fame only of those which cannot be required of any man. Honor is of qualities which everyone has a right to attribute to himself; fame only of those which should be left to others to attribute. Whilst our honor extends as far as people have knowledge of us; fame runs in advance, and makes us known wherever it finds its way. Everyone can make a claim to honor; very few to fame, as being attainable only in virtue of extraordinary achievements.

These achievements may be of two kinds, either actions or works; and so to fame there are two paths open. On the path of actions, a great heart is the chief recommendation; on that of works, a great head. Each of the two paths has its own peculiar advantages and detriments; and the chief difference between them is that actions are fleeting, while works remain. The influence of an action, be it never so noble, can last but a short time; but a work of genius is a living influence, beneficial and ennobling

52

throughout the ages. All that can remain of actions is a memory, and that becomes weak and disfigured by time—a matter of indifference to us, until at last it is extinguished altogether; unless, indeed, history takes it up, and presents it, fossilized, to posterity. Works are immortal in themselves, and once committed to writing, may live for ever. Of Alexander the Great we have but the name and the record; but Plato and Aristotle, Homer and Horace are alive, and as directly at work to-day as they were in their own lifetime. The Vedas, and their Upanishads, are still with us: but of all contemporaneous actions not a trace has come down to us.[24]

Another disadvantage under which actions labor is that they depend upon chance for the possibility of coming into existence; and hence, the fame they win does not flow entirely from their intrinsic value, but also from the circumstances which happened to lend them importance and lustre. Again, the fame of actions, if, as in war, they are purely personal, depends upon the testimony of fewer witnesses; and these are not always present, and even if present, are not always just or unbiased observers. This disadvantage, however, is counterbalanced by the fact that actions have the advantage of being of a practical character, and, therefore, within the range of general human intelligence; so that once the facts have been correctly reported, justice is immediately done; unless, indeed, the motive underlying the action is not at first properly understood or appreciated. No action can be really understood apart from the motive which prompted it.

It is just the contrary with works. Their inception does not depend upon chance, but wholly and entirely upon their author; and whoever they are in and for themselves, that they remain as long as they live. Further, there is a difficulty in properly judging them, which becomes all the harder, the higher their character; often there are no persons competent to understand the work, and often no unbiased or honest critics. Their fame, however, does not depend upon one judge only; they can enter an appeal to another. In the case of actions, as I have said, it is only their memory which comes down to posterity, and then only in the traditional form; but works are handed down themselves, and, except when parts of them have been lost, in the form in which they first appeared. In this case there is no room for any disfigurement of the facts; and any circumstance which may have prejudiced them in their origin, fall away with the lapse of time. Nay, it is often only after the lapse of time that the persons really competent to judge them appear—exceptional critics sitting in judgment on exceptional works, and giving their weighty verdicts in succession. These collectively form a perfectly just appreciation; and though there are cases where it has taken some hundreds of years to form it, no further lapse of time is able to reverse the verdict;—so secure and inevitable is the fame of a great work.

Whether authors ever live to see the dawn of their fame depends upon the chance of circumstance; and the higher and more important their works are, the less likelihood there is of their doing so. That was an incomparable fine saying of Seneca's, that fame follows merit as surely as the body casts a shadow; sometimes falling in front, and sometimes behind. And he goes on to remark that though the envy of contemporaries be shown by universal silence, there will come those who will judge without enmity or favor. From this remark it is manifest that even in Seneca's age there were rascals who understood the art of suppressing merit by maliciously ignoring its existence, and of concealing good work from the public in order to favor the bad: it is an art well understood in our day, too, manifesting itself, both then and now, in an envious conspiracy of silence.

53

As a general rule, the longer a man's fame is likely to last, the later it will be in coming; for all excellent products require time for their development. The fame which lasts to posterity is like an oak, of very slow growth; and that which endures but a little while, like plants which spring up in a year and then die; whilst false fame is like a fungus, shooting up in a night and perishing as soon.

And why? For this reason; the more a man belongs to posterity, in other words, to humanity in general, the more of an alien he is to his contemporaries; since his work is not meant for them as such, but only for them in so far as they form part of mankind at large; there is none of that familiar local color about his productions which would appeal to them; and so what he does, fails of recognition because it is strange.

People are more likely to appreciate the man who serves the circumstances of his own brief hour, or the temper of the moment,—belonging to it, living and dying with it.

The general history of art and literature shows that the highest achievements of the human mind are, as a rule, not favorably received at first; but remain in obscurity until they win notice from intelligence of a high order, by whose influence they are brought into a position which they then maintain, in virtue of the authority thus given them.

If the reason of this should be asked, it will be found that ultimately, a man can really understand and appreciate those things only which are of like nature with himself. The dull person will like what is dull, and the common person what is common; a man whose ideas are mixed will be attracted by confusion of thought; and folly will appeal to him who has no brains at all; but best of all, a man will like his own works, as being of a character thoroughly at one with himself. This is a truth as old as Epicharmus of fabulous memory—

[Greek: Thaumaston ouden esti me tauth outo legein
Kal andanein autoisin autous kal dokein
Kalos pethukenai kal gar ho kuon kuni
Kalloton eimen phainetai koi bous boi
Onos dono kalliston [estin], us dut.]

The sense of this passage—for it should not be lost—is that we should not be surprised if people are pleased with themselves, and fancy that they are in good case; for to a dog the best thing in the world is a dog; to an ox, an ox; to an ass, an ass; and to a sow, a sow.

The strongest arm is unavailing to give impetus to a featherweight; for, instead of speeding on its way and hitting its mark with effect, it will soon fall to the ground, having expended what little energy was given to it, and possessing no mass of its own to be the vehicle of momentum. So it is with great and noble thoughts, nay, with the very masterpieces of genius, when there are none but little, weak, and perverse minds to appreciate them,—a fact which has been deplored by a chorus of the wise in all ages. Jesus, the son of Sirach, for instance, declares that He that telleth a tale to a fool speaketh to one in slumber: when he hath told his tale, he will say, What is the matter?[25] And Hamlet says, A knavish speech sleeps in a fool's ear.[26] And Goethe is of the same opinion, that a dull ear mocks at the wisest word,

Das glücktichste Wort es wird verhöhnt, Wenn der Hörer ein Schiefohr ist:

and again, that we should not be discouraged if people are stupid, for you can make no rings if you throw your stone into a marsh.

Du iwirkest nicht, Alles bleibt so stumpf:
  Sei guter Dinge!
Der Stein in Sumpf
  Macht keine Ringe.

Lichtenberg asks: When a head and a book come into collision, and one sounds hollow, is it always the book? And in another place: Works like this are as a mirror; if an ass looks in, you cannot expect an apostle to look out. We should do well to remember old Gellert's fine and touching lament, that the best gifts of all find the fewest admirers, and that most men mistake the bad for the good,—a daily evil that nothing can prevent, like a plague which no remedy can cure. There is but one thing to be done, though how difficult!—the foolish must become wise,—and that they can never be. The value of life they never know; they see with the outer eye but never with the mind, and praise the trivial because the good is strange to them:—

Nie kennen sie den Werth der Dinge,
  Ihr Auge schliesst, nicht ihr Verstand;
Sie loben ewig das Geringe
  Weil sie das Gute nie gekannt.

To the intellectual incapacity which, as Goethe says, fails to recognize and appreciate the good which exists, must be added something which comes into play everywhere, the moral baseness of mankind, here taking the form of envy. The new fame that a man wins raises him afresh over the heads of his fellows, who are thus degraded in proportion. All conspicuous merit is obtained at the cost of those who possess none; or, as Goethe has it in the Westöstlicher Divan, another's praise is one's own depreciation—

Wenn wir Andern Ehre geben Müssen wir uns selbst entadeln.

We see, then, how it is that, whatever be the form which excellence takes, mediocrity, the common lot of by far the greatest number, is leagued against it in a conspiracy to resist, and if possible, to suppress it. The pass-word of this league is à bas le mérite. Nay more; those who have done something themselves, and enjoy a certain amount of fame, do not care about the appearance of a new reputation, because its success is apt to throw theirs into the shade. Hence, Goethe declares that if we had to depend for our life upon the favor of others, we should never have lived at all; from their desire to appear important themselves, people gladly ignore our very existence:—

Hätte ich gezaudert zu werden,
  Bis man mir's Leben geögnut,
Ich wäre noch nicht auf Erden,
  Wie ihr begreifen könnt,
Wenn ihr seht, wie sie sich geberden,
  Die, um etwas zu scheinen,
  Mich gerne mochten verneinen.

Honor, on the contrary, generally meets with fair appreciation, and is not exposed to the onslaught of envy; nay, every man is credited with the possession of it until the contrary is proved. But fame has to be won in despite of envy, and the tribunal which awards the laurel is composed of judges biased against the applicant from the very first. Honor is something which we are able and ready to share with everyone; fame suffers encroachment and is rendered more unattainable in proportion as more people come by it. Further, the difficulty of winning fame by any given work stands in reverse ratio to the number of people who are likely to read it; and hence it is so much harder to become famous as the author of a learned work than as a writer who aspires only to amuse. It is hardest of all in the case of philosophical works, because the result at which they aim is rather vague, and, at the same time, useless from a material point of view; they appeal chiefly to readers who are working on the same lines themselves.

It is clear, then, from what I have said as to the difficulty of winning fame, that those who labor, not out of love for their subject, nor from pleasure in pursuing it, but under the stimulus of ambition, rarely or never leave mankind a legacy of immortal works. The man who seeks to do what is good and genuine, must avoid what is bad, and be ready to defy the opinions of the mob, nay, even to despise it and its misleaders. Hence the truth of the remark, (especially insisted upon by Osorius de Gloria), that fame shuns those who seek it, and seeks those who shun it; for the one adapt themselves to the taste of their contemporaries, and the others work in defiance of it.

But, difficult though it be to acquire fame, it is an easy thing to keep when once acquired. Here, again, fame is in direct opposition to honor, with which everyone is presumably to be accredited. Honor has not to be won; it must only not be lost. But there lies the difficulty! For by a single unworthy action, it is gone irretrievably. But fame, in the proper sense of the word, can never disappear; for the action or work by which it was acquired can never be undone; and fame attaches to its author, even though he does nothing to deserve it anew. The fame which vanishes, or is outlived, proves itself thereby to be spurious, in other words, unmerited, and due to a momentary overestimate of a man's work; not to speak of the kind of fame which Hegel enjoyed, and which Lichtenberg describes as trumpeted forth by a clique of admiring undergraduates—the resounding echo of empty heads;—such a fame as will make posterity smile when it lights upon a grotesque architecture of words, a fine nest with the birds long ago flown; it will knock at the door of this decayed structure of conventionalities and find it utterly empty!—not even a trace of thought there to invite the passer-by.

The truth is that fame means nothing but what a man is in comparison with others. It is essentially relative in character, and therefore only indirectly valuable; for it vanishes the moment other people become what the famous man is. Absolute value can be predicated only of what a man possesses under any and all circumstances,—here, what a man is directly and in himself. It is the possession of a great heart or a great head, and not the mere fame of it, which is worth having, and conducive to happiness. Not fame, but that which deserves to be famous, is what a man should hold in esteem. This is, as it were, the true underlying substance, and fame is only an accident, affecting its subject chiefly as a kind of external symptom, which serves to confirm his own opinion of himself. Light is not visible unless it meets with something to reflect it; and talent is sure of itself only when its fame is noised abroad. But fame is not a certain symptom of merit; because you can have the one without the other; or, as Lessing nicely puts it, Some people obtain fame, and others deserve it.

It would be a miserable existence which should make its value or want of value depend upon what other people think; but such would be the life of a hero or a genius if its worth consisted in fame, that is, in the applause of the world. Every man lives and exists on his own account, and, therefore, mainly in and for himself; and what he is and the whole manner of his being concern himself more than anyone else; so if he is not worth much in this respect, he cannot be worth much otherwise. The idea which other people form of his existence is something secondary, derivative, exposed to all the chances of fate, and in the end affecting him but very indirectly. Besides, other people's heads are a wretched place to be the home of a man's true happiness—a fanciful happiness perhaps, but not a real one.

And what a mixed company inhabits the Temple of Universal Fame!—generals, ministers, charlatans, jugglers, dancers, singers, millionaires and Jews! It is a temple in which more sincere recognition, more genuine esteem, is given to the several excellencies of such folk, than to superiority of mind, even of a high order, which obtains from the great majority only a verbal acknowledgment.

From the point of view of human happiness, fame is, surely, nothing but a very rare and delicate morsel for the appetite that feeds on pride and vanity—an appetite which, however carefully concealed, exists to an immoderate degree in every man, and is, perhaps strongest of all in those who set their hearts on becoming famous at any cost. Such people generally have to wait some time in uncertainty as to their own value, before the opportunity comes which will put it to the proof and let other people see what they are made of; but until then, they feel as if they were suffering secret injustice.[27]

But, as I explained at the beginning of this chapter, an unreasonable value is set upon other people's opinion, and one quite disproportionate to its real worth. Hobbes has some strong remarks on this subject; and no doubt he is quite right. Mental pleasure, he writes, and ecstacy of any kind, arise when, on comparing ourselves with others, we come to the conclusion that we may think well of ourselves. So we can easily understand the great value which is always attached to fame, as worth any sacrifices if there is the slightest hope of attaining it.

Fame is the spur that the clear spirit doth raise (That hath infirmity of noble mind)
To scorn delights and live laborious days[28]

And again:

How hard it is to climb The heights where Fame's proud temple shines afar!

We can thus understand how it is that the vainest people in the world are always talking about la gloire, with the most implicit faith in it as a stimulus to great actions and great works. But there can he no doubt that fame is something secondary in its character, a mere echo or reflection—as it were, a shadow or symptom—of merit: and, in any case, what excites admiration must be of more value than the admiration itself. The truth is that a man is made happy, not by fame, but by that which brings him fame, by his merits, or to speak more correctly, by the disposition and capacity from which his merits proceed, whether they be moral or intellectual. The best side of a man's nature must of necessity be more important for him than for anyone else: the reflection of it, the opinion which exists in the heads of others, is a matter that can affect him only in a very subordinate degree. He who deserves fame without getting it possesses by far the more important element of happiness, which should console him for the loss of the other. It is not that a man is thought to be great by masses of incompetent and often infatuated people, but that he really is great, which should

57

move us to envy his position; and his happiness lies, not in the fact that posterity will hear of him, but that he is the creator of thoughts worthy to be treasured up and studied for hundreds of years.

Besides, if a man has done this, he possesses something which cannot be wrested from him; and, unlike fame, it is a possession dependent entirely upon himself. If admiration were his chief aim, there would be nothing in him to admire. This is just what happens in the case of false, that is, unmerited, fame; for its recipient lives upon it without actually possessing the solid substratum of which fame is the outward and visible sign. False fame must often put its possessor out of conceit with himself; for the time may come when, in spite of the illusions borne of self-love, he will feel giddy on the heights which he was never meant to climb, or look upon himself as spurious coin; and in the anguish of threatened discovery and well-merited degradation, he will read the sentence of posterity on the foreheads of the wise—like a man who owes his property to a forged will. The truest fame, the fame that comes after death, is never heard of by its recipient; and yet he is called a happy man.

His happiness lay both in the possession of those great qualities which won him fame, and in the opportunity that was granted him of developing them—the leisure he had to act as he pleased, to dedicate himself to his favorite pursuits. It is only work done from the heart that ever gains the laurel.

Greatness of soul, or wealth of intellect, is what makes a man happy—intellect, such as, when stamped on its productions, will receive the admiration of centuries to come,—thoughts which make him happy at the time, and will in their turn be a source of study and delight to the noblest minds of the most remote posterity. The value of posthumous fame lies in deserving it; and this is its own reward. Whether works destined to fame attain it in the lifetime of their author is a chance affair, of no very great importance. For the average man has no critical power of his own, and is absolutely incapable of appreciating the difficulty of a great work. People are always swayed by authority; and where fame is widespread, it means that ninety-nine out of a hundred take it on faith alone. If a man is famed far and wide in his own lifetime, he will, if he is wise, not set too much value upon it, because it is no more than the echo of a few voices, which the chance of a day has touched in his favor.

Would a musician feel flattered by the loud applause of an audience if he knew that they were nearly all deaf, and that, to conceal their infirmity, they set to work to clap vigorously as soon as ever they saw one or two persons applauding? And what would he say if he got to know that those one or two persons had often taken bribes to secure the loudest applause for the poorest player!

It is easy to see why contemporary praise so seldom develops into posthumous fame. D'Alembert, in an extremely fine description of the temple of literary fame, remarks that the sanctuary of the temple is inhabited by the great dead, who during their life had no place there, and by a very few living persons, who are nearly all ejected on their death. Let me remark, in passing, that to erect a monument to a man in his lifetime is as much as declaring that posterity is not to be trusted in its judgment of him. If a man does happen to see his own true fame, it can very rarely be before he is old, though there have been artists and musicians who have been exceptions to this rule, but very few philosophers. This is confirmed by the portraits of people celebrated by their works; for most of them are taken only after their subjects have attained celebrity, generally depicting them as old and grey; more especially if philosophy has been the work of their lives. From the eudaemonistic standpoint, this

58

is a very proper arrangement; as fame and youth are too much for a mortal at one and the same time. Life is such a poor business that the strictest economy must be exercised in its good things. Youth has enough and to spare in itself, and must rest content with what it has. But when the delights and joys of life fall away in old age, as the leaves from a tree in autumn, fame buds forth opportunely, like a plant that is green in winter. Fame is, as it were, the fruit that must grow all the summer before it can be enjoyed at Yule. There is no greater consolation in age than the feeling of having put the whole force of one's youth into works which still remain young.

Finally, let us examine a little more closely the kinds of fame which attach to various intellectual pursuits; for it is with fame of this sort that my remarks are more immediately concerned.

I think it may be said broadly that the intellectual superiority it denotes consists in forming theories, that is, new combinations of certain facts. These facts may be of very different kinds; but the better they are known, and the more they come within everyday experience, the greater and wider will be the fame which is to be won by theorizing about them.

For instance, if the facts in question are numbers or lines or special branches of science, such as physics, zoology, botany, anatomy, or corrupt passages in ancient authors, or undecipherable inscriptions, written, it may be, in some unknown alphabet, or obscure points in history; the kind of fame that may be obtained by correctly manipulating such facts will not extend much beyond those who make a study of them—a small number of persons, most of whom live retired lives and are envious of others who become famous in their special branch of knowledge.

But if the facts be such as are known to everyone, for example, the fundamental characteristics of the human mind or the human heart, which are shared by all alike; or the great physical agencies which are constantly in operation before our eyes, or the general course of natural laws; the kind of fame which is to be won by spreading the light of a new and manifestly true theory in regard to them, is such as in time will extend almost all over the civilized world: for if the facts be such as everyone can grasp, the theory also will be generally intelligible. But the extent of the fame will depend upon the difficulties overcome; and the more generally known the facts are, the harder it will be to form a theory that shall be both new and true: because a great many heads will have been occupied with them, and there will be little or no possibility of saying anything that has not been said before.

On the other hand, facts which are not accessible to everybody, and can be got at only after much difficulty and labor, nearly always admit of new combinations and theories; so that, if sound understanding and judgment are brought to bear upon them—qualities which do not involve very high intellectual power—a man may easily be so fortunate as to light upon some new theory in regard to them which shall be also true. But fame won on such paths does not extend much beyond those who possess a knowledge of the facts in question. To solve problems of this sort requires, no doubt, a great ideal of study and labor, if only to get at the facts; whilst on the path where the greatest and most widespread fame is to be won, the facts may be grasped without any labor at all. But just in proportion as less labor is necessary, more talent or genius is required; and between such qualities and the drudgery of research no comparison is possible, in respect either of their intrinsic value, or of the estimation in which they are held.

And so people who feel that they possess solid intellectual capacity and a sound judgment, and yet cannot claim the highest mental powers, should not be afraid of laborious study; for by its aid they may work themselves above the great mob of humanity who have the facts constantly before their eyes, and reach those secluded spots which are accessible to learned toil.

For this is a sphere where there are infinitely fewer rivals, and a man of only moderate capacity may soon find an opportunity of proclaiming a theory which shall be both new and true; nay, the merit of his discovery will partly rest upon the difficulty of coming at the facts. But applause from one's fellow-students, who are the only persons with a knowledge of the subject, sounds very faint to the far-off multitude. And if we follow up this sort of fame far enough, we shall at last come to a point where facts very difficult to get at are in themselves sufficient to lay a foundation of fame, without any necessity for forming a theory;—travels, for instance, in remote and little-known countries, which make a man famous by what he has seen, not by what he has thought. The great advantage of this kind of fame is that to relate what one has seen, is much easier than to impart one's thoughts, and people are apt to understand descriptions better than ideas, reading the one more readily than the other: for, as Asmus says,

When one goes forth a-voyaging He has a tale to tell.

And yet for all that, a personal acquaintance with celebrated travelers often remind us of a line from Horace—new scenes do not always mean new ideas—

Caelum non animum mutant qui trans mare currunt.[29]

But if a man finds himself in possession of great mental faculties, such as alone should venture on the solution of the hardest of all problems—those which concern nature as a whole and humanity in its widest range, he will do well to extend his view equally in all directions, without ever straying too far amid the intricacies of various by-paths, or invading regions little known; in other words, without occupying himself with special branches of knowledge, to say nothing of their petty details. There is no necessity for him to seek out subjects difficult of access, in order to escape a crowd of rivals; the common objects of life will give him material for new theories at once serious and true; and the service he renders will be appreciated by all those—and they form a great part of mankind—who know the facts of which he treats. What a vast distinction there is between students of physics, chemistry, anatomy, mineralogy, zoology, philology, history, and the men who deal with the great facts of human life, the poet and the philosopher!

[1: Horace, Epist: II., 1, 180.]

[2: Let me remark that people in the highest positions in life, with all their brilliance, pomp, display, magnificence and general show, may well say:—Our happiness lies entirely outside us; for it exists only in the heads of others.]

[3: Scire tuum nihil est nisi te scire hoc sciat alter, (Persins i, 27)—knowledge is no use unless others know that you have it.]

[4: Hist., iv., 6.]

[5: Translator's Note.—It should be remembered that these remarks were written in the earlier part of the present century, and that a German philosopher now-a-days, even though he were as apt to say bitter things as Schopenhauer, could hardly write in a similar strain.]

[6: De finilus iii., 17.]

[7: Disc: iii. 17.]

[8: Heroditus, i. 199.]

[10: De Constantia, 11.]

[11: See C.G. von Waehter's Beiträge zur deutschen Geschichte, especially the chapter on criminal law.]

[12: Translator's Note.—It is true that this expression has another special meaning in the technical terminology of Chivalry, but it is the nearest English equivalent which I can find for the German—ein Bescholtener]

[13: Translator's Note. It must be remembered that Schopenhauer is here describing, or perhaps caricaturing the manners and customs of the German aristocracy of half a century ago. Now, of course, nous avons change tout cela!]

[14: Translator's Note. These and other remarks on dueling will no doubt wear a belated look to English readers; but they are hardly yet antiquated for most parts of the Continent.]

[15:litteraires: par C. Durand. Rouen, 1828.]

[16: Bk. IX.].

[17: Diogenes Laertius, ii., 21.]

[18: Ibid 36.]

[19: Diogenes Laertius, vi. 87, and Apul: Flor: p. 126.]

[20: Cf. Casaubon's Note, Diog. Laert., vi. 33.]

[21: Translator's Note. The story to which Schopenhauer here refers is briefly as follows: Two gentlemen, one of whom was named Desglands, were paying court to the same lady. As they sat at table side by side, with the lady opposite, Desglands did his best to charm her with his conversation; but she pretended not to hear him, and kept looking at his rival. In the agony of jealousy, Desglands, as he was holding a fresh egg in his hand, involuntarily crushed it; the shell broke, and its contents bespattered his rival's face. Seeing him raise his hand, Desglands seized it and whispered: Sir, I take it as given. The next day Desglands appeared with a large piece of black sticking-plaster upon his right cheek. In the duel which followed, Desglands severely wounded his rival; upon which he reduced the size of the plaster. When his rival recovered, they had another duel; Desglands drew blood again, and again made his plaster a little smaller; and so on for five or six times. After every duel Desglands' plaster grew less and less, until at last his rival.]

[Note 22: Knightly honor is the child of pride and folly, and it is needy not pride, which is the heritage of the human race. It is a very remarkable fact that this extreme form of pride should be found exclusively amongst the adherents of the religion which teaches the deepest humility. Still, this pride must not be put down to religion, but, rather, to the feudal system, which made every nobleman a petty sovereign who recognized no human judge, and learned to regard his person as sacred and inviolable, and any attack upon it, or any blow or insulting word, as an offence punishable with death. The principle of knightly honor and of the duel were at first confined to the nobles, and, later on, also to officers in the army, who, enjoying a kind of off-and-on relationship with the upper classes, though they were never incorporated with them, were anxious not to be behind them. It is true that duels were the product of the old ordeals; but the latter are not the foundation, but rather the consequence and application of the principle of honor: the man who recognized no human judge appealed to the divine. Ordeals, however, are not peculiar to Christendom: they may be found in great force among the Hindoos, especially of ancient times; and there are traces of them even now.]

[23: Ritterhetze]

[24: Accordingly it is a poor compliment, though sometimes a fashionable one, to try to pay honor to a work by calling it an action. For a work is something essentially higher in its nature. An action is always something based on motive, and, therefore, fragmentary and fleeting—a part, in fact, of that Will which is the universal and original element in the constitution of the world. But a great and beautiful work has a permanent character, as being of universal significance, and sprung from the Intellect, which rises, like a perfume, above the faults and follies of the world of Will.

The fame of a great action has this advantage, that it generally starts with a loud explosion; so loud, indeed, as to be heard all over Europe: whereas the fame of a great work is slow and gradual in its beginnings; the noise it makes is at first slight, but it goes on growing greater, until at last, after a hundred years perhaps, it attains its full force; but then it remains, because the works remain, for thousands of years. But in the other case, when the first explosion is over, the noise it makes grows less and less, and is heard by fewer and fewer persons; until it ends by the action having only a shadowy existence in the pages of history.]   [25: Ecclesiasticus, xxii., 8.]

[26: Act iv., Sc. 2.]

[27: Our greatest pleasure consists in being admired; but those who admire us, even if they have every reason to do so, are slow to express their sentiments. Hence he is the happiest man who, no matter how, manages sincerely to admire himself—so long as other people leave him alone.]

[28: Milton. Lycidas.]

[29: Epist. I. II.]

Counsels and Maxims

Translator's Note

For convenience of publication, I have divided this translation of Schopenhauer's Aphorismen zur Lebensweisheit into two parts; and for the sake of appearances, a new series of chapters has been begun in the present volume. But it should be understood that there is no such division in the original and that The Wisdom of Life and Counsels and Maxims form a single treatise, devoted to a popular exposition of the author's views on matters of practice. To the former volume I have prefixed some remarks which may help the reader to appreciate the value of Schopenhauer's teaching, and to determine its relation to certain well-known theories of life.

T. B. S.

Introduction

If my object in these pages were to present a complete scheme of counsels and maxims for the guidance of life, I should have to repeat the numerous rules—some of them excellent—which have been drawn up by thinkers of all ages, from Theognis and Solomon[1] down to La Rochefoucauld; and, in so doing, I should inevitably entail upon the reader a vast amount of well-worn commonplace. But the fact is that in this work I make still less claim to exhaust my subject than in any other of my writings.

An author who makes no claims to completeness must also, in a great measure, abandon any attempt at systematic arrangement. For his double loss in this respect, the reader may console himself by reflecting that a complete and systematic treatment of such a subject as the guidance of life could hardly fail to be a very wearisome business. I have simply put down those of my thoughts which appear to be worth communicating—thoughts which, as far as I know, have not been uttered, or, at any rate, not just in the same form, by any one else; so that my remarks may be taken as a supplement to what has been already achieved in the immense field.

However, by way of introducing some sort of order into the great variety of matters upon which advice will be given in the following pages, I shall distribute what I have to say under the following heads: (1) general rules; (2) our relation to ourselves; (3) our relation to others; and finally, (4) rules which concern our manner of life and our worldly circumstances. I shall conclude with some remarks on the changes which the various periods of life produce in us.

General Rules

The first and foremost rule for the wise conduct of life seems to me to be contained in a view to which Aristotle parenthetically refers in the Nichomachean Ethics:[1] [Greek: o phronimoz to alupon dioke e ou to aedu] or, as it may be rendered, not pleasure, but freedom from pain, is what the wise man will aim at.

The truth of this remark turns upon the negative character of happiness,—the fact that pleasure is only the negation of pain, and that pain is the positive element in life. Though I have given a detailed proof of this proposition in my chief work,[2] I may supply one more illustration of it here, drawn from a circumstance of daily occurrence. Suppose that, with the exception of some sore or painful spot, we are physically in a sound and healthy condition: the sore of this one spot, will completely absorb our attention, causing us to lose the sense of general well-being, and destroying all our comfort in life. In the same way, when all our affairs but one turn out as we wish, the single instance in which our aims are frustrated is a constant trouble to us, even though it be something quite trivial. We think a great deal about it, and very little about those other and more important matters in which we have been successful. In both these cases what has met with resistance is the will; in the one case, as it is objectified in the organism, in the other, as it presents itself in the struggle of life; and in both, it is plain that the satisfaction of the will consists in nothing else than that it meets with no resistance. It is, therefore, a satisfaction which is not directly felt; at most, we can become conscious of it only when we reflect upon our condition. But that which checks or arrests the will is something positive; it proclaims its own presence. All pleasure consists in merely removing this check—in other words, in freeing us from its action; and hence pleasure is a state which can never last very long.

This is the true basis of the above excellent rule quoted from Aristotle, which bids us direct our aim, not toward securing what is pleasurable and agreeable in life, but toward avoiding, as far as possible, its innumerable evils. If this were not the right course to take, that saying of Voltaire's, Happiness is but a dream and sorrow is real, would be as false as it is, in fact, true. A man who desires to make up the book of his life and determine where the balance of happiness lies, must put down in his accounts, not the pleasures which he has enjoyed, but the evils which he has escaped. That is the true method of eudaemonology; for all eudaemonology must begin by recognizing that its very name is a euphemism, and that to live happily only means to live less unhappily—to live a tolerable life. There is no doubt that life is given us, not to be enjoyed, but to be overcome—to be got over. There are numerous expressions illustrating this—such as degere vitam, vita defungi; or in Italian, si scampa cosi; or in German, man muss suchen durchzukommen; er wird schon durch die Welt kommen, and so on. In old age it is indeed a consolation to think that the work of life is over and done with. The happiest lot is not to have experienced the keenest delights or the greatest pleasures, but to have brought life to a close without any very great pain,

64

bodily or mental. To measure the happiness of a life by its delights or pleasures, is to apply a false standard. For pleasures are and remain something negative; that they produce happiness is a delusion, cherished by envy to its own punishment. Pain is felt to be something positive, and hence its absence is the true standard of happiness. And if, over and above freedom from pain, there is also an absence of boredom, the essential conditions of earthly happiness are attained; for all else is chimerical.

It follows from this that a man should never try to purchase pleasure at the cost of pain, or even at the risk of incurring it; to do so is to pay what is positive and real, for what is negative and illusory; while there is a net profit in sacrificing pleasure for the sake of avoiding pain. In either case it is a matter of indifference whether the pain follows the pleasure or precedes it. While it is a complete inversion of the natural order to try and turn this scene of misery into a garden of pleasure, to aim at joy and pleasure rather than at the greatest possible freedom from pain—and yet how many do it!—there is some wisdom in taking a gloomy view, in looking upon the world as a kind of Hell, and in confining one's efforts to securing a little room that shall not be exposed to the fire. The fool rushes after the pleasures of life and finds himself their dupe; the wise man avoids its evils; and even if, notwithstanding his precautions, he falls into misfortunes, that is the fault of fate, not of his own folly. As far as he is successful in his endeavors, he cannot be said to have lived a life of illusion; for the evils which he shuns are very real. Even if he goes too far out of his way to avoid evils, and makes an unnecessary sacrifice of pleasure, he is, in reality, not the worse off for that; for all pleasures are chimerical, and to mourn for having lost any of them is a frivolous, and even ridiculous proceeding.

The failure to recognize this truth—a failure promoted by optimistic ideas—is the source of much unhappiness. In moments free from pain, our restless wishes present, as it were in a mirror, the image of a happiness that has no counterpart in reality, seducing us to follow it; in doing so we bring pain upon ourselves, and that is something undeniably real. Afterwards, we come to look with regret upon that lost state of painlessness; it is a paradise which we have gambled away; it is no longer with us, and we long in vain to undo what has been done.

One might well fancy that these visions of wishes fulfilled were the work of some evil spirit, conjured up in order to entice us away from that painless state which forms our highest happiness. A careless youth may think that the world is meant to be enjoyed, as though it were the abode of some real or positive happiness, which only those fail to attain who are not clever enough to overcome the difficulties that lie in the way. This false notion takes a stronger hold on him when he comes to read poetry and romance, and to be deceived by outward show—the hypocrisy that characterizes the world from beginning to end; on which I shall have something to say presently. The result is that his life is the more or less deliberate pursuit of positive happiness; and happiness he takes to be equivalent to a series of definite pleasures. In seeking for these pleasures he encounters danger—a fact which should not be forgotten. He hunts for game that does not exist; and so he ends by suffering some very real and positive misfortune—pain, distress, sickness, loss, care, poverty, shame, and all the thousand ills of life. Too late he discovers the trick that has been played upon him.

But if the rule I have mentioned is observed, and a plan of life is adopted which proceeds by avoiding pain—in other words, by taking measures of precaution against want, sickness, and distress in all its forms, the aim is a real one, and something may be achieved which will be great in proportion as the plan is not disturbed by striving after the chimera of positive happiness. This agrees with the opinion expressed by Goethe in the Elective Affinities, and there put into the mouth of Mittler— the man who is always trying to make other people happy: To desire to get rid of an evil is a definite object, but to desire a better fortune than one has is blind folly. The same truth is contained in that fine French proverb: le mieux est l'ennemi du bien— leave well alone. And, as I have remarked in my chief work,[3] this is the leading thought underlying the philosophical system of the Cynics. For what was it led the Cynics to repudiate pleasure in every form, if it was not the fact that pain is, in a greater or less degree, always bound up with pleasure? To go out of the way of pain seemed to them so much easier than to secure pleasure. Deeply impressed as they were by the negative nature of pleasure and the positive nature of pain, they consistently devoted all their efforts to the avoidance of pain. The first step to that end was, in their opinion, a complete and deliberate repudiation of pleasure, as something which served only to entrap the victim in order that he might be delivered over to pain.

We are all born, as Schiller says, in Arcadia. In other words, we come into the world full of claims to happiness and pleasure, and we cherish the fond hope of making them good. But, as a rule, Fate soon teaches us, in a rough and ready way that we really possess nothing at all, but that everything in the world is at its command, in virtue of an unassailable right, not only to all we have or acquire, to wife or child, but even to our very limbs, our arms, legs, eyes and ears, nay, even to the nose in the middle of our face. And in any case, after some little time, we learn by experience that happiness and pleasure are a fata morgana, which, visible from afar, vanish as we approach; that, on the other hand, suffering and pain are a reality, which makes its presence felt without any intermediary, and for its effect, stands in no need of illusion or the play of false hope.

If the teaching of experience bears fruit in us, we soon give up the pursuit of pleasure and happiness, and think much more about making ourselves secure against the attacks of pain and suffering. We see that the best the world has to offer is an existence free from pain—a quiet, tolerable life; and we confine our claims to this, as to something we can more surely hope to achieve. For the safest way of not being very miserable is not to expect to be very happy. Merck, the friend of Goethe's youth, was conscious of this truth when he wrote: It is the wretched way people have of setting up a claim to happiness—and, that to, in a measure corresponding with their desires—that ruins everything in this world. A man will make progress if he can get rid of this claim,[4] and desire nothing but what he sees before him. Accordingly it is advisable to put very moderate limits upon our expectations of pleasure, possessions, rank, honor and so on; because it is just this striving and struggling to be happy, to dazzle the world, to lead a life full of pleasure, which entail great misfortune. It is prudent and wise, I say, to reduce one's claims, if only for the reason that it is extremely easy to be very unhappy; while to be very happy is not indeed difficult, but quite impossible. With justice sings the poet of life's wisdom:

Auream quisquis mediocritatem
Diligit, tutus caret obsoleti
Sordibus tecti, caret invidenda
Sobrius aula.

Savius ventis agitatur ingens
Pinus: et celsae graviori casu
Decidunt turres; feriuntque summos
Fulgura monies.[5]

the golden mean is best—to live free from the squalor of a mean abode, and yet not be a mark for envy. It is the tall pine which is cruelly shaken by the wind, the highest summits that are struck in the storm, and the lofty towers that fall so heavily.

He who has taken to heart the teaching of my philosophy—who knows, therefore, that our whole existence is something which had better not have been, and that to disown and disclaim it is the highest wisdom—he will have no great expectations from anything or any condition in life: he will spend passion upon nothing in the world, nor lament over-much if he fails in any of his undertakings. He will feel the deep truth of what Plato[6] says: [Greek: oute ti ton anthropinon haxion on megalaes spondaes]—nothing in human affairs is worth any great anxiety; or, as the Persian poet has it,

Though from thy grasp all worldly things should flee, Grieve not for them, for they are nothing worth:

And though a world in thy possession be,
Joy not, for worthless are the things of earth.
Since to that better world 'tis given to thee
To pass, speed on, for this is nothing worth.[7]

The chief obstacle to our arriving at these salutary views is that hypocrisy of the world to which I have already alluded—an hypocrisy which should be early revealed to the young. Most of the glories of the world are mere outward show, like the scenes on a stage: there is nothing real about them. Ships festooned and hung with pennants, firing of cannon, illuminations, beating of drums and blowing of trumpets, shouting and applauding—these are all the outward sign, the pretence and suggestion,—as it were the hieroglyphic,—of joy: but just there, joy is, as a rule, not to be found; it is the only guest who has declined to be present at the festival. Where this guest may really be found, he comes generally without invitation; he is not formerly announced, but slips in quietly by himself sans facon; often making his appearance under the most unimportant and trivial circumstances, and in the commonest company—anywhere, in short, but where the society is brilliant and distinguished. Joy is like the gold in the Australian mines—found only now and then, as it were, by the caprice of chance, and according to no rule or law; oftenest in very little grains, and very seldom in heaps. All that outward show which I have described, is only an attempt to make people believe that it is really joy which has come to the festival; and to produce this impression upon the spectators is, in fact, the whole object of it.

With mourning it is just the same. That long funeral procession, moving up so slowly; how melancholy it looks! what an endless row of carriages! But look into them—they are all empty; the coachmen of the whole town are the sole escort the dead man has to his grave. Eloquent picture of the friendship and esteem of the world! This is the falsehood, the hollowness, the hypocrisy of human affairs!

Take another example—a roomful of guests in full dress, being received with great ceremony. You could almost believe that this is a noble and distinguished company; but, as a matter of fact, it is compulsion, pain and boredom who are the real guests. For where many are invited, it is a rabble—even if they all wear stars. Really good society is everywhere of necessity very small. In brilliant festivals and noisy entertainments, there is always, at bottom, a sense of emptiness prevalent. A false tone is there: such gatherings are in strange contrast with the misery and barrenness of our existence. The contrast brings the true condition into greater relief. Still, these gatherings are effective from the outside; and that is just their purpose. Chamfort[8] makes the excellent remark that society—les cercles, les salons, ce qu'on appelle le monde—is like a miserable play, or a bad opera, without any interest in itself, but supported for a time by mechanical aid, costumes and scenery.

And so, too, with academies and chairs of philosophy. You have a kind of sign-board hung out to show the apparent abode of wisdom: but wisdom is another guest who declines the invitation; she is to be found elsewhere. The chiming of bells, ecclesiastical millinery, attitudes of devotion, insane antics—these are the pretence, the false show of piety. And so on. Everything in the world is like a hollow nut; there is little kernel anywhere, and when it does exist, it is still more rare to find it in the shell. You may look for it elsewhere, and find it, as a rule, only by chance.

Section 2

To estimate a man's condition in regard to happiness, it is necessary to ask, not what things please him, but what things trouble him; and the more trivial these things are in themselves, the happier the man will be. To be irritated by trifles, a man must be well off; for in misfortunes trifles are unfelt.

Section 3

Care should be taken not to build the happiness of life upon a broad foundation—not to require a great many things in order to be happy. For happiness on such a foundation is the most easily undermined; it offers many more opportunities for accidents; and accidents are always happening. The architecture of happiness follows a plan in this respect just the opposite of that adopted in every other case, where the broadest foundation offers the greatest security. Accordingly, to reduce your claims to the lowest possible degree, in comparison with your means,—of whatever kind these may be—is the surest way of avoiding extreme misfortune.

To make extensive preparations for life—no matter what form they may take—is one of the greatest and commonest of follies. Such preparations presuppose, in the first place, a long life, the full and complete term of years appointed to man—and how few reach it! and even if it be reached, it is still too short for all the plans that have been made; for to carry them out requites more time than was thought necessary at the beginning. And then how many mischances and obstacles stand in the way! how seldom the goal is ever reached in human affairs!

And lastly, even though the goal should be reached, the changes which Time works in us have been left out of the reckoning: we forget that the capacity whether for achievement or for enjoyment does not last a whole lifetime. So we often toil for things which are no longer suited to us when we attain them; and again, the years we spend in preparing for some work, unconsciously rob us of the power for carrying it out.

How often it happens that a man is unable to enjoy the wealth which he acquired at so much trouble and risk, and that the fruits of his labor are reserved for others; or that he is incapable of filling the position which he has won after so many years of toil and struggle. Fortune has come too late for him; or, contrarily, he has come too late for fortune,—when, for instance, he wants to achieve great things, say, in art or literature: the popular taste has changed, it may be; a new generation has grown up, which takes no interest in his work; others have gone a shorter way and got the start of him. These are the facts of life which Horace must have had in view, when he lamented the uselessness of all advice:—

quid eternis minorem
Consiliis animum fatigas?[9]

The cause of this commonest of all follies is that optical illusion of the mind from which everyone suffers, making life, at its beginning, seem of long duration; and at its end, when one looks back over the course of it, how short a time it seems! There is some advantage in the illusion; but for it, no great work would ever be done.

Our life is like a journey on which, as we advance, the landscape takes a different view from that which it presented at first, and changes again, as we come nearer. This is just what happens—especially with our wishes. We often find something else, nay, something better than what we are looking for; and what we look for, we often find on a very different path from that on which we began a vain search. Instead of finding, as we expected, pleasure, happiness, joy, we get experience, insight, knowledge—a real and permanent blessing, instead of a fleeting and illusory one.

This is the thought that runs through Wilhelm Meister, like the bass in a piece of music. In this work of Goethe's, we have a novel of the intellectual kind, and, therefore, superior to all others, even to Sir Walter Scott's, which are, one and all, ethical; in other words, they treat of human nature only from the side of the will. So, too, in the Zauberfloete—that grotesque, but still significant, and even hieroglyphic—the same thought is symbolized, but in great, coarse lines, much in the way in which scenery is painted. Here the symbol would be complete if Tamino were in the end to be cured of his desire to possess Tainina, and received, in her stead, initiation into the mysteries of the Temple of Wisdom. It is quite right for Papageno, his necessary contrast, to succeed in getting his Papagena.

Men of any worth or value soon come to see that they are in the hands of Fate, and gratefully submit to be moulded by its teachings. They recognize that the fruit of life is experience, and not happiness; they become accustomed and content to exchange hope for insight; and, in the end, they can say, with Petrarch, that all they care for is to learn:—

Altro diletto che 'mparar, non provo.

It may even be that they to some extent still follow their old wishes and aims, trifling with them, as it were, for the sake of appearances; all the while really and seriously looking for nothing but instruction; a process which lends them an air of genius, a trait of something contemplative and sublime.

In their search for gold, the alchemists discovered other things—gunpowder, china, medicines, the laws of nature. There is a sense in which we are all alchemists.

1. *vii. (11) 12.*
2. *Welt als Wille und Vorstellung. Vol. I., p. 58.*
3. *Welt als Wille und Vorstellung, vol. ii., ch. 16*
4. *Letters to and from Merck.*
5. *Horace. Odes II. x.*
6. *Republic, x. 604.*
7. *Translator's Note. From the Anvar-i Suhaili—The Lights of Canopus—being the Persian version of the Table of Bidpai. Translated by E.B. Eastwick, ch. iii. Story vi., p. 289.*
8. *Translator's Note. Nicholas "Chamfort" (1741-94), a French miscellaneous writer, whose brilliant conversation, power of sarcasm, and epigrammic force, coupled with an extraordinary career, render him one of the most interesting and remarkable men of his time. Schopenhauer undoubtedly owed much to this writer, to whom he constantly refers.*
9. *Odes II. xi.*

Our Relation to Ourselves

Section 4

The mason employed on the building of a house may be quite ignorant of its general design; or at any rate, he may not keep it constantly in mind. So it is with man: in working through the days and hours of his life, he takes little thought of its character as a whole.

If there is any merit or importance attaching to a man's career, if he lays himself out carefully for some special work, it is all the more necessary and advisable for him to turn his attention now and then to its plan, that is to say, the miniature sketch of its general outlines. Of course, to do that, he must have applied the maxim [Greek: Gnothi seauton]; he must have made some little progress in the art of understanding himself. He must know what is his real, chief, and foremost object in life,—what it is that he most wants in order to be happy; and then, after that, what occupies the second and third place in his thoughts; he must find out what, on the whole, his vocation really is—the part he has to play, his general relation to the world. If he maps out important work for himself on great lines, a glance at this miniature plan of his life will, more than anything else stimulate, rouse and ennoble him, urge him on to action and keep him from false paths.

Again, just as the traveler, on reaching a height, gets a connected view over the road he has taken, with its many turns and windings; so it is only when we have completed a period in our life, or approach the end of it altogether, that we recognize the true connection between all our actions,—what it is we have achieved, what work we have done. It is only then that we see the precise chain of cause and effect, and the exact value of all our efforts. For as long as we are actually engaged in the work of life, we always act in accordance with the nature of our character, under the influence of motive, and within the limits of our capacity,—in a word, from beginning to end, under a law of necessity; at every moment we do just what appears to us right and proper. It is only afterwards, when we come to look back at the whole course of our life and its general result, that we see the why and wherefore of it all.

When we are actually doing some great deed, or creating some immortal work, we are not conscious of it as such; we think only of satisfying present aims, of fulfilling the intentions we happen to have at the time, of doing the right thing at the moment. It is only when we come to view our life as a connected whole that our character and capacities show themselves in their true light; that we see how, in particular instances, some happy inspiration, as it were, led us to choose the only true path out of a thousand which might have brought us to ruin. It was our genius that guided us, a force felt in the affairs of the intellectual as in those of the world; and working by its defect just in the same way in regard to evil and disaster.

Section 5

Another important element in the wise conduct of life is to preserve a proper proportion between our thought for the present and our thought for the future; in order not to spoil the one by paying over-great attention to the other. Many live too long in the present—frivolous people, I mean; others, too much in the future, ever anxious and full of care. It is seldom that a man holds the right balance between the two extremes. Those who strive and hope and live only in the future, always looking ahead and impatiently anticipating what is coming, as something which will make them happy when they get it, are, in spite of their very clever airs, exactly like those donkeys one sees in Italy, whose pace may be hurried by fixing a stick on their heads with a wisp of hay at the end of it; this is always just in front of them, and they keep on trying to get it. Such people are in a constant state of illusion as to their whole existence; they go on living ad interim, until at last they die.

Instead, therefore, of always thinking about our plans and anxiously looking to the future, or of giving ourselves up to regret for the past, we should never forget that the present is the only reality, the only certainty; that the future almost always turns out contrary to our expectations; that the past, too, was very different from what we suppose it to have been. But the past and the future are, on the whole, of less consequence than we think. Distance, which makes objects look small to the outward eye, makes them look big to the eye of thought. The present alone is true and actual; it is the only time which possesses full reality, and our existence lies in it exclusively. Therefore we should always be glad of it, and give it the welcome it deserves, and enjoy every hour that is bearable by its freedom from pain and annoyance with a full consciousness of its value. We shall hardly be able to do this if we make a wry face over the failure of our hopes in the past or over our anxiety for the future. It is the height of folly to refuse the present hour of happiness, or wantonly to spoil it by vexation at by-gones or uneasiness about what is to come. There is a time, of course, for forethought, nay, even for repentance; but when it is over let us think of what is past as of something to which we have said farewell, of necessity subduing our hearts—

[Greek: alla ta men protuchthai easomen achnumenoi per tumhon eni staethessi philon damasntes hanankae],[1]

and of the future as of that which lies beyond our power, in the lap of the gods—

[Greek: all aetoi men tauta theon en gounasi keitai].[2]

But in regard to the present let us remember Seneca's advice, and live each day as if it were our whole life,—singulas dies singulas vitas puta: let us make it as agreeable as possible, it is the only real time we have.

Only those evils which are sure to come at a definite date have any right to disturb us; and how few there are which fulfill this description. For evils are of two kinds; either they are possible only, at most probable; or they are inevitable. Even in the case of evils which are sure to happen, the time at which they will happen is uncertain. A man who is always preparing for either class of evil will not have a moment of peace left him. So, if we are not to lose all comfort in life through the fear of evils, some of which are uncertain in themselves, and others, in the time at which they will occur, we should look upon the one kind as never likely to happen, and the other as not likely to happen very soon.

Now, the less our peace of mind is disturbed by fear, the more likely it is to be agitated by desire and expectation. This is the true meaning of that song of Goethe's which is such a favorite with everyone: Ich hab' mein' Sach' auf nichts gestellt. It is only after a man has got rid of all pretension, and taken refuge in mere unembellished existence, that he is able to attain that peace of mind which is the foundation of human happiness. Peace of mind! that is something essential to any enjoyment of the present moment; and unless its separate moments are enjoyed, there is an end of life's happiness as a whole. We should always collect that To-day comes only once, and never returns. We fancy that it will come again to-morrow; but To-morrow is another day, which, in its turn, comes once only. We are apt to forget that every day is an integral, and therefore irreplaceable portion of life, and to look upon life as though it were a collective idea or name which does not suffer if one of the individuals it covers is destroyed.

We should be more likely to appreciate and enjoy the present, if, in those good days when we are well and strong, we did not fail to reflect how, in sickness and sorrow, every past hour that was free from pain and privation seemed in our memory so infinitely to be envied—as it were, a lost paradise, or some one who was only then seen to have acted as a friend. But we live through our days of happiness without noticing them; it is only when evil comes upon us that we wish them back. A thousand gay and pleasant hours are wasted in ill-humor; we let them slip by unenjoyed, and sigh for them in vain when the sky is overcast. Those present moments that are bearable, be they never so trite and common,—passed by in indifference, or, it may be, impatiently pushed away,—those are the moments we should honor; never failing to remember that the ebbing tide is even how hurrying them into the past, where memory will store them transfigured and shining with an imperishable light,—in some after-time, and above all, when our days are evil, to raise the veil and present them as the object of our fondest regret.

Section 6

Limitations always make for happiness. We are happy in proportion as our range of vision, our sphere of work, our points of contact with the world, are restricted and circumscribed. We are more likely to feel worried and anxious if these limits are wide; for it means that our cares, desires and terrors are increased and intensified. That is why the blind are not so unhappy as we might be inclined to suppose; otherwise there would not be that gentle and almost serene expression of peace in their faces.

Another reason why limitation makes for happiness is that the second half of life proves even more dreary that the first. As the years wear on, the horizon of our aims and our points of contact with the world become more extended. In childhood our horizon is limited to the narrowest sphere about us; in youth there is already a very considerable widening of our view; in manhood it comprises the whole range of our activity, often stretching out over a very distant sphere,—the care, for instance, of a State or a nation; in old age it embraces posterity.

But even in the affairs of the intellect, limitation is necessary if we are to be happy. For the less the will is excited, the less we suffer. We have seen that suffering is something positive, and that happiness is only a negative condition. To limit the sphere of outward activity is to relieve the will of external stimulus: to limit the sphere of our intellectual efforts is to relieve the will of internal sources of excitement. This latter kind of limitation is attended by the disadvantage that it opens the door to boredom, which is a direct source of countless sufferings; for to banish boredom, a man will have recourse to any means that may be handy—dissipation, society, extravagance, gaming, and drinking, and the like, which in their turn bring mischief, ruin and misery in their train. Difficiles in otio quies—it is difficult to keep quiet if you have nothing to do. That limitation in the sphere of outward activity is conducive, nay, even necessary to human happiness, such as it is, may be seen in the fact that the only kind of poetry which depicts men in a happy state of life—Idyllic poetry, I mean,—always aims, as an intrinsic part of its treatment, at representing them in very simple and restricted circumstances. It is this feeling, too, which is at the bottom of the pleasure we take in what are called genre pictures.

Simplicity, therefore, as far as it can be attained, and even monotony, in our manner of life, if it does not mean that we are bored, will contribute to happiness; just because, under such circumstances, life, and consequently the burden which is the essential concomitant of life, will be least felt. Our existence will glide on peacefully like a stream which no waves or whirlpools disturb.

Section 7

Whether we are in a pleasant or a painful state depends, ultimately, upon the kind of matter that pervades and engrosses our consciousness. In this respect, purely intellectual occupation, for the mind that is capable of it, will, as a rule, do much more in the way of happiness than any form of practical life, with its constant alternations of success and failure, and all the shocks and torments it produces. But it must be confessed that for such occupation a pre-eminent amount of intellectual capacity is necessary. And in this connection it may be noted that, just as a life devoted to outward activity will distract and divert a man from study, and also deprive him of that quiet concentration of mind which is necessary for such work; so, on the other hand, a long course of thought will make him more or less unfit for the noisy pursuits of real life. It is advisable, therefore, to suspend mental work for a while, if circumstances happen which demand any degree of energy in affairs of a practical nature.

Section 8

To live a life that shall be entirely prudent and discreet, and to draw from experience all the instruction it contains, it is requisite to be constantly thinking back,—to make a kind of recapitulation of what we have done, of our impressions and sensations, to compare our former with our present judgments—what we set before us and struggle to achieve, with the actual result and satisfaction we have obtained. To do this is to get a repetition of the private lessons of experience,—lessons which are given to every one.

Experience of the world may be looked upon as a kind of text, to which reflection and knowledge form the commentary. Where there is great deal of reflection and intellectual knowledge, and very little experience, the result is like those books which have on each page two lines of text to forty lines of commentary. A great deal of experience with little reflection and scant knowledge, gives us books like those of the editio Bipontina[3] where there are no notes and much that is unintelligible.

The advice here given is on a par with a rule recommended by Pythagoras,—to review, every night before going to sleep, what we have done during the day. To live at random, in the hurly-burly of business or pleasure, without ever reflecting upon the past,—to go on, as it were, pulling cotton off the reel of life,—is to have no clear idea of what we are about; and a man who lives in this state will have chaos in his emotions and certain confusion in his thoughts; as is soon manifest by the abrupt and fragmentary character of his conversation, which becomes a kind of mincemeat. A man will be all the more exposed to this fate in proportion as he lives a restless life in the world, amid a crowd of various impressions and with a correspondingly small amount of activity on the part of his own mind.

And in this connection it will be in place to observe that, when events and circumstances which have influenced us pass away in the course of time, we are unable to bring back and renew the particular mood or state of feeling which they aroused in us: but we can remember what we were led to say and do in regard to them; and thus form, as it were, the result, expression and measure of those events. We should, therefore, be careful to preserve the memory of our thoughts at important points in our life; and herein lies the great advantage of keeping a journal.

Section 9

To be self-sufficient, to be all in all to oneself, to want for nothing, to be able to say omnia mea mecum porto—that is assuredly the chief qualification for happiness. Hence Aristotle's remark, [Greek: hae eudaimonia ton autarchon esti][4]—to be happy means to be self-sufficient—cannot be too often repeated. It is, at bottom, the same thought as is present in the very well-turned sentence from Chamfort:

Le bonheur n'est pas chose aisee: il est tres difficile de le trouver en nous, et impossible de le trouver ailleurs.

For while a man cannot reckon with certainty upon anyone but himself, the burdens and disadvantages, the dangers and annoyances, which arise from having to do with others, are not only countless but unavoidable.

There is no more mistaken path to happiness than worldliness, revelry, high life: for the whole object of it is to transform our miserable existence into a succession of joys, delights and pleasures,—a process which cannot fail to result in disappointment and delusion; on a par, in this respect, with its obligato accompaniment, the interchange of lies.[5]

All society necessarily involves, as the first condition of its existence, mutual accommodation and restraint upon the part of its members. This means that the larger it is, the more insipid will be its tone. A man can be himself only so long as he is alone; and if he does not love solitude, he will not love freedom; for it is only when he is alone that he is really free. Constraint is always present in society, like a companion of whom there is no riddance; and in proportion to the greatness of a man's individuality, it will be hard for him to bear the sacrifices which all intercourse with others demands, Solitude will be welcomed or endured or avoided, according as a man's personal value is large or small,—the wretch feeling, when he is alone, the whole burden of his misery; the great intellect delighting in its greatness; and everyone, in short, being just what he is.

Further, if a man stands high in Nature's lists, it is natural and inevitable that he should feel solitary. It will be an advantage to him if his surroundings do not interfere with this feeling; for if he has to see a great deal of other people who are not of like character with himself, they will exercise a disturbing influence upon him, adverse to his peace of mind; they will rob him, in fact, of himself, and give him nothing to compensate for the loss.

But while Nature sets very wide differences between man and man in respect both of morality and of intellect, society disregards and effaces them; or, rather, it sets up artificial differences in their stead,—gradations of rank and position, which are very often diametrically opposed to those which Nature establishes. The result of this arrangement is to elevate those whom Nature has placed low, and to depress the few who stand high. These latter, then, usually withdraw from society, where, as soon as it is at all numerous, vulgarity reigns supreme.

What offends a great intellect in society is the equality of rights, leading to equality of pretensions, which everyone enjoys; while at the same time, inequality of capacity means a corresponding disparity of social power. So-called good society recognizes every kind of claim but that of intellect, which is a contraband article; and people are expected to exhibit an unlimited amount of patience towards every form of folly and stupidity, perversity and dullness; whilst personal merit has to beg pardon, as it were, for being present, or else conceal itself altogether. Intellectual superiority offends by its very existence, without any desire to do so.

The worst of what is called good society is not only that it offers us the companionship of people who are unable to win either our praise or our affection, but that it does not allow of our being that which we naturally are; it compels us, for the sake of harmony, to shrivel up, or even alter our shape altogether. Intellectual conversation, whether grave or humorous, is only fit for intellectual society; it is downright abhorrent to ordinary people, to please whom it is absolutely necessary to be commonplace and dull. This demands an act of severe self-denial; we have to forfeit three-fourths of ourselves in order to become like other people. No doubt their company may be set down against our loss in this respect; but the more a man is worth, the more he will find that what he gains does not cover what he loses, and that the balance is on the debit side of the account; for the people with whom he deals are generally bankrupt,—that is to say, there is nothing to be got from their society which can compensate either for its boredom, annoyance and disagreeableness, or for the self-denial which it renders necessary. Accordingly, most society is so constituted as to offer a good profit to anyone who will exchange it for solitude.

Nor is this all. By way of providing a substitute for real—I mean intellectual—superiority, which is seldom to be met with, and intolerable when it is found, society has capriciously adopted a false kind of superiority, conventional in its character, and resting upon arbitrary principles,—a tradition, as it were, handed down in the higher circles, and, like a password, subject to alteration; I refer to bon-ton fashion. Whenever this kind of superiority comes into collision with the real kind, its weakness is manifest. Moreover, the presence of good tone means the absence of good sense.

No man can be in perfect accord with any one but himself—not even with a friend or the partner of his life; differences of individuality and temperament are always bringing in some degree of discord, though it may be a very slight one. That genuine, profound peace of mind, that perfect tranquillity of soul, which, next to health, is the highest blessing the earth can give, is to be attained only in solitude, and, as a permanent mood, only in complete retirement; and then, if there is anything great and rich in the man's own self, his way of life is the happiest that may be found in this wretched world.

Let me speak plainly. However close the bond of friendship, love, marriage—a man, ultimately, looks to himself, to his own welfare alone; at most, to his child's too. The less necessity there is for you to come into contact with mankind in general, in the relations whether of business or of personal intimacy, the better off you are. Loneliness and solitude have their evils, it is true; but if you cannot feel them all at once, you can at least see where they lie; on the other hand, society is insidious in this respect; as in offering you what appears to be the pastime of pleasing social intercourse, it works great and often irreparable mischief. The young should early be trained to bear being left alone; for it is a source of happiness and peace of mind.

It follows from this that a man is best off if he be thrown upon his own resources and can be all in all to himself; and Cicero goes so far as to say that a man who is in this condition cannot fail to be very happy—nemo potest non beatissimus esse qui est totus aptus ex sese, quique in se uno ponit omnia.[6] The more a man has in himself, the less others can be to him. The feeling of self-sufficiency! it is that which restrains those whose personal value is in itself great riches, from such considerable sacrifices as are demanded by intercourse with the world, let alone, then, from actually practicing self-denial by going out of their way to seek it. Ordinary people are sociable and complaisant just from the very opposite feeling;—to bear others' company is easier for them than to bear their own. Moreover, respect is not paid in this world to that which has real merit; it is reserved for that which has none. So retirement is at once a proof and a result of being distinguished by the possession of meritorious qualities. It will therefore show real wisdom on the part of any one who is worth anything in himself, to limit his requirements as may be necessary, in order to preserve or extend his freedom, and,—since a man must come into some relations with his fellow-men—to admit them to his intimacy as little as possible.

I have said that people are rendered sociable by their ability to endure solitude, that is to say, their own society. They become sick of themselves. It is this vacuity of soul which drives them to intercourse with others,—to travels in foreign countries. Their mind is wanting in elasticity; it has no movement of its own, and so they try to give it some,—by drink, for instance. How much drunkenness is due to this cause alone! They are always looking for some form of excitement, of the strongest kind

76

they can bear—the excitement of being with people of like nature with themselves; and if they fail in this, their mind sinks by its own weight, and they fall into a grievous lethargy.[7] Such people, it may be said, possess only a small fraction of humanity in themselves; and it requires a great many of them put together to make up a fair amount of it,—to attain any degree of consciousness as men. A man, in the full sense of the word,—a man par excellence—does not represent a fraction, but a whole number: he is complete in himself.

Ordinary society is, in this respect, very like the kind of music to be obtained from an orchestra composed of Russian horns. Each horn has only one note; and the music is produced by each note coming in just at the right moment. In the monotonous sound of a single horn, you have a precise illustration of the effect of most people's minds. How often there seems to be only one thought there! and no room for any other. It is easy to see why people are so bored; and also why they are sociable, why they like to go about in crowds—why mankind is so gregarious. It is the monotony of his own nature that makes a man find solitude intolerable. Omnis stultitia laborat fastidio sui: folly is truly its own burden. Put a great many men together, and you may get some result—some music from your horns!

A man of intellect is like an artist who gives a concert without any help from anyone else, playing on a single instrument—a piano, say, which is a little orchestra in itself. Such a man is a little world in himself; and the effect produced by various instruments together, he produces single-handed, in the unity of his own consciousness. Like the piano, he has no place in a symphony: he is a soloist and performs by himself,—in solitude, it may be; or, if in company with other instruments, only as principal; or for setting the tone, as in singing. However, those who are fond of society from time to time may profit by this simile, and lay it down as a general rule that deficiency of quality in those we meet may be to some extent compensated by an increase in quantity. One man's company may be quite enough, if he is clever; but where you have only ordinary people to deal with, it is advisable to have a great many of them, so that some advantage may accrue by letting them all work together,--on the analogy of the horns; and may Heaven grant you patience for your task!

That mental vacuity and barrenness of soul to which I have alluded, is responsible for another misfortune. When men of the better class form a society for promoting some noble or ideal aim, the result almost always is that the innumerable mob of humanity comes crowding in too, as it always does everywhere, like vermin—their object being to try and get rid of boredom, or some other defect of their nature; and anything that will effect that, they seize upon at once, without the slightest discrimination. Some of them will slip into that society, or push themselves in, and then either soon destroy it altogether, or alter it so much that in the end it comes to have a purpose the exact opposite of that which it had at first.

This is not the only point of view from which the social impulse may be regarded. On cold days people manage to get some warmth by crowding together; and you can warm your mind in the same way—by bringing it into contact with others. But a man who has a great deal of intellectual warmth in himself will stand in no need of such resources. I have written a little fable illustrating this: it may be found elsewhere.[8] As a general rule, it may be said that a man's sociability stands very nearly in inverse ratio to his intellectual value: to say that "so and so" is very unsociable, is almost tantamount to saying that he is a man of great capacity.

Solitude is doubly advantageous to such a man. Firstly, it allows him to be with himself, and, secondly, it prevents him being with others—an advantage of great moment; for how much constraint, annoyance, and even danger there is in all intercourse with the world. Tout notre mal, says La Bruyere, vient de ne pouvoir etre seul. It is really a very risky, nay, a fatal thing, to be sociable; because it means contact with natures, the great majority of which are bad morally, and dull or perverse, intellectually. To be unsociable is not to care about such people; and to have enough in oneself to dispense with the necessity of their company is a great piece of good fortune; because almost all our sufferings spring from having to do with other people; and that destroys the peace of mind, which, as I have said, comes next after health in the elements of happiness. Peace of mind is impossible without a considerable amount of solitude. The Cynics renounced all private property in order to attain the bliss of having nothing to trouble them; and to renounce society with the same object is the wisest thing a man can do. Bernardin de Saint Pierre has the very excellent and pertinent remark that to be sparing in regard to food is a means of health; in regard to society, a means of tranquillity—la diete des ailmens nous rend la sante du corps, et celle des hommes la tranquillite de l'ame. To be soon on friendly, or even affectionate, terms with solitude is like winning a gold mine; but this is not something which everybody can do. The prime reason for social intercourse is mutual need; and as soon as that is satisfied, boredom drives people together once more. If it were not for these two reasons, a man would probably elect to remain alone; if only because solitude is the sole condition of life which gives full play to that feeling of exclusive importance which every man has in his own eyes,—as if he were the only person in the world! a feeling which, in the throng and press of real life, soon shrivels up to nothing, getting, at every step, a painful dementi. From this point of view it may be said that solitude is the original and natural state of man, where, like another Adam, he is as happy as his nature will allow.

But still, had Adam no father or mother? There is another sense in which solitude is not the natural state; for, at his entrance into the world, a man finds himself with parents, brothers, sisters, that is to say, in society, and not alone. Accordingly it cannot be said that the love of solitude is an original characteristic of human nature; it is rather the result of experience and reflection, and these in their turn depend upon the development of intellectual power, and increase with the years.

Speaking generally, sociability stands in inverse ratio with age. A little child raises a piteous cry of fright if it is left alone for only a few minutes; and later on, to be shut up by itself is a great punishment. Young people soon get on very friendly terms with one another; it is only the few among them of any nobility of mind who are glad now and then to be alone;—but to spend the whole day thus would be disagreeable. A grown-up man can easily do it; it is little trouble to him to be much alone, and it becomes less and less trouble as he advances in years. An old man who has outlived all his friends, and is either indifferent or dead to the pleasures of life, is in his proper element in solitude; and in individual cases the special tendency to retirement and seclusion will always be in direct proportion to intellectual capacity.

For this tendency is not, as I have said, a purely natural one; it does not come into existence as a direct need of human nature; it is rather the effect of the experience we go through, the product of reflection upon what our needs really are; proceeding, more especially, from the insight we attain into the wretched stuff of which most people are made, whether you look at their morals or their intellects. The worst of it all is that, in the individual, moral and intellectual shortcomings are closely connected and play into each other's hands, so that all manner of disagreeable results are obtained, which make intercourse with most people not only unpleasant but intolerable. Hence, though the world contains many things which are thoroughly bad, the worst thing in it is society. Even Voltaire, that sociable Frenchman, was obliged to admit that there are everywhere crowds of people not worth talking to: *la terre est couverte de gens qui ne meritent pas qu'on leur parle.* And Petrarch gives a similar reason for wishing to be alone—that tender spirit! so strong and constant in his love of seclusion. The streams, the plains and woods know well, he says, how he has tried to escape the perverse and stupid people who have missed the way to heaven:—

Cercato ho sempre solitaria vita
(Le rive il sanno, e le campagne e i boschi)
Per fuggir quest' ingegni storti e loschi
Che la strada del ciel' hanno smarrita.

He pursues the same strain in that delightful book of his, DeVita Solitaria, which seems to have given Zimmerman the idea of his celebrated work on Solitude. It is the secondary and indirect character of the love of seclusion to which Chamfort alludes in the following passage, couched in his sarcastic vein: On dit quelquefois d'un homme qui vit seul, il n'aime pas la societe. C'est souvent comme si on disait d'un homme qu'il n'aime pas la promenade, sous le pretexte qu'il ne se promene pas volontiers le soir dans le foret de Bondy.

You will find a similar sentiment expressed by the Persian poet Sadi, in his Garden of Roses. Since that time, he says, we have taken leave of society, preferring the path of seclusion; for there is safety in solitude. Angelus Silesius,[9] a very gentle and Christian writer, confesses to the same feeling, in his own mythical language. Herod, he says, is the common enemy; and when, as with Joseph, God warns us of danger, we fly from the world to solitude, from Bethlehem to Egypt; or else suffering and death await us!—

Herodes ist ein Feind; der Joseph der Verstand, Dem machte Gott die Gefahr im
Traum (in Geist) bekannt;
Die Welt ist Bethlehem, Aegypten Einsamkeit,
Fleuch, meine Seele! fleuch, sonst stirbest du vor Leid.

Giordano Bruno also declares himself a friend of seclusion. Tanti uomini, he says, che in terra hanno voluto gustare vita celeste, dissero con una voce, "ecce elongavi fugiens et mansi in solitudine"—those who in this world have desired a foretaste of the divine life, have always proclaimed with one voice:

Lo! then would I wander far off;
I would lodge in the wilderness.[10]

And in the work from which I have already quoted, Sadi says of himself: In disgust with my friends at Damascus, I withdrew into the desert about Jerusalem, to seek the society of the beasts of the field. In short, the same thing has been said by all whom Prometheus has formed out of better clay. What pleasure could they find in the company of people with whom their only common ground is just what is lowest and least noble in their own nature—the part of them that is commonplace, trivial and vulgar?

What do they want with people who cannot rise to a higher level, and for whom nothing remains but to drag others down to theirs? for this is what they aim at. It is an aristocratic feeling that is at the bottom of this propensity to seclusion and solitude.

Rascals are always sociable—more's the pity! and the chief sign that a man has any nobility in his character is the little pleasure he takes in others' company. He prefers solitude more and more, and, in course of time, comes to see that, with few exceptions, the world offers no choice beyond solitude on one side and vulgarity on the other. This may sound a hard thing to say; but even Angelus Silesius, with all his Christian feelings of gentleness and love, was obliged to admit the truth of it. However painful solitude may be, he says, be careful not to be vulgar; for then you may find a desert everywhere:—

Die Einsamkeit ist noth: doch sei nur nicht gemein, So kannst du ueberall in einer Wueste sein.

It is natural for great minds—the true teachers of humanity—to care little about the constant company of others; just as little as the schoolmaster cares for joining in the gambols of the noisy crowd of boys which surround him. The mission of these great minds is to guide mankind over the sea of error to the haven of truth—to draw it forth from the dark abysses of a barbarous vulgarity up into the light of culture and refinement. Men of great intellect live in the world without really belonging to it; and so, from their earliest years, they feel that there is a perceptible difference between them and other people. But it is only gradually, with the lapse of years, that they come to a clear understanding of their position. Their intellectual isolation is then reinforced by actual seclusion in their manner of life; they let no one approach who is not in some degree emancipated from the prevailing vulgarity.

From what has been said it is obvious that the love of solitude is not a direct, original impulse in human nature, but rather something secondary and of gradual growth. It is the more distinguishing feature of nobler minds, developed not without some conquest of natural desires, and now and then in actual opposition to the promptings of Mephistopheles—bidding you exchange a morose and soul-destroying solitude for life amongst men, for society; even the worst, he says, will give a sense of human fellowship:—

Hoer' auf mit deinem Gram zu spielen, Der, wie ein Geier, dir am Leben frisst:

Die schlechteste Gesellschaft laesst dich fuehlen
Dass du ein Mensch mit Menschen bist.[11]

To be alone is the fate of all great minds—a fate deplored at times, but still always chosen as the less grievous of two evils. As the years increase, it always becomes easier to say, Dare to be wise—sapere aude. And after sixty, the inclination to be alone grows into a kind of real, natural instinct; for at that age everything combines in favor of it. The strongest impulse—the love of woman's society—has little or no effect; it is the sexless condition of old age which lays the foundation of a certain self-sufficiency, and that gradually absorbs all desire for others' company. A thousand illusions and follies are overcome; the active years of life are in most cases gone; a man has no more expectations or plans or intentions. The generation to which he belonged has passed away, and a new race has sprung up which looks upon him as essentially outside its sphere of activity. And then the years pass more quickly as we

80

become older, and we want to devote our remaining time to the intellectual rather than to the practical side of life. For, provided that the mind retains its faculties, the amount of knowledge and experience we have acquired, together with the facility we have gained in the use of our powers, makes it then more than ever easy and interesting to us to pursue the study of any subject. A thousand things become clear which were formerly enveloped in obscurity, and results are obtained which give a feeling of difficulties overcome. From long experience of men, we cease to expect much from them; we find that, on the whole, people do not gain by a nearer acquaintance; and that—apart from a few rare and fortunate exceptions—we have come across none but defective specimens of human nature which it is advisable to leave in peace. We are no more subject to the ordinary illusions of life; and as, in individual instances, we soon see what a man is made of, we seldom feel any inclination to come into closer relations with him. Finally, isolation—our own society—has become a habit, as it were a second nature to us, more especially if we have been on friendly terms with it from our youth up. The love of solitude which was formerly indulged only at the expense of our desire for society, has now come to be the simple quality of our natural disposition—the element proper to our life, as water to a fish. This is why anyone who possesses a unique individuality—unlike others and therefore necessarily isolated—feels that, as he becomes older, his position is no longer so burdensome as when he was young.

For, as a matter of fact, this very genuine privilege of old age is one which can be enjoyed only if a man is possessed of a certain amount of intellect; it will be appreciated most of all where there is real mental power; but in some degree by every one. It is only people of very barren and vulgar nature who will be just as sociable in their old age as they were in their youth. But then they become troublesome to a society to which they are no longer suited, and, at most, manage to be tolerated; whereas, they were formerly in great request.

There is another aspect of this inverse proportion between age and sociability—the way in which it conduces to education. The younger that people are, the more in every respect they have to learn; and it is just in youth that Nature provides a system of mutual education, so that mere intercourse with others, at that time of life, carries instruction with it. Human society, from this point of view, resembles a huge academy of learning, on the Bell and Lancaster system, opposed to the system of education by means of books and schools, as something artificial and contrary to the institutions of Nature. It is therefore a very suitable arrangement that, in his young days, a man should be a very diligent student at the place of learning provided by Nature herself.

But there is nothing in life which has not some drawback—nihil est ab omni parte beatum, as Horace says; or, in the words of an Indian proverb, no lotus without a stalk. Seclusion, which has so many advantages, has also its little annoyances and drawbacks, which are small, however, in comparison with those of society; hence anyone who is worth much in himself will get on better without other people than with them. But amongst the disadvantages of seclusion there is one which is not so easy to see as the rest. It is this: when people remain indoors all day, they become physically very sensitive to atmospheric changes, so that every little draught is enough to make them ill; so with our temper; a long course of seclusion makes it so sensitive that the most trivial incidents, words, or even looks, are sufficient to disturb or to vex and offend us—little things which are unnoticed by those who live in the turmoil of life.

When you find human society disagreeable and feel yourself justified in flying to solitude, you can be so constituted as to be unable to bear the depression of it for any length of time, which will probably be the case if you are young. Let me advise you, then, to form the habit of taking some of your solitude with you into society, to learn to be to some extent alone even though you are in company; not to say at once what you think, and, on the other hand, not to attach too precise a meaning to what others say; rather, not to expect much of them, either morally or intellectually, and to strengthen yourself in the feeling of indifference to their opinion, which is the surest way of always practicing a praiseworthy toleration. If you do that, you will not live so much with other people, though you may appear to move amongst them: your relation to them will be of a purely objective character. This precaution will keep you from too close contact with society, and therefore secure you against being contaminated or even outraged by it.[12] Society is in this respect like a fire—the wise man warming himself at a proper distance from it; not coming too close, like the fool, who, on getting scorched, runs away and shivers in solitude, loud in his complaint that the fire burns.

Section 10

Envy is natural to man; and still, it is at once a vice and a source of misery.[13] We should treat it as the enemy of our happiness, and stifle it like an evil thought. This is the advice given by Seneca; as he well puts it, we shall be pleased with what we have, if we avoid the self-torture of comparing our own lot with some other and happier one—nostra nos sine comparatione delectent; nunquam erit felix quem torquebit felicior.[14] And again, quum adspexeris quot te antecedent, cogita quot sequantur[15]—if a great many people appear to be better off than yourself, think how many there are in a worse position. It is a fact that if real calamity comes upon us, the most effective consolation—though it springs from the same source as envy— is just the thought of greater misfortunes than ours; and the next best is the society of those who are in the same luck as we—the partners of our sorrows.

So much for the envy which we may feel towards others. As regards the envy which we may excite in them, it should always be remembered that no form of hatred is so implacable as the hatred that comes from envy; and therefore we should always carefully refrain from doing anything to rouse it; nay, as with many another form of vice, it is better altogether to renounce any pleasure there may be in it, because of the serious nature of its consequences.

Aristocracies are of three kinds: (1) of birth and rank; (2) of wealth; and (3) of intellect. The last is really the most distinguished of the three, and its claim to occupy the first position comes to be recognized, if it is only allowed time to work. So eminent a king as Frederick the Great admitted it—les ames privilegiees rangent a l'egal des souverains, as he said to his chamberlain, when the latter expressed his surprise that Voltaire should have a seat at the table reserved for kings and princes, whilst ministers and generals were relegated to the chamberlain's.

Every one of these aristocracies is surrounded by a host of envious persons. If you belong to one of them, they will be secretly embittered against you; and unless they are restrained by fear, they will always be anxious to let you understand that you are

82

no better than they. It is by their anxiety to let you know this, that they betray how greatly they are conscious that the opposite is the truth.

The line of conduct to be pursued if you are exposed to envy, is to keep the envious persons at a distance, and, as far as possible, avoid all contact with them, so that there may be a wide gulf fixed between you and them; if this cannot be done, to bear their attacks with the greatest composure. In the latter case, the very thing that provokes the attack will also neutralize it. This is what appears to be generally done.

The members of one of these aristocracies usually get on very well with those of another, and there is no call for envy between them, because their several privileges effect an equipoise.

Section 11

Give mature and repeated consideration to any plan before you proceed to carry it out; and even after you have thoroughly turned it over in your mind, make some concession to the incompetency of human judgment; for it may always happen that circumstances which cannot be investigated or foreseen, will come in and upset the whole of your calculation. This is a reflection that will always influence the negative side of the balance—a kind of warning to refrain from unnecessary action in matters of importance—quieta non movere. But having once made up your mind and begun your work, you must let it run its course and abide the result—not worry yourself by fresh reflections on what is already accomplished, or by a renewal of your scruples on the score of possible danger: free your mind from the subject altogether, and refuse to go into it again, secure in the thought that you gave it mature attention at the proper time. This is the same advice as is given by an Italian proverb—legala bene e poi lascia la andare—which Goethe has translated thus: See well to your girths, and then ride on boldly.[16]

And if, notwithstanding that, you fail, it is because human affairs are the sport of chance and error. Socrates, the wisest of men, needed the warning voice of his good genius, or [Greek: daimonion], to enable him to do what was right in regard to his own personal affairs, or at any rate, to avoid mistakes; which argues that the human intellect is incompetent for the purpose. There is a saying—which is reported to have originated with one of the Popes—that when misfortune happens to us, the blame of it, at least in some degree, attaches to ourselves. If this is not true absolutely and in every instance, it is certainly true in the great majority of cases. It even looks as if this truth had a great deal to do with the effort people make as far as possible to conceal their misfortunes, and to put the best face they can upon them, for fear lest their misfortunes may show how much they are to blame.

Section 12

In the case of a misfortune which has already happened and therefore cannot be altered, you should not allow yourself to think that it might have been otherwise; still less, that it might have been avoided by such and such means; for reflections of this kind will only add to your distress and make it intolerable, so that you will become a tormentor to yourself—[Greek: heautontimoroumeaeos]. It is better to follow the example of King David; who, as long as his son lay on the bed of sickness, assailed Jehovah with unceasing supplications and entreaties for his recovery; but when he was dead, snapped his fingers and thought no more of it. If you are not light-hearted enough for that, you can take refuge in fatalism, and have the great truth revealed to you that everything which happens is the result of necessity, and therefore inevitable.

However good this advice may be, it is one-sided and partial. In relieving and quieting us for the moment, it is no doubt effective enough; but when our misfortunes have resulted—as is usually the case—from our own carelessness or folly, or, at any rate, partly by our own fault, it is a good thing to consider how they might have been avoided, and to consider it often in spite of its being a tender subject—a salutary form of self-discipline, which will make us wiser and better men for the future. If we have made obvious mistakes, we should not try, as we generally do, to gloss them over, or to find something to excuse or extenuate them; we should admit to ourselves that we have committed faults, and open our eyes wide to all their enormity, in order that we may firmly resolve to avoid them in time to come. To be sure, that means a great deal of self-inflicted pain, in the shape of discontent, but it should be remembered that to spare the rod is to spoil the child—[Greek: ho mae dareis anthropos ou paideuetai].[17]

Section 13

In all matters affecting our weal or woe, we should be careful not to let our imagination run away with us, and build no castles in the air. In the first place, they are expensive to build, because we have to pull them down again immediately, and that is a source of grief. We should be still more on our guard against distressing our hearts by depicting possible misfortunes. If these were misfortunes of a purely imaginary kind, or very remote and unlikely, we should at once see, on awaking from our dream, that the whole thing was mere illusion; we should rejoice all the more in a reality better than our dreams, or at most, be warned against misfortunes which, though very remote, were still possible. These, however, are not the sort of playthings in which imagination delights; it is only in idle hours that we build castles in the air, and they are always of a pleasing description. The matter which goes to form gloomy dreams are mischances which to some extent really threaten us, though it be from some distance; imagination makes us look larger and nearer and more terrible than they are in reality. This is a kind of dream which cannot be so readily shaken off on awaking as a pleasant one; for a pleasant dream is soon dispelled by reality, leaving, at most, a feeble hope lying in the lap of possibility. Once we have abandoned ourselves to a fit of the blues, visions are conjured up which do not so easily vanish again; for it is always just possible that the visions may be realized. But we are not always able to estimate the exact degree of possibility: possibility may easily pass into probability; and thus we deliver ourselves up to torture. Therefore we should be careful not to be over-anxious on any matter affecting our weal or our woe, not to carry our anxiety to unreasonable or injudicious limits; but coolly and dispassionately to deliberate upon the matter, as though it were an abstract question which did not touch us in particular. We should give no play to imagination here; for imagination is not judgment—it only conjures up visions, inducing an unprofitable and often very painful mood.

The rule on which I am here insisting should be most carefully observed towards evening. For as darkness makes us timid and apt to see terrifying shapes everywhere, there is something similar in the effect of indistinct thought; and uncertainty always brings with it a sense of danger. Hence, towards evening, when our powers of thought and judgment are relaxed,—at the hour, as it were, of subjective darkness,—the intellect becomes tired, easily confused, and unable to get at the bottom of things; and if, in that state, we meditate on matters of personal interest to ourselves, they soon assume a dangerous and terrifying aspect. This is mostly the case at night, when we are in bed; for then the mind is fully relaxed, and the power of judgment quite unequal to its duties; but imagination is still awake. Night gives a black look to everything, whatever it may be. This is why our thoughts, just before we go to sleep, or as we lie awake through the hours of the night, are usually such confusions and perversions of facts as dreams themselves; and when our thoughts at that time are concentrated upon our own concerns, they are generally as black and monstrous as possible. In the morning all such nightmares vanish like dreams: as the Spanish proverb has it, noche tinta, bianco el dia—the night is colored, the day is white. But even towards nightfall, as soon as the candles are lit, the mind, like the eye, no longer sees things so clearly as by day: it is a time unsuited to serious meditation, especially on unpleasant subjects. The morning is the proper time for that—as indeed for all efforts without exception, whether mental or bodily. For the morning is the youth of the day, when everything is bright, fresh, and easy of attainment; we feel strong then, and all our faculties are completely at our disposal. Do not shorten the morning by getting up late, or waste it in unworthy occupations or in talk; look upon it as the quintessence of life, as to a certain extent sacred. Evening is like old age: we are languid, talkative, silly. Each day is a little life: every waking and rising a little birth, every fresh morning a little youth, every going to rest and sleep a little death.

But condition of health, sleep, nourishment, temperature, weather, surroundings, and much else that is purely external, have, in general, an important influence upon our mood and therefore upon our thoughts. Hence both our view of any matter and our capacity for any work are very much subject to time and place. So it is best to profit by a good mood—for how seldom it comes!—

Nehmt die gute Stimmung wahr,
Denn sie kommt so selten.[18]

We are not always able to form new ideas about; our surroundings, or to command original thoughts: they come if they will, and when they will. And so, too, we cannot always succeed in completely considering some personal matter at the precise time at which we have determined beforehand to consider it, and just when we set ourselves to do so. For the peculiar train of thought which is favorable to it may suddenly become active without any special call being made upon it, and we may then follow it up with keen interest. In this way reflection, too, chooses its own time.

This reining-in of the imagination which I am recommending, will also forbid us to summon up the memory of the past misfortune, to paint a dark picture of the injustice or harm that has been done us, the losses we have sustained, the insults, slights and annoyances to which we have been exposed: for to do that is to rouse into fresh life all those hateful passions long laid asleep—the anger and resentment which disturb and pollute our nature. In an excellent parable, Proclus, the Neoplatonist, points out how in every town the mob dwells side by side with those who are rich and distinguished: so, too, in every man, be he never so noble and dignified, there is, in the depth of his nature, a mob of low and vulgar desires which constitute him an animal. It will not do to let this mob revolt or even so much as peep forth from its hiding-place; it is hideous of mien, and its rebel leaders are those flights of imagination which I have been describing. The smallest annoyance, whether it comes from our fellow-men or from the things around us, may swell up into a monster of dreadful aspect, putting us at our wits' end—and all because we go on brooding over our troubles and painting them in the most glaring colors and on the largest scale. It is much better to take a very calm and prosaic view of what is disagreeable; for that is the easiest way of bearing it.

If you hold small objects close to your eyes, you limit your field of vision and shut out the world. And, in the same way, the people or the things which stand nearest, even though they are of the very smallest consequence, are apt to claim an amount of attention much beyond their due, occupying us disagreeably, and leaving no room for serious thoughts and affairs of importance. We ought to work against this tendency.

Section 14

The sight of things which do not belong to us is very apt to raise the thought: Ah, if that were only mine! making us sensible of our privation. Instead of that we should do better by more frequently putting to ourselves the opposite case: Ah, if that were not mine. What I mean is that we should sometimes try to look upon our possessions in the light in which they would appear if we had lost them; whatever they may be, property, health, friends, a wife or child or someone else we love, our horse or our dog—it is usually only when we have lost them that we begin to find out their value. But if we come to look at things in the way I recommend, we shall be doubly the gainers; we shall at once get more pleasure out of them than we did before, and we shall do everything in our power to prevent the loss of them; for instance, by not risking our property, or angering our friends, or exposing our wives to temptation, or being careless about our children's health, and so on.

We often try to banish the gloom and despondency of the present by speculating upon our chances of success in the future; a process which leads us to invent a great many chimerical hopes. Every one of them contains the germ of illusion, and disappointment is inevitable when our hopes are shattered by the hard facts of life.

It is less hurtful to take the chances of misfortune as a theme for speculation; because, in doing so, we provide ourselves at once with measures of precaution against it, and a pleasant surprise when it fails to make its appearance. Is it not a fact that we always feel a marked improvement in our spirits when we begin to get over a period of anxiety? I may go further and say that there is some use in occasionally looking upon terrible misfortunes—such as might happen to us—as though they had actually happened, for then the trivial reverses which subsequently come in reality, are much easier to bear. It is a source of consolation to look back upon those great misfortunes which never happened. But in following out this rule, care must be taken not to neglect what I have said in the preceding section.

Section 15

The things which engage our attention—whether they are matters of business or ordinary events—are of such diverse kinds, that, if taken quite separately and in no fixed order or relation, they present a medley of the most glaring contrasts, with nothing in common, except that they one and all affect us in particular. There must be a corresponding abruptness in the thoughts and anxieties which these various matters arouse in us, if our thoughts are to be in keeping with their various subjects. Therefore, in setting about anything, the first step is to withdraw our attention from everything else: this will enable us to attend to each matter at its own time, and to enjoy or put up with it, quite apart from any thought of our remaining interests. Our thoughts must be arranged, as it were, in little drawers, so that we may open one without disturbing any of the others.

In this way we can keep the heavy burden of anxiety from weighing upon us so much as to spoil the little pleasures of the present, or from robbing us of our rest; otherwise the consideration of one matter will interfere with every other, and attention to some important business may lead us to neglect many affairs which happen to be of less moment. It is most important for everyone who is capable of higher and nobler thoughts to keep their mind from being so completely engrossed with private affairs and vulgar troubles as to let them take up all his attention and crowd out worthier matter; for that is, in a very real sense, to lose sight of the true end of life— propter vitam vivendi perdere causas.

Of course for this—as for so much else—self-control is necessary; without it, we cannot manage ourselves in the way I have described. And self-control may not appear so very difficult, if we consider that every man has to submit to a great deal of very severe control on the part of his surroundings, and that without it no form of existence is possible. Further, a little self-control at the right moment may prevent much subsequent compulsion at the hands of others; just as a very small section of a circle close to the centre may correspond to a part near the circumference a hundred times as large. Nothing will protect us from external compulsion so much as the control of ourselves; and, as Seneca says, to submit yourself to reason is the way to make everything else submit to you—si tibi vis omnia subjicere, te subjice rationi. Self-control, too, is something which we have in our own power; and if the worst comes to the worst, and it touches us in a very sensitive part, we can always relax its severity. But other people will pay no regard to our feelings, if they have to use compulsion, and we shall be treated without pity or mercy. Therefore it will be prudent to anticipate compulsion by self-control.

Section 16

We must set limits to our wishes, curb our desires, moderate our anger, always remembering that an individual can attain only an infinitesimal share in anything that is worth having; and that, on the other hand, everyone must incur many of the ills of life; in a word, we must bear and forbear—abstinere et sustinere; and if we fail to observe this rule, no position of wealth or power will prevent us from feeling wretched. This is what Horace means when he recommends us to study carefully and inquire diligently what will best promote a tranquil life—not to be always agitated by fruitless desires and fears and hopes for things, which, after all, are not worth very much:—

Inter cuncta leges et percontabere doctos
Qua ratione queas traducere leniter aevum;

Ne te semper inops agitet vexetque cupido,
Ne pavor, et rerum mediocriter utilium spes.[19]

Section 17

Life consists in movement, says Aristotle; and he is obviously right. We exist, physically, because our organism is the seat of constant motion; and if we are to exist intellectually, it can only be by means of continual occupation—no matter with what so long as it is some form of practical or mental activity. You may see that this is so by the way in which people who have no work or nothing to think about, immediately begin to beat the devil's tattoo with their knuckles or a stick or anything that comes handy. The truth is, that our nature is essentially restless in its character: we very soon get tired of having nothing to do; it is intolerable boredom. This impulse to activity should be regulated, and some sort of method introduced into it, which of itself will enhance the satisfaction we obtain. Activity!—doing something, if possible creating something, at any rate learning something—how fortunate it is that men cannot exist without that! A man wants to use his strength, to see, if he can, what effect it will produce; and he will get the most complete satisfaction of this desire if he can make or construct something—be it a book or a basket. There is a direct pleasure in seeing work grow under one's hands day by day, until at last it is finished. This is the pleasure attaching to a work of art or a manuscript, or even mere manual labor; and, of course, the higher the work, the greater pleasure it will give.

From this point of view, those are happiest of all who are conscious of the power to produce great works animated by some significant purpose: it gives a higher kind of interest—a sort of rare flavor—to the whole of their life, which, by its absence from the life of the ordinary man, makes it, in comparison, something very insipid. For richly endowed natures, life and the world have a special interest beyond the mere everyday personal interest which so many others share; and something higher than that—a formal interest. It is from life and the world that they get the material for their works; and as soon as they are freed from the pressure of personal needs, it is to the diligent collection of material that they devote their whole existence. So with their intellect: it is to some extent of a two-fold character, and devoted partly to the ordinary affairs of every day—those matters of will which are common to them and the rest of mankind, and partly to their peculiar work—the pure and objective contemplation of existence. And while, on the stage of the world, most men play their little part and then pass away, the genius lives a double life, at once an actor and a spectator.

Let everyone, then, do something, according to the measure of his capacities. To have no regular work, no set sphere of activity—what a miserable thing it is! How often long travels undertaken for pleasure make a man downright unhappy; because the absence of anything that can be called occupation forces him, as it were, out of his right element. Effort, struggles with difficulties! that is as natural to a man as grubbing in the ground is to a mole. To have all his wants satisfied is something intolerable—the feeling of stagnation which comes from pleasures that last too long. To overcome difficulties is to experience the full delight of existence, no matter where the obstacles are encountered; whether in the affairs of life, in commerce or business; or in mental effort—the spirit of inquiry that tries to master its subject. There is always something pleasurable in the struggle and the victory. And if a man has no opportunity to excite himself, he will do what he can to create one, and according to his individual bent, he will hunt or play Cup and Ball: or led on by this unsuspected element in his nature, he will pick a quarrel with some one, or hatch a plot or intrigue, or take to swindling and rascally courses generally—all to put an end to a state of repose which is intolerable. As I have remarked, *difficilis in otio quies*—it is difficult to keep quiet if you have nothing to do.

Section 18

A man should avoid being led on by the phantoms of his imagination. This is not the same thing as to submit to the guidance of ideas clearly thought out: and yet these are rules of life which most people pervert. If you examine closely into the circumstances which, in any deliberation, ultimately turn the scale in favor of some particular course, you will generally find that the decision is influenced, not by any clear arrangement of ideas leading to a formal judgment, but by some fanciful picture which seems to stand for one of the alternatives in question.

In one of Voltaire's or Diderot's romances,—I forget the precise reference,—the hero, standing like a young Hercules at the parting of ways, can see no other representation of Virtue than his old tutor holding a snuff-box in his left hand, from which he takes a pinch and moralizes; whilst Vice appears in the shape of his mother's chambermaid. It is in youth, more especially, that the goal of our efforts comes to be a fanciful picture of happiness, which continues to hover before our eyes sometimes for half and even for the whole of our life—a sort of mocking spirit; for when we think our dream is to be realized, the picture fades away, leaving us the knowledge that nothing of what it promised is actually accomplished. How often this is so with the visions of domesticity—the detailed picture of what our home will be like; or, of life among our fellow-citizens or in society; or, again, of living in the country—the kind of house we shall have, its surroundings, the marks of honor and respect that will be paid to us, and so on,—whatever our hobby may be; *chaque fou a sa marotte.* It is often the same, too, with our dreams about one we love. And this is all quite natural; for the visions we conjure up affect us directly, as though they were real objects; and so they exercise a more immediate influence upon our will than an abstract idea, which gives merely a vague, general outline, devoid of details; and the details are just the real part of it. We can be only indirectly affected by an abstract idea, and yet it is the abstract idea alone which will do as much as it promises; and it is the function of education to teach us to put our trust in it. Of course the abstract idea must be occasionally explained—paraphrased, as it were—by the aid of pictures; but discreetly, *cum grano salis.*

Section 19

The preceding rule may be taken as a special case of the more general maxim, that a man should never let himself be mastered by the impressions of the moment, or indeed by outward appearances at all, which are incomparably more powerful in their effects than the mere play of thought or a train of ideas; not because these momentary impressions are rich in virtue of the data they supply,—it is often just the contrary,—but because they are something palpable to the senses and direct in their working; they forcibly invade our mind, disturbing our repose and shattering our resolutions.

It is easy to understand that the thing which lies before our very eyes will produce the whole of its effect at once, but that time and leisure are necessary for the working of thought and the appreciation of argument, as it is impossible to think of everything at one and the same moment. This is why we are so allured by pleasure, in spite of all our determination to resist it; or so much annoyed by a criticism, even though we know that its author it totally incompetent to judge; or so irritated by an insult, though it comes from some very contemptible quarter. In the same way, to mention no other instances, ten reasons for thinking that there is no danger may be out-weighed by one mistaken notion that it is actually at hand. All this shows the radical unreason of human nature. Women frequently succumb altogether to this predomi-nating influence of present impressions, and there are few men so overweighted with reason as to escape suffering from a similar cause.

If it is impossible to resist the effects of some external influence by the mere play of thought, the best thing to do is to neutralize it by some contrary influence; for ex-ample, the effect of an insult may be overcome by seeking the society of those who have a good opinion of us; and the unpleasant sensation of imminent danger may be avoided by fixing our attention on the means of warding it off.

Leibnitz[20] tells of an Italian who managed to bear up under the tortures of the rack by never for a moment ceasing to think of the gallows which would have await-ed him, had he revealed his secret; he kept on crying out: I see it! I see it!— afterwards explaining that this was part of his plan.

It is from some such reason as this, that we find it so difficult to stand alone in a matter of opinion,—not to be made irresolute by the fact that everyone else disa-grees with us and acts accordingly, even though we are quite sure that they are in the wrong. Take the case of a fugitive king who is trying to avoid capture; how much con-solation he must find in the ceremonious and submissive attitude of a faithful follow-er, exhibited secretly so as not to betray his master's strict incognito; it must be al-most necessary to prevent him doubting his own existence.

Section 20

In the first part of this work I have insisted upon the great value of health as the chief and most important element in happiness. Let me emphasize and confirm what I have there said by giving a few general rules as to its preservation.

The way to harden the body is to impose a great deal of labor and effort upon it in the days of good health,—to exercise it, both as a whole and in its several parts, and to habituate it to withstand all kinds of noxious influences. But on the appearance of an illness or disorder, either in the body as a whole or in many of its parts, a contrary course should be taken, and every means used to nurse the body, or the part of it which is affected, and to spare it any effort; for what is ailing and debilitated cannot be hardened.

The muscles may be strengthened by a vigorous use of them; but not so the nerves; they are weakened by it. Therefore, while exercising the muscles in every way that is suitable, care should be taken to spare the nerves as much as possible. The eyes, for instance, should be protected from too strong a light,—especially when it is reflected light,—from any straining of them in the dark, or from the long-continued examination of minute objects; and the ears from too loud sounds. Above all, the brain should never be forced, or used too much, or at the wrong time; let it have a rest during digestion; for then the same vital energy which forms thoughts in the brain has a great deal of work to do elsewhere,—I mean in the digestive organs, where it prepares chyme and chyle. For similar reasons, the brain should never be used during, or immediately after, violent muscular exercise. For the motor nerves are in this respect on a par with the sensory nerves; the pain felt when a limb is wounded has its seat in the brain; and, in the same way, it is not really our legs and arms which work and move,—it is the brain, or, more strictly, that part of it which, through the medium of the spine, excites the nerves in the limbs and sets them in motion. Accordingly, when our arms and legs feel tired, the true seat of this feeling is in the brain. This is why it is only in connection with those muscles which are set in motion consciously and voluntarily,—in other words, depend for their action upon the brain,—that any feeling of fatigue can arise; this is not the case with those muscles which work involuntarily, like the heart. It is obvious, then, that injury is done to the brain if violent muscular exercise and intellectual exertion are forced upon it at the same moment, or at very short intervals.

What I say stands in no contradiction with the fact that at the beginning of a walk, or at any period of a short stroll, there often comes a feeling of enhanced intellectual vigor. The parts of the brain that come into play have had no time to become tired; and besides, slight muscular exercise conduces to activity of the respiratory organs, and causes a purer and more oxydated supply of arterial blood to mount to the brain.

It is most important to allow the brain the full measure of sleep which is required to restore it; for sleep is to a man's whole nature what winding up is to a clock.[21] This measure will vary directly with the development and activity of the brain; to overstep the measure is mere waste of time, because if that is done, sleep gains only so much in length as it loses in depth.[22]

It should be clearly understood that thought is nothing but the organic function of the brain; and it has to obey the same laws in regard to exertion and repose as any other organic function. The brain can be ruined by overstrain, just like the eyes. As the function of the stomach is to digest, so it is that of the brain to think. The notion of a soul,—as something elementary and immaterial, merely lodging in the brain and needing nothing at all for the performance of its essential function, which consists in always and unweariedly thinking—has undoubtedly driven many people to foolish practices, leading to a deadening of the intellectual powers; Frederick the Great, even, once tried to form the habit of doing without sleep altogether. It would be well if professors of philosophy refrained from giving currency to a notion which is attended by practical results of a pernicious character; but then this is just what professorial philosophy does, in its old-womanish endeavor to keep on good terms with the catechism. A man should accustom himself to view his intellectual capacities in no other light than that of physiological functions, and to manage them accordingly—nursing or exercising them as the case may be; remembering that every kind of physical suffering, malady or disorder, in whatever part of the body it occurs, has its effect upon the mind. The best advice that I know on this subject is given by Cabanis in his Rapports du physique et du moral de l'homme.[23]

Through neglect of this rule, many men of genius and great scholars have become weak-minded and childish, or even gone quite mad, as they grew old. To take no other instances, there can be no doubt that the celebrated English poets of the early part of this century, Scott, Wordsworth, Southey, became intellectually dull and incapable towards the end of their days, nay, soon after passing their sixtieth year; and that their imbecility can be traced to the fact that, at that period of life, they were all led on? by the promise of high pay, to treat literature as a trade and to write for money. This seduced them into an unnatural abuse of their intellectual powers; and a man who puts his Pegasus into harness, and urges on his Muse with the whip, will have to pay a penalty similar to that which is exacted by the abuse of other kinds of power.

And even in the case of Kant, I suspect that the second childhood of his last four years was due to overwork in later life, and after he had succeeded in becoming a famous man.

Every month of the year has its own peculiar and direct influence upon health and bodily condition generally; nay, even upon the state of the mind. It is an influence dependent upon the weather.

Notes

1. *Iliad, xix, 65.*
2. *Ibid, xvii, 514*
3. *Translator's Note. A series of Greek, Latin and French classics published at Zweibraecken in the Palatinate, from and after the year 1779. Cf. Butter, Ueber die Bipontiner und die editiones Bipontinae.*
4. *Eudem. Eth. VII. ii. 37.*
5. *As our body is concealed by the clothes we wear, so our mind is veiled in lies. The veil is always there, and it is only through it that we can sometimes guess at what a man really thinks; just as from his clothes we arrive at the general shape of his body.*
6. *Paradoxa Stoidorum: II.*
7. *It is a well-known fact, that we can more easily bear up under evils which fall upon a great many people besides ourselves. As boredom seems to be an evil of this kind, people band together to offer it a common resistance. The love of life is at bottom only the fear of death; and, in the same way, the social impulse does not rest directly upon the love of society, but upon the fear of solitude; it is not alone the charm of being in others' company that people seek, it is the dreary oppression of being alone—the monotony of their own consciousness—that they would avoid. They will do anything to escape it,—even tolerate bad companions, and put up with the feeling of constraint which all society involves, in this case a very burdensome one. But if aversion to such society conquers the aversion to being alone, they become accustomed to solitude and hardened to its immediate effects. They no longer find solitude to be such a very bad thing, and settle down comfortably to it without any hankering after society;—and this, partly because it is only indirectly that they need others' company, and partly because they have become accustomed to the benefits of being alone.*
8. *Translator's Note. The passage to which Schopenhauer refers is Parerga: vol. ii. Sec. 413 (4th edition). The fable is of certain porcupines, who huddled together for warmth on a cold day; but as they began to prick one another with their quills, they were obliged to disperse. However the cold drove them together again, when just the same thing happened. At last, after many turns of huddling and dispersing, they discovered that they would be best off by remaining at a little distance from one another. In the same way, the need of society drives the human porcupines together—only to be mutually repelled by the many prickly and disagreeable qualities of their nature. The moderate distance which they at last discover to be the only tolerable condition of intercourse, is the code of politeness and fine manners; and those who transgress it are roughly told—in the English phrase—to keep their distance. By this arrangement the mutual need of*

warmth is only very moderately satisfied,—but then people do not get pricked. A man who has some heat in himself prefers to remain outside, where he will neither prick other people nor get pricked himself.

9. *Translator's Note. Angelus Silesius, pseudonym for Johannes Scheffler, a physician and mystic poet of the seventeenth century (1624-77).*

10. *Psalms, lv. 7.*

11. *Goethe's Faust, Part I., 1281-5.*

12. *This restricted, or, as it were, entrenched kind of sociability has been dramatically illustrated in a play—well worth reading—of Moratin's, entitled El Cafe o sea la Comedia Nuova (The Cafe or the New Comedy), chiefly by one of the characters, Don Pedro and especially in the second and third scenes of the first act.*

13. *Envy shows how unhappy people are; and their constant attention to what others do and leave undone, how much they are bored.*

14. *De Ira: iii., 30.*

15. *Epist. xv.*

16. *It may be observed, in passing, that a great many of the maxims which Goethe puts under the head of Proverbial, are translations from the Italian.*

17. *Menander. Monost: 422.*

18. *Goethe.*

19. *Epist. I. xviii. 97.*

20. *Nouveaux Essais. Liv. I. ch. 2. Sec. 11.*

21. *Of. Welt als Wille und Vorstellung, 4th Edition. Bk. II. pp. 236-40.*

22. *Cf. loc: cit: p. 275. Sleep is a morsel of death borrowed to keep up and renew the part of life which is exhausted by the day—le sommeil est un emprunt fait a la mort. Or it might be said that sleep is the interest we have to pay on the capital which is called in at death; and the higher the rate of interest and the more regularly it is paid, the further the date of redemption is postponed.*

23. *Translator's Note. The work to which Schopenhauer here refers is a series of essays by Cabanis, a French philosopher (1757-1808), treating of mental and moral phenomena on a physiological basis. In his later days, Cabanis completely abandoned his materialistic standpoint.*

Our Relation to Others

Section 21

In making his way through life, a man will find it useful to be ready and able to do two things: to look ahead and to overlook: the one will protect him from loss and injury, the other from disputes and squabbles.

No one who has to live amongst men should absolutely discard any person who has his due place in the order of nature, even though he is very wicked or contemptible or ridiculous. He must accept him as an unalterable fact—unalterable, because the necessary outcome of an eternal, fundamental principle; and in bad cases he should remember the words of Mephistopheles: es muss auch solche Kaeuze geben[1]—there must be fools and rogues in the world. If he acts otherwise, he will be committing an injustice, and giving a challenge of life and death to the man he discards. No one can alter his own peculiar individuality, his moral character, his intellectual capacity, his temperament or physique; and if we go so far as to condemn a man from every point of view, there will be nothing left him but to engage us in deadly conflict; for we are practically allowing him the right to exist only on condition that he becomes another man—which is impossible; his nature forbids it.

So if you have to live amongst men, you must allow everyone the right to exist in accordance with the character he has, whatever it turns out to be: and all you should strive to do is to make use of this character in such a way as its kind and nature permit, rather than to hope for any alteration in it, or to condemn it off-hand for what it is. This is the true sense of the maxim—Live and let live. That, however, is a task which is difficult in proportion as it is right; and he is a happy man who can once for all avoid having to do with a great many of his fellow creatures.

The art of putting up with people may be learned by practicing patience on inanimate objects, which, in virtue of some mechanical or general physical necessity, oppose a stubborn resistance to our freedom of action—a form of patience which is required every day. The patience thus gained may be applied to our dealings with men, by accustoming ourselves to regard their opposition, wherever we encounter it, as the inevitable outcome of their nature, which sets itself up against us in virtue of the same rigid law of necessity as governs the resistance of inanimate objects. To become indignant at their conduct is as foolish as to be angry with a stone because it rolls into your path. And with many people the wisest thing you can do, is to resolve to make use of those whom you cannot alter.

Section 22

It is astonishing how easily and how quickly similarity, or difference of mind and disposition, makes itself felt between one man and another as soon as they begin to talk: every little trifle shows it. When two people of totally different natures are conversing, almost everything said by the one will, in a greater or less degree, displease the other, and in many cases produce positive annoyance; even though the conversation turn upon the most out-of-the-way subject, or one in which neither of the parties has any real interest. People of similar nature, on the other hand, immediately come to feel a kind of general agreement; and if they are cast very much in the same mould, complete harmony or even unison will flow from their intercourse.

This explain two circumstances. First of all, it shows why it is that common, ordinary people are so sociable and find good company wherever they go. Ah! those good, dear, brave people. It is just the contrary with those who are not of the common run; and the less they are so, the more unsociable they become; so that if, in their isolation, they chance to come across some one in whose nature they can find even a single sympathetic chord, be it never so minute, they show extraordinary pleasure in his society. For one man can be to another only so much as the other is to him. Great minds are like eagles, and build their nest in some lofty solitude.

Secondly, we are enabled to understand how it is that people of like disposition so quickly get on with one another, as though they were drawn together by magnetic force—kindred souls greeting each other from afar. Of course the most frequent opportunity of observing this is afforded by people of vulgar tastes and inferior intellect, but only because their name is legion; while those who are better off in this respect and of a rarer nature, are not often to be met with: they are called rare because you can seldom find them.

94

Take the case of a large number of people who have formed themselves into a league for the purpose of carrying out some practical object; if there be two rascals among them, they will recognize each other as readily as if they bore a similar badge, and will at once conspire for some misfeasance or treachery. In the same way, if you can imagine—per impossible—a large company of very intelligent and clever people, amongst whom there are only two blockheads, these two will be sure to be drawn together by a feeling of sympathy, and each of them will very soon secretly rejoice at having found at least one intelligent person in the whole company. It is really quite curious to see how two such men, especially if they are morally and intellectually of an inferior type, will recognize each other at first sight; with what zeal they will strive to become intimate; how affably and cheerily they will run to greet each other, just as though they were old friends;—it is all so striking that one is tempted to embrace the Buddhist doctrine of metempsychosis and presume that they were on familiar terms in some former state of existence.

Still, in spite of all this general agreement, men are kept apart who might come together; or, in some cases, a passing discord springs up between them. This is due to diversity of mood. You will hardly ever see two people exactly in the same frame of mind; for that is something which varies with their condition of life, occupation, surroundings, health, the train of thought they are in at the moment, and so on. These differences give rise to discord between persons of the most harmonious disposition. To correct the balance properly, so as to remove the disturbance—to introduce, as it were, a uniform temperature,—is a work demanding a very high degree of culture. The extent to which uniformity of mood is productive of good-fellowship may be measured by its effects upon a large company. When, for instance, a great many people are gathered together and presented with some objective interest which works upon all alike and influences them in a similar way, no matter what it be—a common danger or hope, some great news, a spectacle, a play, a piece of music, or anything of that kind—you will find them roused to a mutual expression of thought, and a display of sincere interest. There will be a general feeling of pleasure amongst them; for that which attracts their attention produces a unity of mood by overpowering all private and personal interests.

And in default of some objective interest of the kind I have mentioned, recourse is usually had to something subjective. A bottle of wine is not an uncommon means of introducing a mutual feeling of fellowship; and even tea and coffee are used for a like end.

The discord which so easily finds its way into all society as an effect of the different moods in which people happen to be for the moment, also in part explains why it is that memory always idealizes, and sometimes almost transfigures, the attitude we have taken up at any period of the past—a change due to our inability to remember all the fleeting influences which disturbed us on any given occasion. Memory is in this respect like the lens of a camera obscura: it contracts everything within its range, and so produces a much finer picture than the actual landscape affords. And, in the case of a man, absence always goes some way towards securing this advantageous light; for though the idealizing tendency of the memory requires times to complete its work, it begins it at once. Hence it is a prudent thing to see your friends and acquaintances only at considerable intervals of time; and on meeting them again, you will observe that memory has been at work.

Section 23

No man can see over his own height. Let me explain what I mean.

You cannot see in another man any more than you have in yourself; and your own intelligence strictly determines the extent to which he comes within its grasp. If your intelligence is of a very low order, mental qualities in another, even though they be of the highest kind, will have no effect at all upon you; you will see nothing in their possessor except the meanest side of his individuality—in other words, just those parts of his character and disposition which are weak and defective. Your whole estimate of the man will be confined to his defects, and his higher mental qualities will no more exist for you than colors exist for those who cannot see.

Intellect is invisible to the man who has none. In any attempt to criticise another's work, the range of knowledge possessed by the critic is as essential a part of his verdict as the claims of the work itself.

Hence intercourse with others involves a process of leveling down. The qualities which are present in one man, and absent in another, cannot come into play when they meet; and the self-sacrifice which this entails upon one of the parties, calls forth no recognition from the other.

Consider how sordid, how stupid, in a word, how vulgar most men are, and you will see that it is impossible to talk to them without becoming vulgar yourself for the time being. Vulgarity is in this respect like electricity; it is easily distributed. You will then fully appreciate the truth and propriety of the expression, to make yourself cheap; and you will be glad to avoid the society of people whose only possible point of contact with you is just that part of your nature of which you have least reason to be proud. So you will see that, in dealing with fools and blockheads, there is only one way of showing your intelligence—by having nothing to do with them. That means, of course, that when you go into society, you may now and then feel like a good dancer who gets an invitation to a ball, and on arriving, finds that everyone is lame:—with whom is he to dance?

Section 24

I feel respect for the man—and he is one in a hundred—who, when he is waiting or sitting unoccupied, refrains from rattling or beating time with anything that happens to be handy,—his stick, or knife and fork, or whatever else it may be. The probability is that he is thinking of something.

With a large number of people, it is quite evident that their power of sight completely dominates over their power of thought; they seem to be conscious of existence only when they are making a noise; unless indeed they happen to be smoking, for this serves a similar end. It is for the same reason that they never fail to be all eyes and ears for what is going on around them.

Section 25

La Rochefoucauld makes the striking remark that it is difficult to feel deep veneration and great affection for one and the same person. If this is so, we shall have to choose whether it is veneration or love that we want from our fellow-men.

Their love is always selfish, though in very different ways; and the means used to gain it are not always of a kind to make us proud. A man is loved by others mainly in the degree in which he moderates his claim on their good feeling and intelligence: but he must act genuinely in the matter and without dissimulation—not merely out of forbearance, which is at bottom a kind of contempt. This calls to mind a very true observation of Helvetius[2]: the amount of intellect necessary to please us, is a most accurate measure of the amount of intellect we have ourselves. With these remarks as premises, it is easy to draw the conclusion.

Now with veneration the case is just the opposite; it is wrung from men reluctantly, and for that very reason mostly concealed. Hence, as compared with love, veneration gives more real satisfaction; for it is connected with personal value, and the same is not directly true of love, which is subjective in its nature, whilst veneration is objective. To be sure, it is more useful to be loved than to be venerated.

Section 26

Most men are so thoroughly subjective that nothing really interests them but themselves. They always think of their own case as soon as ever any remark is made, and their whole attention is engrossed and absorbed by the merest chance reference to anything which affects them personally, be it never so remote: with the result that they have no power left for forming an objective view of things, should the conversation take that turn; neither can they admit any validity in arguments which tell against their interest or their vanity. Hence their attention is easily distracted. They are so readily offended, insulted or annoyed, that in discussing any impersonal matter with them, no care is too great to avoid letting your remarks bear the slightest possible reference to the very worthy and sensitive individuals whom you have before you; for anything you may say will perhaps hurt their feelings. People really care about nothing that does not affect them personally. True and striking observations, fine, subtle and witty things are lost upon them: they cannot understand or feel them. But anything that disturbs their petty vanity in the most remote and indirect way, or reflects prejudicially upon their exceedingly precious selves—to that, they are most tenderly sensitive. In this respect they are like the little dog whose toes you are so apt to tread upon inadvertently—you know it by the shrill bark it sets up: or, again, they resemble a sick man covered with sores and boils, with whom the greatest care must be taken to avoid unnecessary handling. And in some people this feeling reaches such a pass that, if they are talking with anyone, and he exhibits, or does not sufficiently conceal, his intelligence and discernment, they look upon it as a downright insult; although for the moment they hide their ill will, and the unsuspecting author of it afterwards ruminates in vain upon their conduct, and racks his brain to discover what he could possibly have done to excite their malice and hatred.

But it is just as easy to flatter and win them over; and this is why their judgment is usually corrupt, and why their opinions are swayed, not by what is really true and right, but by the favor of the party or class to which they belong. And the ultimate reason of it all is, that in such people force of will greatly predominates over knowledge; and hence their meagre intellect is wholly given up to the service of the will, and can never free itself from that service for a moment.

Astrology furnishes a magnificent proof of this miserable subjective tendency in men, which leads them to see everything only as bearing upon themselves, and to think of nothing that is not straightway made into a personal matter. The aim of astrology is to bring the motions of the celestial bodies into relation with the wretched Ego and to establish a connection between a comet in the sky and squabbles and rascalities on earth.[3]

Section 27

When any wrong statement is made, whether in public or in society, or in books, and well received—or, at any rate, not refuted—that that is no reason why you should despair or think there the matter will rest. You should comfort yourself with the reflection that the question will be afterwards gradually subjected to examination; light will be thrown upon it; it will be thought over, considered, discussed, and generally in the end the correct view will be reached; so that, after a time—the length of which will depend upon the difficulty of the subject—everyone will come to understand that which a clear head saw at once.

In the meantime, of course, you must have patience. He who can see truly in the midst of general infatuation is like a man whose watch keeps good time, when all clocks in the town in which he lives are wrong. He alone knows the right time; but what use is that to him? for everyone goes by the clocks which speak false, not even excepting those who know that his watch is the only one that is right.

Section 28

Men are like children, in that, if you spoil them, they become naughty.

Therefore it is well not to be too indulgent or charitable with anyone. You may take it as a general rule that you will not lose a friend by refusing him a loan, but that you are very likely to do so by granting it; and, for similar reasons, you will not readily alienate people by being somewhat proud and careless in your behaviour; but if you are very kind and complaisant towards them, you will often make them arrogant and intolerable, and so a breach will ensue.

There is one thing that, more than any other, throws people absolutely off their balance—the thought that you are dependent upon them. This is sure to produce an insolent and domineering manner towards you. There are some people, indeed, who become rude if you enter into any kind of relation with them; for instance, if you have occasion to converse with them frequently upon confidential matters, they soon come to fancy that they can take liberties with you, and so they try and transgress the laws of politeness. This is why there are so few with whom you care to become more intimate, and why you should avoid familiarity with vulgar people. If a man comes to think that I am more dependent upon him than he is upon me, he at once feels as though I had stolen something from him; and his endeavor will be to have his vengeance and get it back. The only way to attain superiority in dealing with men, is to let it be seen that you are independent of them.

And in this view it is advisable to let everyone of your acquaintance—whether man or woman—feel now and then that you could very well dispense with their company. This will consolidate friendship. Nay, with most people there will be no harm in occasionally mixing a grain of disdain with your treatment of them; that will make them value your friendship all the more. Chi non istima vien stimato, as a subtle Italian proverb has it—to disregard is to win regard. But if we really think very highly of a person, we should conceal it from him like a crime. This is not a very gratifying thing to do, but it is right. Why, a dog will not bear being treated too kindly, let alone a man!

Section 29

It is often the case that people of noble character and great mental gifts betray a strange lack of worldly wisdom and a deficiency in the knowledge of men, more especially when they are young; with the result that it is easy to deceive or mislead them; and that, on the other hand, natures of the commoner sort are more ready and successful in making their way in the world.

The reason of this is that, when a man has little or no experience, he must judge by his own antecedent notions; and in matters demanding judgment, an antecedent notion is never on the same level as experience. For, with the commoner sort of people, an antecedent notion means just their own selfish point of view. This is not the case with those whose mind and character are above the ordinary; for it is precisely in this respect—their unselfishness—that they differ from the rest of mankind; and as they judge other people's thoughts and actions by their own high standard, the result does not always tally with their calculation.

But if, in the end, a man of noble character comes to see, as the effect of his own experience, or by the lessons he learns from others, what it is that may be expected of men in general,—namely, that five-sixths of them are morally and intellectually so constituted that, if circumstances do not place you in relation with them, you had better get out of their way and keep as far as possible from having anything to do with them,—still, he will scarcely ever attain an adequate notion of their wretchedly mean and shabby nature: all his life long he will have to be extending and adding to the inferior estimate he forms of them; and in the meantime he will commit a great many mistakes and do himself harm.

Then, again, after he has really taken to heart the lessons that have been taught him, it will occasionally happen that, when he is in the society of people whom he does not know, he will be surprised to find how thoroughly reasonable they all appear to be, both in their conversation and in their demeanor—in fact, quite honest, sincere, virtuous and trustworthy people, and at the same time shrewd and clever.

But that ought not to perplex him. Nature is not like those bad poets, who, in setting a fool or a knave before us, do their work so clumsily, and with such evident design, that you might almost fancy you saw the poet standing behind each of his characters, and continually disavowing their sentiments, and telling you in a tone of warning: This is a knave; that is a fool; do not mind what he says. But Nature goes to work like Shakespeare and Goethe, poets who make every one of their characters—even if it is the devil himself!—appear to be quite in the right for the moment that they come before us in their several parts; the characters are described so objectively that they excite our interest and compel us to sympathize with their point of view; for, like the works of Nature, every one of these characters is evolved as the result of some hidden law or principle, which makes all they say and do appear natural and therefore necessary. And you will always be the prey or the plaything of the devils and fools in this world, if you expect to see them going about with horns or jangling their bells.

And it should be borne in mind that, in their intercourse with others, people are like the moon, or like hunchbacks; they show you only one of their sides. Every man has an innate talent for mimicry,—for making a mask out of his physiognomy, so that he can always look as if he really were what he pretends to be; and since he makes his calculations always within the lines of his individual nature, the appearance he puts on suits him to a nicety, and its effect is extremely deceptive. He dons his mask whenever his object is to flatter himself into some one's good opinion; and you may pay just as much attention to it as if it were made of wax or cardboard, never forgetting that excellent Italian proverb: non e si tristo cane che non meni la coda,—there is no dog so bad but that he will wag his tail.

In any case it is well to take care not to form a highly favorable opinion of a person whose acquaintance you have only recently made, for otherwise you are very likely to be disappointed; and then you will be ashamed of yourself and perhaps even suffer some injury. And while I am on the subject, there is another fact that deserves mention. It is this. A man shows his character just in the way in which he deals with trifles,—for then he is off his guard. This will often afford a good opportunity of observing the boundless egoism of man's nature, and his total lack of consideration for others; and if these defects show themselves in small things, or merely in his general demeanor, you will find that they also underlie his action in matters of importance, although he may disguise the fact. This is an opportunity which should not be missed. If in the little affairs of every day,—the trifles of life, those matters to which the rule de minimis non applies,—a man is inconsiderate and seeks only what is advantageous or convenient to himself, to the prejudice of others' rights; if he appropriates to himself that which belongs to all alike, you may be sure there is no justice in his heart, and that he would be a scoundrel on a wholesale scale, only that law and compulsion bind his hands. Do not trust him beyond your door. He who is not afraid to break the laws of his own private circle, will break those of the State when he can do so with impunity.

If the average man were so constituted that the good in him outweighed the bad, it would be more advisable to rely upon his sense of justice, fairness, gratitude, fidelity, love or compassion, than to work upon his fears; but as the contrary is the case, and it is the bad that outweighs the good, the opposite course is the more prudent one.

If any person with whom we are associated or have to do, exhibits unpleasant or annoying qualities, we have only to ask ourselves whether or not this person is of so much value to us that we can put up with frequent and repeated exhibitions of the same qualities in a somewhat aggravated form.[4] In case of an affirmative answer to this question, there will not be much to be said, because talking is very little use. We must let the matter pass, with or without some notice; but we should nevertheless remember that we are thereby exposing ourselves to a repetition of the offence. If the answer is in the negative, we must break with our worthy friend at once and forever; or in the case of a servant, dismiss him. For he will inevitably repeat the offence, or do something tantamount to it, should the occasion return, even though for the moment he is deep and sincere in his assurances of the contrary. There is nothing, absolutely nothing, that a man cannot forget,—but not himself, his own character. For character is incorrigible; because all a man's actions emanate from an inward principle, in virtue of which he must always do the same thing under like circumstances; and he cannot do otherwise. Let me refer to my prize essay on the so-called

Freedom of the Will, the perusal of which will dissipate any delusions the reader may have on this subject.

To become reconciled to a friend with whom you have broken, is a form of weakness; and you pay the penalty of it when he takes the first opportunity of doing precisely the very thing which brought about the breach; nay, he does it the more boldly, because he is secretly conscious that you cannot get on without him. This is also applicable to servants whom you have dismissed, and then taken into your service again.

For the same reason, you should just as little expect people to continue to act in a similar way under altered circumstances. The truth is that men alter their demeanor and sentiments just as fast as their interest changes; and their resign in this respect is a bill drawn for short payment that the man must be still more short-sighted who accepts the bill without protesting it. Accordingly, suppose you want to know how a man will behave in an office into which you think of putting him; you should not build upon expectations, on his promises or assurances. For, even allowing that he is quite sincere, he is speaking about a matter of which he has no knowledge. The only way to calculate how he will behave, is to consider the circumstances in which he will be placed, and the extent to which they will conflict with his character.

If you wish to get a clear and profound insight—and it is very needful—into the true but melancholy elements of which most men are made, you will find in a very instructive thing to take the way they behave in the pages of literature as a commentary to their doings in practical life, and vice versa. The experience thus gained will be very useful in avoiding wrong ideas, whether about yourself or about others. But if you come across any special trait of meanness or stupidity—in life or in literature,—you must be careful not to let it annoy or distress you, but to look upon it merely as an addition to your knowledge—a new fact to be considered in studying the character of humanity. Your attitude towards it will be that of the mineralogist who stumbles upon a very characteristic specimen of a mineral.

Of course there are some facts which are very exceptional, and it is difficult to understand how they arise, and how it is that there come to be such enormous differences between man and man; but, in general, what was said long ago is quite true, and the world is in a very bad way. In savage countries they eat one another, in civilized they deceive one another; and that is what people call the way of the world! What are States and all the elaborate systems of political machinery, and the rule of force, whether in home or in foreign affairs,—what are they but barriers against the boundless iniquity of mankind? Does not all history show that whenever a king is firmly planted on a throne, and his people reach some degree of prosperity, he uses it to lead his army, like a band of robbers, against adjoining countries? Are not almost all wars ultimately undertaken for purposes of plunder? In the most remote antiquity, and to some extent also in the Middle Ages, the conquered became slaves,—in other words, they had to work for those who conquered them; and where is the difference between that and paying war-taxes, which represent the product of our previous work?

All war, says Voltaire, is a matter of robbery; and the Germans should take that as a warning.

No man is so formed that he can be left entirely to himself, to go his own ways; everyone needs to be guided by a preconceived plan, and to follow certain general rules. But if this is carried too far, and a man tries to take on a character which is not natural or innate in him, but it artificially acquired and evolved merely by a process of reasoning, he will very soon discover that Nature cannot be forced, and that if you drive it out, it will return despite your efforts:—

Naturam expelles furca, tamen usque recurret.

To understand a rule governing conduct towards others, even to discover it for oneself and to express it neatly, is easy enough; and still, very soon afterwards, the rule may be broken in practice. But that is no reason for despair; and you need not fancy that as it is impossible to regulate your life in accordance with abstract ideas and maxims, it is better to live just as you please. Here, as in all theoretical instruction that aims at a practical result, the first thing to do is to understand the rule; the second thing is to learn the practice of it. The theory may be understood at once by an effort of reason, and yet the practice of it acquired only in course of time.

A pupil may lean the various notes on an instrument of music, or the different position in fencing; and when he makes a mistake, as he is sure to do, however hard he tries, he is apt to think it will be impossible to observe the rules, when he is set to read music at sight or challenged to a furious duel. But for all that, gradual practice makes him perfect, through a long series of slips, blunders and fresh efforts. It is just the same in other things; in learning to write and speak Latin, a man will forget the grammatical rules; it is only by long practice that a blockhead turns into a courtier, that a passionate man becomes shrewd and worldly-wise, or a frank person reserved, or a noble person ironical. But though self-discipline of this kind is the result of long habit, it always works by a sort of external compulsion, which Nature never ceases to resist and sometimes unexpectedly overcomes. The difference between action in accordance with abstract principles, and action as the result of original, innate tendency, is the same as that between a work of art, say a watch—where form and movement are impressed upon shapeless and inert matter—and a living organism, where form and matter are one, and each is inseparable from the other.

There is a maxim attributed to the Emperor Napoleon, which expresses this relation between acquired and innate character, and confirms what I have said: everything that is unnatural is imperfect;—a rule of universal application, whether in the physical or in the moral sphere. The only exception I can think of to this rule is aventurine,[5] a substance known to mineralogists, which in its natural state cannot compare with the artificial preparation of it.

And in this connection let me utter a word of protest against any and every form of affectation. It always arouses contempt; in the first place, because it argues deception, and the deception is cowardly, for it is based on fear; and, secondly, it argues self-condemnation, because it means that a man is trying to appear what he is not, and therefore something which he things better than he actually is. To affect a quality, and to plume yourself upon it, is just to confess that you have not got it. Whether it is courage, or learning, or intellect, or wit, or success with women, or riches, or social position, or whatever else it may be that a man boasts of, you may conclude by his boasting about it that that is precisely the direction in which he is rather weak; for if a man really possesses any faculty to the full, it will not occur to him to make a great show of affecting it; he is quite content to know that he has it. That is the application of the Spanish proverb: herradura que chacolotea clavo le falta—a clattering hoof means a nail gone. To be sure, as I said at first, no man ought to let the reins go quite loose, and show himself just as he is; for there are many evil and bestial sides to our nature which require to be hidden away out of sight; and this justifies the negative attitude of dissimulation, but it does not justify a positive feigning of qualities which are not there. It should also be remembered that affectation is recognized at once, even before it is clear what it is that is being affected. And, finally, affectation cannot last very long, and one day the mask will fall off. Nemo potest personam diu ferre fictam, says Seneca;[6] ficta cito in naturam suam recidunt—no one can persevere long in a fictitious character; for nature will soon reassert itself.

Section 31

A man bears the weight of his own body without knowing it, but he soon feels the weight of any other, if he tries to move it; in the same way, a man can see other people's shortcoming's and vices, but he is blind to his own. This arrangement has one advantage: it turns other people into a kind of mirror, in which a man can see clearly everything that is vicious, faulty, ill-bred and loathsome in his own nature; only, it is generally the old story of the dog barking at is own image; it is himself that he sees and not another dog, as he fancies.

He who criticises others, works at the reformation of himself. Those who form the secret habit of scrutinizing other people's general behavior, and passing severe judgment upon what they do and leave undone, thereby improve themselves, and work out their own perfection: for they will have sufficient sense of justice, or at any rate enough pride and vanity, to avoid in their own case that which they condemn so harshly elsewhere. But tolerant people are just the opposite, and claim for themselves the same indulgence that they extend to others—hanc veniam damus petimusque vicissim. It is all very well for the Bible to talk about the mote in another's eye and the beam in one's own. The nature of the eye is to look not at itself but at other things; and therefore to observe and blame faults in another is a very suitable way of becoming conscious of one's own. We require a looking-glass for the due dressing of our morals.

The same rule applies in the case of style and fine writing. If, instead of condemning, you applaud some new folly in these matters, you will imitate it. That is just why literary follies have such vogue in Germany. The Germans are a very tolerant people—everybody can see that! Their maxim is—Hanc veniam damns petimusque vicissim.

Section 32

When he is young, a man of noble character fancies that the relations prevailing amongst mankind, and the alliances to which these relations lead, are at bottom and essentially, ideal in their nature; that is to say, that they rest upon similarity of disposition or sentiment, or taste, or intellectual power, and so on.

But, later on, he finds out that it is a real foundation which underlies these alliances; that they are based upon some material interest. This is the true foundation of almost all alliances: nay, most men have no notion of an alliance resting upon any other basis. Accordingly we find that a man is always measured by the office he holds, or by his occupation, nationality, or family relations—in a word, by the position and character which have been assigned him in the conventional arrangements of life, where he is ticketed and treated as so much goods. Reference to what he is in himself, as a man—to the measure of his own personal qualities—is never made unless for convenience' sake: and so that view of a man is something exceptional, to be set aside and ignored, the moment that anyone finds it disagreeable; and this is what usually happens. But the more of personal worth a man has, the less pleasure he will take in these conventional arrangements; and he will try to withdraw from the sphere in which they apply. The reason why these arrangements exist at all, is simply that in this world of ours misery and need are the chief features: therefore it is everywhere the essential and paramount business of life to devise the means of alleviating them.

Section 33

As paper-money circulates in the world instead of real coin, so, is the place of true esteem and genuine friendship, you have the outward appearance of it—a mimic show made to look as much like the real thing as possible.

On the other hand, it may be asked whether there are any people who really deserve the true coin. For my own part, I should certainly pay more respect to an honest dog wagging his tail than to a hundred such demonstrations of human regard.

True and genuine friendship presupposes a strong sympathy with the weal and woe of another—purely objective in its character and quite disinterested; and this in its turn means an absolute identification of self with the object of friendship. The egoism of human nature is so strongly antagonistic to any such sympathy, that true friendship belongs to that class of things—the sea-serpent, for instance,—with regard to which no one knows whether they are fabulous or really exist somewhere or other.

Still, in many cases, there is a grain of true and genuine friendship in the relation of man to man, though generally, of course, some secret personal interest is at the bottom of them—some one among the many forms that selfishness can take. But in a world where all is imperfect, this grain of true feeling is such an ennobling influence that it gives some warrant for calling those relations by the name of friendship, for they stand far above the ordinary friendships that prevail amongst mankind. The latter are so constituted that, were you to hear how your dear friends speak of you behind your back, you would never say another word to them.

Apart from the case where it would be a real help to you if your friend were to make some great sacrifice to serve you, there is no better means of testing the genuineness of his feelings than the way in which he receives the news of a misfortune that has just happened to you. At that moment the expression of his features will either show that his one thought is that of true and sincere sympathy for you; or else the absolute composure of his countenance, or the passing trace of something other than sympathy, will confirm the well-known maxim of La Rochefoucauld: Dans l'adversite de nos meilleurs amis, nous trouvons toujours quelque chose qui ne nous deplait pas. Indeed, at such a moment, the ordinary so-called friend will find it hard to suppress the signs of a slight smile of pleasure. There are few ways by which you can make more certain of putting people into a good humor than by telling them of some trouble that has recently befallen you, or by unreservedly disclosing some personal weakness of yours. How characteristic this is of humanity!

Distance and long absence are always prejudicial to friendship, however disinclined a man may be to admit. Our regard for people whom we do not see—even though they be our dearest friends—gradually dries up in the course of years, and they become abstract notions; so that our interest in them grows to be more and more intellectual,—nay, it is kept up only as a kind of tradition; whilst we retain a lively and deep interest in those who are constantly before our eyes, even if they be only pet animals. This shows how much men are limited by their senses, and how true is the remark that Goethe makes in Tasso about the dominant influence of the present moment:—

Die Gegenwart ist eine maechtige Goettin[7]

Friends of the house are very rightly so called; because they are friends of the house rather than of its master; in other words, they are more like cats than dogs.

Your friends will tell you that they are sincere; your enemies are really so. Let your enemies' censure be like a bitter medicine, to be used as a means of self-knowledge.

A friend in need, as the saying goes, is rare. Nay, it is just the contrary; no sooner have you made a friend than he is in need, and asks for a loan.

Section 34

A man must be still a greenhorn in the ways of the world, if he imagines that he can make himself popular in society by exhibiting intelligence and discernment. With the immense majority of people, such qualities excite hatred and resentment, which are rendered all the harder to bear by the fact that people are obliged to suppress—even from themselves—the real reason of their anger.

What actually takes place is this. A man feels and perceives that the person with whom he is conversing is intellectually very much his superior.[8]

He thereupon secretly and half unconsciously concludes that his interlocutor must form a proportionately low and limited estimate of his abilities. That is a method of reasoning—an enthymeme—which rouses the bitterest feelings of sullen and rancorous hatred. And so Gracian is quite right in saying that the only way to win affection from people is to show the most animal-like simplicity of demeanor—para ser bien quisto, el unico medio vestirse la piel del mas simple de los brutos.[9]

To show your intelligence and discernment is only an indirect way of reproaching other people for being dull and incapable. And besides, it is natural for a vulgar man to be violently agitated by the sight of opposition in any form; and in this case envy comes in as the secret cause of his hostility. For it is a matter of daily observation that people take the greatest pleasure in that which satisfies their vanity; and vanity cannot be satisfied without comparison with others. Now, there is nothing of which a man is prouder than of intellectual ability, for it is this that gives him his commanding place in the animal world. It is an exceedingly rash thing to let any one see that you are decidedly superior to him in this respect, and to let other people see it too; because he will then thirst for vengeance, and generally look about for an opportunity of taking it by means of insult, because this is to pass from the sphere of intellect to that of will—and there, all are on an equal footing as regards the feeling of hostility. Hence, while rank and riches may always reckon upon deferential treatment in society, that is something which intellectual ability can never expect; to be ignored is the greatest favor shown to it; and if people notice it at all, it is because they regard it as a piece of impertinence, or else as something to which its possessor has no legitimate right, and upon which he dares to pride himself; and in retaliation and revenge for his conduct, people secretly try and humiliate him in some other way; and if they wait to do this, it is only for a fitting opportunity. A man may be as humble as possible in his demeanor, and yet hardly ever get people to overlook his crime in standing intellectually above them. In the Garden of Roses, Sadi makes the remark:—You should know that foolish people are a hundredfold more averse to meeting the wise than the wise are indisposed for the company of the foolish.

On the other hand, it is a real recommendation to be stupid. For just as warmth is agreeable to the body, so it does the mind good to feel its superiority; and a man will seek company likely to give him this feeling, as instinctively as he will approach the fireplace or walk in the sun if he wants to get warm. But this means that he will be disliked on account of his superiority; and if a man is to be liked, he must really be inferior in point of intellect; and the same thing holds good of a woman in point of beauty. To give proof of real and unfeigned inferiority to some of the people you meet—that is a very difficult business indeed!

Consider how kindly and heartily a girl who is passably pretty will welcome one who is downright ugly. Physical advantages are not thought so much of in the case of man, though I suppose you would rather a little man sat next to you than one who was bigger than yourself. This is why, amongst men, it is the dull and ignorant, and amongst women, the ugly, who are always popular and in request.[10] It is likely to be said of such people that they are extremely good-natured, because every one wants to find a pretext for caring about them—a pretext which will blind both himself and other people to the real reason why he likes them. This is also why mental superiority of any sort always tends to isolate its possessor; people run away from him out of pure hatred, and say all manner of bad things about him by way of justifying their action. Beauty, in the case of women, has a similar effect: very pretty girls have no friends of their own sex, and they even find it hard to get another girl to keep them company. A handsome woman should always avoid applying for a position as companion, because the moment she enters the room, her prospective mistress will scowl at her beauty, as a piece of folly with which, both for her own and for her daughter's sake, she can very well dispense. But if the girl has advantages of rank, the case is very different; because rank, unlike personal qualities which work by the force of mere contrast, produces its effect by a process of reflection; much in the same way as the particular hue of a person's complexion depends upon the prevailing tone of his immediate surroundings.

Section 35

Our trust in other people often consists in great measure of pure laziness, selfishness and vanity on our own part: I say laziness, because, instead of making inquiries ourselves, and exercising an active care, we prefer to trust others; selfishness, because we are led to confide in people by the pressure of our own affairs; and vanity, when we ask confidence for a matter on which we rather pride ourselves. And yet, for all that, we expect people to be true to the trust we repose in them.

But we ought not to become angry if people put no trust in us: because that really means that they pay honesty the sincere compliment of regarding it as a very rare thing,—so rare, indeed, as to leave us in doubt whether its existence is not merely fabulous.

Section 36

Politeness,—which the Chinese hold to be a cardinal virtue,—is based upon two considerations of policy. I have explained one of these considerations in my Ethics; the other is as follows:—Politeness is a tacit agreement that people's miserable defects, whether moral or intellectual, shall on either side be ignored and not made the subject of reproach; and since these defects are thus rendered somewhat less obtrusive, the result is mutually advantageous.[11]

It is a wise thing to be polite; consequently, it is a stupid thing to be rude. To make enemies by unnecessary and willful incivility, is just as insane a proceeding as to set your house on fire. For politeness is like a counter—an avowedly false coin, with which it is foolish to be stingy. A sensible man will be generous in the use of it. It is customary in every country to end a letter with the words:—your most obedient servant—votre tres-humble serviteur—suo devotissimo servo_. (The Germans are the only people who suppress the word servant—Diener—because, of course, it is not true!) However, to carry politeness to such an extent as to damage your prospects, is like giving money where only counters are expected.

Wax, a substance naturally hard and brittle, can be made soft by the application of a little warmth, so that it will take any shape you please. In the same way, by being polite and friendly, you can make people pliable and obliging, even though they are apt to be crabbed and malevolent. Hence politeness is to human nature what warmth is to wax.

Of course, it is no easy matter to be polite; in so far, I mean, as it requires us to show great respect for everybody, whereas most people deserve none at all; and again in so far as it demands that we should feign the most lively interest in people, when we must be very glad that we have nothing to do with them. To combine politeness with pride is a masterpiece of wisdom.

We should be much less ready to lose our temper over an insult,—which, in the strict sense of the word, means that we have not been treated with respect,—if, on the one hand, we have not such an exaggerated estimate of our value and dignity—that is to say, if we were not so immensely proud of ourselves; and, on the other hand, if we had arrived at any clear notion of the judgment which, in his heart, one man generally passes upon another. If most people resent the slightest hint that any blame attaches to them, you may imagine their feelings if they were to overhear what their acquaintance say about them. You should never lose sight of the fact that ordinary politeness is only a grinning mask: if it shifts its place a little, or is removed for a moment, there is no use raising a hue and cry. When a man is downright rude, it is as though he had taken off all his clothes, and stood before you in puris naturalibus. Like most men in this condition, he does not present a very attractive appearance.

Section 37

You ought never to take any man as a model for what you should do or leave undone; because position and circumstances are in no two cases alike, and difference of character gives a peculiar, individual tone to what a man does. Hence duo cum faciunt idem, non est idem—two persons may do the same thing with a different result. A man should act in accordance with his own character, as soon as he has carefully deliberated on what he is about to do.

The outcome of this is that originality cannot be dispensed with in practical matters: otherwise, what a man does will not accord with what he is.

Section 38

Never combat any man's opinion; for though you reached the age of Methuselah, you would never have done setting him right upon all the absurd things that he believes.

It is also well to avoid correcting people's mistakes in conversation, however good your intentions may be; for it is easy to offend people, and difficult, if not impossible, to mend them.

If you feel irritated by the absurd remarks of two people whose conversation you happen to overhear, you should imagine that you are listening to a dialogue of two fools in a comedy. Probatum est.

The man who comes into the world with the notion that he is really going to instruct in matters of the highest importance, may thank his stars if he escapes with a whole skin.

Section 39

If you want your judgment to be accepted, express it coolly and without passion. All violence has its seat in the will; and so, if your judgment is expressed with vehemence, people will consider it an effort of will, and not the outcome of knowledge, which is in its nature cold and unimpassioned. Since the will is the primary and radical element in human nature, and intellect merely supervenes as something secondary, people are more likely to believe that the opinion you express with so much vehemence is due to the excited state of your will, rather than that the excitement of the will comes only from the ardent nature of your opinion.

Section 40

Even when you are fully justified in praising yourself, you should never be seduced into doing so. For vanity is so very common, and merit so very uncommon, that even if a man appears to be praising himself, though very indirectly, people will be ready to lay a hundred to one that he is talking out of pure vanity, and that he has not sense enough to see what a fool he is making of himself.

Still, for all that, there may be some truth in Bacon's remark that, as in the case of calumny, if you throw enough dirt, some of it will stick, so it it also in regard to self-praise; with the conclusion that self-praise, in small doses, is to be recommended.[12]

Section 41

If you have reason to suspect that a person is telling you a lie, look as though you believed every word he said. This will give him courage to go on; he will become more vehement in his assertions, and in the end betray himself.

Again, if you perceive that a person is trying to conceal something from you, but with only partial success, look as though you did not believe him, This opposition on your part will provoke him into leading out his reserve of truth and bringing the whole force of it to bear upon your incredulity.

Section 42

You should regard all your private affairs as secrets, and, in respect of them, treat your acquaintances, even though you are on good terms with them, as perfect strangers, letting them know nothing more than they can see for themselves. For in course of time, and under altered circumstances, you may find it a disadvantage that they know even the most harmless things about you.

And, as a general rule, it is more advisable to show your intelligence by saying nothing than by speaking out; for silence is a matter of prudence, whilst speech has something in it of vanity. The opportunities for displaying the one or the other quality occur equally often; but the fleeting satisfaction afforded by speech is often preferred to the permanent advantage secured by silence.

The feeling of relief which lively people experience in speaking aloud when no one is listening, should not be indulged, lest it grow into a habit; for in this way thought establishes such very friendly terms with speech, that conversation is apt to become a process of thinking aloud. Prudence exacts that a wide gulf should be fixed between what we think and what we say.

At times we fancy that people are utterly unable to believe in the truth of some statement affecting us personally, whereas it never occurs to them to doubt it; but if we give them the slightest opportunity of doubting it, they find it absolutely impossible to believe it any more. We often betray ourselves into revealing something, simply because we suppose that people cannot help noticing it,—just as a man will throw himself down from a great height because he loses his head, in other words, because he fancies that he cannot retain a firm footing any longer; the torment of his position is so great, that he thinks it better to put an end to it at once. This is the kind of insanity which is called acrophobia.

But it should not be forgotten how clever people are in regard to affairs which do not concern them, even though they show no particularly sign of acuteness in other matters. This is a kind of algebra in which people are very proficient: give them a single fact to go upon, and they will solve the most complicated problems. So, if you wish to relate some event that happened long ago, without mentioning any names, or otherwise indicating the persons to whom you refer, you should be very careful not to introduce into your narrative anything that might point, however distantly, to some definite fact, whether it is a particular locality, or a date, or the name of some one who was only to a small extent implicated, or anything else that was even remotely connected with the event; for that at once gives people something positive to go upon, and by the aid of their talent for this sort of algebra, they will discover all the rest. Their curiosity in these matters becomes a kind of enthusiasm: their will spurs on their intellect, and drives it forward to the attainment of the most remote results. For however unsusceptible and different people may be to general and universal truths, they are very ardent in the matter of particular details.

In keeping with what I have said, it will be found that all those who profess to give instructions in the wisdom of life are specially urgent in commending the practice of

109

silence, and assign manifold reasons why it should be observed; so it is not necessary for me to enlarge upon the subject any further. However, I may just add one or two little known Arabian proverbs, which occur to me as peculiarly appropriate:—

Do not tell a friend anything that you would conceal from an enemy.

A secret is in my custody, if I keep it; but should it escape me, it is I who am the prisoner.

The tree of silence bears the fruit of peace.

Section 43

Money is never spent to so much advantage as when you have been cheated out of it; for at one stroke you have purchased prudence.

Section 44

If possible, no animosity should be felt for anyone. But carefully observe and remember the manner in which a man conducts himself, so that you may take the measure of his value,—at any rate in regard to yourself,—and regulate your bearing towards him accordingly; never losing sight of the fact that character is unalterable, and that to forget the bad features in a man's disposition is like throwing away hard-won money. Thus you will protect yourself against the results of unwise intimacy and foolish friendship.

Give way neither to love nor to hate, is one-half of worldly wisdom: say nothing and believe nothing, the other half. Truly, a world where there is need of such rules as this and the following, is one upon which a man may well turn his back.

Section 45

To speak angrily to a person, to show your hatred by what you say or by the way you look, is an unnecessary proceeding—dangerous, foolish, ridiculous, and vulgar.

Anger and hatred should never be shown otherwise than in what you do; and feelings will be all the more effective in action, in so far as you avoid the exhibition of them in any other way. It is only cold-blooded animals whose bite is poisonous.

Section 46

To speak without emphasizing your words—parler sans accent—is an old rule with those who are wise in the world's ways. It means that you should leave other people to discover what it is that you have said; and as their minds are slow, you can make your escape in time. On the other hand, to emphasize your meaning—parler avec accent—is to address their feelings; and the result is always the opposite of what you expect. If you are polite enough in your manner and courteous in your tone there are many people whom you may abuse outright, and yet run no immediate risk of offending them.

110

Notes

1. *Goethe's Faust, Part I.*
2. *Translator's Note. Helvetius, Claude-Adrien (1715-71), a French philosophical writer much esteemed by Schopenhauer. His chief work, De l'Esprit, excited great interest and opposition at the time of its publication, on account of the author's pronounced materialism.*
3. *See, for instance, Stobasus, Eclog. I. xxii. 9.*
4. *To forgive and forget means to throw away dearly bought experience.*
5. *Translator's Note. Aventurine is a rare kind of quartz; and the same name is given to a brownish-colored glass much resembling it, which is manufactured at Murano. It is so called from the fact that the glass was discovered by chance (arventura).*
6. *De Clementia, I. 1.*
7. *Act iv., se. 4.*
8. *Cf. Welt als Wills und Vorstellung, Bk. II. p. 256 (4th Edit.), where I quote from Dr. Johnson, and from Merck, the friend of Goethe's youth. The former says: There is nothing by which a man exasperates most people more, than by displaying a superior ability of brilliancy in conversation. They seem pleased at the time, but their envy makes them curse him at their hearts. (Boswells Life of Johnson aetat: 74).*
9. *Translator's Note.—Balthazar Graeian, Oraculo manual, y arte de prudencia, 240. Gracian (1584-1658) was a Spanish prose writer and Jesuit, whose works deal chiefly with the observation of character in the various phenomena of life. Schopenhauer, among others, had a great admiration for his worldly philosophy, and translated his Oraculo manual—a system of rules for the conduct of life—into German. The same book was translated into English towards the close of the seventeenth century.*
10. *If you desire to get on in the world, friends and acquaintances are by far the best passport to fortune. The possession of a great deal of ability makes a man proud, and therefore not apt to flatter those who have very little, and from whom, on that account, the possession of great ability should be carefully concealed. The consciousness of small intellectual power has just the opposite effect, and is very compatible with a humble, affable and companionable nature, and with respect for what is mean and wretched. This is why an inferior sort of man has so many friends to befriend and encourage him. These remarks are applicable not only to advancement in political life, but to all competition for places of honor and dignity, nay, even for reputation in the world of science, literature and art. In learned societies, for example, mediocrity—that very acceptable quality—is always to the fore, whilst merit meets with tardy recognition, or with none at all. So it is in everything.*
11. *Translator's Note.—In the passage referred to (Grundlage der Moral, collected works, Vol. IV., pp. 187 and 198), Schopenhauer explains politeness as a conventional and systematic attempt to mask the egoism of human nature in the small affairs of life,—an egoism so repulsive that some such device is necessary for the purpose of concealing its ugliness. The relation which politeness bears to the true love of one's neighbor is analogous to that existing between justice as an affair of legality, and justice as the real integrity of the heart.*
12. *Translator's Note.—Schopenhauer alludes to the following passage in Bacon's De Augmentis Scientiarum, Bk. viii., ch. 2: Sicut enim dici solet de calumnia, audacter calumniare, semper aliquid haeret; sic dici potest de jactantia, (nisi plane deformis fuerit et ridicula), audacter te vendita, semper aliquid haeret. Haerebit certe apud populum, licet prudentiores subrideant. Itaque existimatio parta apud plurimos paucorum fastidium abunde compensabit.*

111

Worldly Fortune

Section 47

However varied the forms that human destiny may take, the same elements are always present; and so life is everywhere much of a piece, whether it passed in the cottage or in the palace, in the barrack or in the cloister. Alter the circumstance as much as you please! point to strange adventures, successes, failures! life is like a sweet-shop, where there is a great variety of things, odd in shape and diverse in color—one and all made from the same paste. And when men speak of some one's success, the lot of the man who has failed is not so very different as it seems. The inequalities in the world are like the combinations in a kaleidoscope; at every turn a fresh picture strikes the eye; and yet, in reality, you see only the same bits of glass as you saw before.

Section 48

An ancient writer says, very truly, that there are three great powers in the world; Sagacity, Strength, and Luck,—[Greek: sunetos, kratos, tuchu.] I think the last is the most efficacious.

A man's life is like the voyage of a ship, where luck—secunda aut adversa fortuna—acts the part of the wind, and speeds the vessel on its way or drives it far out of its course. All that the man can do for himself is of little avail; like the rudder, which, if worked hard and continuously, may help in the navigation of the ship; and yet all may be lost again by a sudden squall. But if the wind is only in the right quarter, the ship will sail on so as not to need any steering. The power of luck is nowhere better expressed than in a certain Spanish proverb: Da Ventura a tu hijo, y echa lo en el mar—give your son luck and throw him into the sea.

Still, chance, it may be said, is a malignant power, and as little as possible should be left to its agency. And yet where is there any giver who, in dispensing gifts, tells us quite clearly that we have no right to them, and that we owe them not to any merit on our part, but wholly to the goodness and grace of the giver—at the same time allowing us to cherish the joyful hope of receiving, in all humility, further undeserved gifts from the same hands—where is there any giver like that, unless it be Chance? who understands the kingly art of showing the recipient that all merit is powerless and unavailing against the royal grace and favor.

On looking back over the course of his life,—that labyrinthine way of error,—a man must see many points where luck failed him and misfortune came; and then it is easy to carry self-reproach to an unjust excess. For the course of a man's life is in no wise entirely of his own making; it is the product of two factors—the series of things that happened, and his own resolves in regard to them, and these two are constantly interacting upon and modifying each other. And besides these, another influence is at work in the very limited extent of a man's horizon, whether it is that he cannot see very far ahead in respect of the plans he will adopt, or that he is still less able to predict the course of future events: his knowledge is strictly confined to present plans and present events. Hence, as long as a man's goal is far off, he cannot steer straight for it; he must be content to make a course that is approximately right; and in following the direction in which he thinks he ought to go, he will often have occasion to tack.

All that a man can do is to form such resolves as from time to time accord with the circumstances in which he is placed, in the hope of thus managing to advance a step nearer towards the final goal. It is usually the case that the position in which we stand, and the object at which we aim, resemble two tendencies working with dissimilar strength in different directions; and the course of our life is represented by their diagonal, or resultant force.

Terence makes the remark that life is like a game at dice, where if the number that turns up is not precisely the one you want, you can still contrive to use it equally:—in vita est hominum quasi cum ludas tesseris; si illud quod maxime opus est jactu non cadit, illud quod cecidit forte, id arte ut corrigas.[1] Or, to put the matter more shortly, life is a game of cards, when the cards are shuffled and dealt by fate. But for my present purpose, the most suitable simile would be that of a game of chess, where the plan we determined to follow is conditioned by the play of our rival,—in life, by the caprice of fate. We are compelled to modify our tactics, often to such an extent that, as we carry them out, hardly a single feature of the original plan can be recognized.

But above and beyond all this, there is another influence that makes itself felt in our lives. It is a trite saying—only too frequently true—that we are often more foolish than we think. On the other hand, we are often wiser than we fancy ourselves to be. This, however, is a discovery which only those can make, of whom it is really true; and it takes them a long time to make it. Our brains are not the wisest part of us. In the great moments of life, when a man decides upon an important step, his action is directed not so much by any clear knowledge of the right thing to do, as by an inner impulse—you may almost call it an instinct—proceeding from the deepest foundations of his being. If, later on, he attempts to criticise his action by the light of hard and fast ideas of what is right in the abstract—those unprofitable ideas which are learnt by rote, or, it may be, borrowed from other people; if he begins to apply general rules, the principles which have guided others, to his own case, without sufficiently weighing the maxim that one man's meat is another's poison, then he will run great risk of doing himself an injustice. The result will show where the right course lay. It is only when a man has reached the happy age of wisdom that he is capable of just judgment in regard either to his own actions or to those of others.

It may be that this impulse or instinct is the unconscious effect of a kind of prophetic dream which is forgotten when we awake—lending our life a uniformity of tone, a dramatic unity, such as could never result from the unstable moments of consciousness, when we are so easily led into error, so liable to strike a false note. It is in virtue of some such prophetic dream that a man feels himself called to great achievements in a special sphere, and works in that direction from his youth up out of an inner and secret feeling that that is his true path, just as by a similar instinct the bee is led to build up its cells in the comb. This is the impulse which Balthazar Gracian calls la gran sinderesis[2]—the great power of moral discernment: it is something that a man instinctively feels to be his salvation without which he were lost.

To act in accordance with abstract principles is a difficult matter, and a great deal of practice will be required before you can be even occasionally successful; it of tens happens that the principles do not fit in with your particular case. But every man has certain innate concrete principles—a part, as it were, of the very blood that flows in his veins, the sum or result, in fact, of all his thoughts, feelings and volitions. Usually he has no knowledge of them in any abstract form; it is only when he looks back upon the course his life has taken, that he becomes aware of having been always led on by them—as though they formed an invisible clue which he had followed unawares.

Section 49

That Time works great changes, and that all things are in their nature fleeting—these are truths that should never be forgotten. Hence, in whatever case you may be, it is well to picture to yourself the opposite: in prosperity, to be mindful of misfortune; in friendship, of enmity; in good weather, of days when the sky is overcast; in love, of hatred; in moments of trust, to imagine the betrayal that will make you regret your confidence; and so, too, when you are in evil plight, to have a lively sense of happier times—what a lasting source of true worldly wisdom were there! We should then always reflect, and not be so very easily deceived; because, in general, we should anticipate the very changes that the years will bring.

Perhaps in no form of knowledge is personal experience so indispensable as in learning to see that all things are unstable and transitory in this world. There is nothing that, in its own place and for the time it lasts, is not a product of necessity, and therefore capable of being fully justified; and it is this fact that makes circumstances of every year, every month, even of every day, seem as though they might maintain their right to last to all eternity. But we know that this can never be the case, and that in a world where all is fleeting, change alone endures. He is a prudent man who is not only undeceived by apparent stability, but is able to forecast the lines upon which movement will take place.[3]

But people generally think that present circumstances will last, and that matters will go on in the future as they have clone in the past. Their mistakes arises from the fact that they do not understand the cause of the things they see—causes which, unlike the effects they produce, contain in themselves the germ of future change. The effects are all that people know, and they hold fast to them on the supposition that those unknown causes, which were sufficient to bring them about, will also be able to maintain them as they are. This is a very common error; and the fact that it is common is not without its advantage, for it means that people always err in unison; and hence the calamity which results from the error affects all alike, and is therefore easy to bear; whereas, if a philosopher makes a mistake, he is alone in his error, and so at a double disadvantage.[4]

But in saying that we should anticipate the effects of time, I mean that we should mentally forecast what they are likely to be; I do not mean that we should practically forestall them, by demanding the immediate performance of promises which time alone can fulfill. The man who makes his demand will find out that there is no worse or more exacting usurer than Time; and that, if you compel Time to give money in advance, you will have to pay a rate of interest more ruinous than any Jew would require. It is possible, for instance, to make a tree burst forth into leaf, blossom, or even bear fruit within a few days, by the application of unslaked lime and artificial heat; but after that the tree will wither away. So a young man may abuse his strength—it may be only for a few weeks—by trying to do at nineteen what he could easily manage at thirty, and Time may give him the loan for which he asks; but the interest he will have to pay comes out of the strength of his later years; nay, it is part of his very life itself.

There are some kinds of illness in which entire restoration to health is possible only by letting the complaint run its natural course; after which it disappears without leaving any trace of its existence. But if the sufferer is very impatient, and, while he is still affected, insists that he is completely well, in this case, too, Time will grant the loan, and the complaint may be shaken off; but life-long weakness and chronic mischief will be the interest paid upon it.

Again, in time of war or general disturbance, a man may require ready money at once, and have to sell out his investments in land or consols for a third or even a still smaller fraction of the sum he would have received from them, if he could have waited for the market to right itself, which would have happened in due course; but he compels Time to grant him a loan, and his loss is the interest he has to pay. Or perhaps he wants to go on a long journey and requires the money: in one or two years he could lay by a sufficient sum out of his income, but he cannot afford to wait; and so he either borrows it or deducts it from his capital; in other words, he gets Time to lend him the money in advance. The interest he pays is a disordered state of his accounts, and permanent and increasing deficits, which he can never make good.

Such is Time's usury; and all who cannot wait are its victims. There is no more thriftless proceeding than to try and mend the measured pace of Time. Be careful, then, not to become its debtor.

Section 50

In the daily affairs of life, you will have very many opportunities of recognizing a characteristic difference between ordinary people of prudence and discretion. In estimating the possibility of danger in connection with any undertaking, an ordinary man will confine his inquiries to the kind of risk that has already attended such undertakings in the past; whereas a prudent person will look ahead, and consider everything that might possibly happen in the future, having regard to a certain Spanish maxim: lo que no acaece en un ano, acaece en un rato—a thing may not happen in a year, and yet may happen within two minutes.

The difference in question is, of course, quite natural; for it requires some amount of discernment to calculate possibilities; but a man need only have his senses about him to see what has already happened.

Do not omit to sacrifice to evil spirits. What I mean is, that a man should not hesitate about spending time, trouble, and money, or giving up his comfort, or restricting his aims and denying himself, if he can thereby shut the door on the possibility of misfortune. The most terrible misfortunes are also the most improbable and remote—the least likely to occur. The rule I am giving is best exemplified in the practice of insurance,—a public sacrifice made on the altar of anxiety. Therefore take out your policy of insurance!

Section 51

Whatever fate befalls you, do not give way to great rejoicings or great lamentations; partly because all things are full of change, and your fortune may turn at any moment; partly because men are so apt to be deceived in their judgment as to what is good or bad for them.

Almost every one in his turn has lamented over something which afterwards turned out to be the very best thing for him that could have happened—or rejoiced at an event which became the source of his greatest sufferings. The right state of mind has been finely portrayed by Shakespeare:

I have felt so many quirks of joy and grief That the first face of neither, on the start, Can woman me unto't.[5]

And, in general, it may be said that, if a man takes misfortunes quietly, it is because he knows that very many dreadful things may happen in the course of life; and so he looks upon the trouble of the moment as only a very small part of that which might come. This is the Stoic temper—never to be unmindful of the sad fate of humanity—condicionis humanoe oblitus; but always to remember that our existence is full of woe and misery: and that the ills to which we are exposed are innumerable. Wherever he be, a man need only cast a look around, to revive the sense of human misery: there before his eyes he can see mankind struggling and floundering in torment,—all for the sake of a wretched existence, barren and unprofitable!

If he remembers this, a man will not expect very much from life, but learn to accommodate himself to a world where all is relative and no perfect state exists;—always looking misfortune in the face, and if he cannot avoid it, meeting it with courage.

It should never be forgotten that misfortune, be it great or small, is the element in which we live. But that is no reason why a man should indulge in fretful complaints, and, like Beresford,[6] pull a long face over the Miseries of Human Life,—and not a single hour is free from them; or still less, call upon the Deity at every flea-bite—in pulicis morsu Deum invocare. Our aim should be to look well about us, to ward off misfortune by going to meet it, to attain such perfection and refinement in averting the disagreeable things of life,—whether they come from our fellow-men or from the physical world,—that, like a clever fox, we may slip out of the way of every mishap, great or small; remembering that a mishap is generally only our own awkwardness in disguise.

The main reason why misfortune falls less heavily upon us, if we have looked upon its occurrence as not impossible, and, as the saying is, prepared ourselves for it, may be this: if, before this misfortune comes, we have quietly thought over it as something which may or may not happen, the whole of its extent and range is known to us, and we can, at least, determine how far it will affect us; so that, if it really arrives, it does not depress us unduly—its weight is not felt to be greater than it actually is. But if no preparation has been made to meet it, and it comes unexpectedly, the mind is in a state of terror for the moment and unable to measure the full extent of the calamity; it seems so far-reaching in its effects that the victim might well think there was no limit to them; in any case, its range is exaggerated. In the same way, darkness and uncertainty always increase the sense of danger. And, of course, if we have thought over the possibility of misfortune, we have also at the same time considered the sources to which we shall look for help and consolation; or, at any rate, we have accustomed ourselves to the idea of it.

There is nothing that better fits us to endure the misfortunes of life with composure, than to know for certain that everything that happens—from the smallest up to the greatest facts of existence—happens of necessity.[7] A man soon accommodates himself to the inevitable—to something that must be; and if he knows that nothing can happen except of necessity, he will see that things cannot be other that they are, and that even the strangest chances in the world are just as much a product of necessity as phenomena which obey well-known rules and turn out exactly in accordance with expectation. Let me here refer to what I have said elsewhere on the soothing effect of the knowledge that all things are inevitable and a product of necessity.[8]

If a man is steeped in the knowledge of this truth, he will, first of all, do what he can, and then readily endure what he must.

We may regard the petty vexations of life that are constantly happening, as designed to keep us in practice for bearing great misfortunes, so that we may not become completely enervated by a career of prosperity. A man should be as Siegfried, armed cap-a-pie, towards the small troubles of every day—those little differences we have with our fellow-men, insignificant disputes, unbecoming conduct in other people, petty gossip, and many other similar annoyances of life; he should not feel them at all, much less take them to heart and brood over them, but hold them at arm's length and push them out of his way, like stones that lie in the road, and upon no account think about them and give them a place in his reflections.

Section 52

What people commonly call Fate is, as a general rule, nothing but their own stupid and foolish conduct. There is a fine passage in Homer,[9] illustrating the truth of this remark, where the poet praises [GREEK: maetis]—shrewd council; and his advice is worthy of all attention. For if wickedness is atoned for only in another world, stupidity gets its reward here—although, now and then, mercy may be shown to the offender.

It is not ferocity but cunning that strikes fear into the heart and forebodes danger; so true it is that the human brain is a more terrible weapon than the lion's paw.

The most finished man of the world would be one who was never irresolute and never in a hurry.

Section 53

Courage comes next to prudence as a quality of mind very essential to happiness. It is quite true that no one can endow himself with either, since a man inherits prudence from his mother and courage from his father; still, if he has these qualities, he can do much to develop them by means of resolute exercise.

In this world, where the game is played with loaded dice, a man must have a temper of iron, with armor proof to the blows of fate, and weapons to make his way against men. Life is one long battle; we have to fight at every step; and Voltaire very rightly says that if we succeed, it is at the point of the sword, and that we die with the weapon in our hand—on ne reussit dans ce monde qua la pointe de l'epee, et on meurt les armes a la main. It is a cowardly soul that shrinks or grows faint and despondent as soon as the storm begins to gather, or even when the first cloud appears on the horizon. Our motto should be No Surrender; and far from yielding to the ills of life, let us take fresh courage from misfortune:—

Tu ne cede malis sed contra audentior ito.[10]

As long as the issue of any matter fraught with peril is still in doubt, and there is yet some possibility left that all may come right, no one should ever tremble or think of anything but resistance,—just as a man should not despair of the weather if he can see a bit of blue sky anywhere. Let our attitude be such that we should not quake even if the world fell in ruins about us:—

Si fractus illabatur orbis
Impavidum ferient ruinae.[11]

Our whole life itself—let alone its blessings—would not be worth such a cowardly trembling and shrinking of the heart. Therefore, let us face life courageously and show a firm front to every ill:—

Quocirca vivite fortes Fortiaque adversis opponite pectora rebus.

Still, it is possible for courage to be carried to an excess and to degenerate into rashness. It may even be said that some amount of fear is necessary, if we are to exist at all in the world, and cowardice is only the exaggerated form of it. This truth has been very well expressed by Bacon, in his account of Terror Panicus; and the etymological account which he gives of its meaning, is very superior to the ancient explanation preserved for us by Plutarch.[12] He connects the expression with Pan the personification of Nature;[13] and observes that fear is innate in every living thing, and, in fact, tends to its preservation, but that it is apt to come into play without due cause, and that man is especially exposed to it. The chief feature of this Panie Terror is that there is no clear notion of any definite danger bound up with it; that it presumes rather than knows that danger exists; and that, in case of need, it pleads fright itself as the reason for being afraid.

Notes

1. He seems to have been referring to a game something like backgammon.
2. *Translator's Note.*—This obscure word appears to be derived from the Greek sugtaereo (*N.T. and Polyb.*) meaning "to observe strictly." It occurs in The Doctor and Student, a series of dialogues between a doctor of divinity and a student on the laws of England, first published in 1518; and is there (Dialog. I. ch. 13) explained as "a natural power of the soule, set in the highest part thereof, moving and stirring it to good, and abhoring evil." This passage is copied into Milton's Commonplace Book, edit. Horwood, Sec. 79. The word is also found in the Dictionary of the Spanish Academy (vol. vi. of the year 1739) in the sense of an innate discernment of moral principles, where a quotation is given from Madre Maria de Jesus, abbess of the convent of the Conception at Agreda, a mystical writer of the seventeenth century, frequently consulted by Philip IV.,—and again in the Bolognese Dictionary of 1824, with a similar meaning, illustrated from the writings of Salvini (1653-1729). For these references I am indebted to the kindness of Mr. Norman Maccoll.
3. Chance plays so great a part in all human affairs that when a man tries to ward off a remote danger by present sacrifice, the danger often vanishes under some new and unforeseen development of events; and then the sacrifice, in addition to being a complete loss, brings about such an altered state of things as to be in itself a source of positive danger in the face of this new development. In taking measures of precaution, then, it is well not to look too far ahead, but to reckon with chance; and often to oppose a courageous front to a danger, in the hope that, like many a dark thunder-cloud, it may pass away without breaking.

4. *I may remark, parenthetically, that all this is a confirmation of the principle laid down in Die Welt als Wille und Vorstellung (Bk. I. p. 94: 4th edit.), that error always consists in making a wrong inference, that is, in ascribing a given effect to something that did not cause it.*

5. *All's Well that Ends Well, Act. ii. Sc. 2.*

6. *Translator's Note.—Rev. James Beresford (1764-1840), miscellaneous writer. The full title of this, his chief work, is "The Miseries of Human Life; or the last groans of Timothy Testy and Samuel Sensitive, with a few supplementary sighs from Mrs. Testy."*

7. *This is a truth which I have firmly established in my prize-essay on the Freedom of the Will, where the reader will find a detailed explanation of the grounds on which it rests. Cf. especially p. 60. [Schopenhauer's Works, 4th Edit., vol. iv.—Tr.]*

8. *Cf. Welt als Wille und Vorstellung, Bk. I. p. 361 (4th edit.).*

9. *Iliad, xxiii. 313, sqq.*

10. *Virgil, Aeneid, vi. 95.*

11. *Horace, Odes iii. 3.*

12. *De Iside et Osiride ch. 14.*

13. *De Sapientia Veterum, C. 6. Natura enim rerum omnibus viventibus indidit mentum ac formidinem, vitae atque essentiae suae conservatricem, ac mala ingruentia vitantem et depellentem. Verumtamen eaden natura modum tenere nescia est: sed timoribus salutaribus semper vanos et innanes admiscet; adeo ut omnia (si intus conspici darentur) Panicis terroribus plenissima sint praesertim humana*

The Ages of Life

There is a very fine saying of Voltaire's to the effect that every age of life has its own peculiar mental character, and that a man will feel completely unhappy if his mind is not in accordance with his years:—

Qui n'a pas l'esprit de son age,
De son age atout le malheur.

It will, therefore, be a fitting close to our speculations upon the nature of happiness, if we glance at the chances which the various periods of life produce in us.

Our whole life long it is the present, and the present alone, that we actually possess: the only difference is that at the beginning of life we look forward to a long future, and that towards the end we look back upon a long past; also that our temperament, but not our character, undergoes certain well-known changes, which make the present wear a different color at each period of life.

I have elsewhere stated that in childhood we are more given to using our intellect than our will; and I have explained why this is so.[1] It is just for this reason that the first quarter of life is so happy: as we look back upon it in after years, it seems a sort of lost paradise. In childhood our relations with others are limited, our wants are few,—in a word, there is little stimulus for the will; and so our chief concern is the extension of our knowledge. The intellect—like the brain, which attains its full size in the seventh year,[2] is developed early, though it takes time to mature; and it explores the whole world of its surroundings in its constant search for nutriment: it is

119

then that existence is in itself an ever fresh delight, and all things sparkle with the charm of novelty.

This is why the years of childhood are like a long poem. For the function of poetry, as of all art, is to grasp the Idea—in the Platonic sense; in other words, to apprehend a particular object in such a way as to perceive its essential nature, the characteristics it has in common with all other objects of the same kind; so that a single object appears as the representative of a class, and the results of one experience hold good for a thousand.

It may be thought that my remarks are opposed to fact, and that the child is never occupied with anything beyond the individual objects or events which are presented to it from time to time, and then only in so far as they interest and excite its will for the moment; but this is not really the case. In those early years, life—in the full meaning of the word, is something so new and fresh, and its sensations are so keen and unblunted by repetition, that, in the midst of all its pursuits and without any clear consciousness of what it is doing, the child is always silently occupied in grasping the nature of life itself,—in arriving at its fundamental character and general outline by means of separate scenes and experiences; or, to use Spinoza's phraseology, the child is learning to see the things and persons about it sub specie aeternitatis,—as particular manifestations of universal law.

The younger we are, then, the more does every individual object represent for us the whole class to which it belongs; but as the years increase, this becomes less and less the case. That is the reason why youthful impressions are so different from those of old age. And that it also why the slight knowledge and experience gained in childhood and youth afterwards come to stand as the permanent rubric, or heading, for all the knowledge acquired in later life,—those early forms of knowledge passing into categories, as it were, under which the results of subsequent experience are classified; though a clear consciousness of what is being done, does not always attend upon the process.

In this way the earliest years of a man's life lay the foundation of his view of the world, whether it be shallow or deep; and although this view may be extended and perfected later on, it is not materially altered. It is an effect of this purely objective and therefore poetical view of the world,—essential to the period of childhood and promoted by the as yet undeveloped state of the volitional energy—that, as children, we are concerned much more with the acquisition of pure knowledge than with exercising the power of will. Hence that grave, fixed look observable in so many children, of which Raphael makes such a happy use in his depiction of cherubs, especially in the picture of the Sistine Madonna. The years of childhood are thus rendered so full of bliss that the memory of them is always coupled with longing and regret.

While we thus eagerly apply ourselves to learning the outward aspect of things, as the primitive method of understanding the objects about us, education aims at instilling into us ideas. But ideas furnish no information as to the real and essential nature of objects, which, as the foundation and true content of all knowledge, can be reached only by the process called intuition. This is a kind of knowledge which can in no wise be instilled into us from without; we must arrive at it by and for ourselves.

Hence a man's intellectual as well as his moral qualities proceed from the depths of his own nature, and are not the result of external influences; and no educational scheme—of Pestalozzi, or of any one else—can turn a born simpleton into a man of sense. The thing is impossible! He was born a simpleton, and a simpleton he will die.

It is the depth and intensity of this early intuitive knowledge of the external world that explain why the experiences of childhood take such a firm hold on the memory. When we were young, we were completely absorbed in our immediate surroundings; there was nothing to distract our attention from them; we looked upon the objects about us as though they were the only ones of their kind, as though, indeed, nothing else existed at all. Later on, when we come to find out how many things there are in the world, this primitive state of mind vanishes, and with it our patience.

I have said elsewhere[3] that the world, considered as object,—in other words, as it is presented to us objectively,—wears in general a pleasing aspect; but that in the world, considered as subject,—that is, in regard to its inner nature, which is will,— pain and trouble predominate. I may be allowed to express the matter, briefly, thus: the world is glorious to look at, but dreadful in reality.

Accordingly, we find that, in the years of childhood, the world is much better known to us on its outer or objective side, namely, as the presentation of will, than on the side of its inner nature, namely, as the will itself. Since the objective side wears a pleasing aspect, and the inner or subjective side, with its tale of horror, remains as yet unknown, the youth, as his intelligence develops, takes all the forms of beauty that he sees, in nature and in art, for so many objects of blissful existence; they are so beautiful to the outward eye that, on their inner side, they must, he thinks, be much more beautiful still. So the world lies before him like another Eden; and this is the Arcadia in which we are all born.

A little later, this state of mind gives birth to a thirst for real life—the impulse to do and suffer—which drives a man forth into the hurly-burly of the world. There he learns the other side of existence—the inner side, the will, which is thwarted at every step. Then comes the great period of disillusion, a period of very gradual growth; but once it has fairly begun, a man will tell you that he has got over all his false notions— l'age des illusions est passe; and yet the process is only beginning, and it goes on ex- tending its sway and applying more and more to the whole of life.

So it may be said that in childhood, life looks like the scenery in a theatre, as you view it from a distance; and that in old age it is like the same scenery when you come up quite close to it.

And, lastly, there is another circumstance that contributes to the happiness of childhood. As spring commences, the young leaves on the trees are similar in color and much the same in shape; and in the first years of life we all resemble one another and harmonize very well. But with puberty divergence begins; and, like the radii of a circle, we go further and further apart.

The period of youth, which forms the remainder of this earlier half of our exist- ence—and how many advantages it has over the later half!—is troubled and made miserable by the pursuit of happiness, as though there were no doubt that it can be met with somewhere in life,—a hope that always ends in failure and leads to discon- tent. An illusory image of some vague future bliss—born of a dream and shaped by fancy—floats before our eyes; and we search for the reality in vain. So it is that the young man is generally dissatisfied with the position in which he finds himself, what- ever it may be; he ascribes his disappointment solely to the state of things that meets him on his first introduction to life, when he had expected something very different; whereas it is only the vanity and wretchedness of human life everywhere that he is now for the first time experiencing.

It would be a great advantage to a young man if his early training could eradicate the idea that the world has a great deal to offer him. But the usual result of education is to strengthen this delusion; and our first ideas of life are generally taken from fiction rather than from fact.

In the bright dawn of our youthful days, the poetry of life spreads out a gorgeous vision before us, and we torture ourselves by longing to see it realized. We might as well wish to grasp the rainbow! The youth expects his career to be like an interesting romance; and there lies the germ of that disappointment which I have been describing.[4] What lends a charm to all these visions is just the fact that they are visionary and not real, and that in contemplating them we are in the sphere of pure knowledge, which is sufficient in itself and free from the noise and struggle of life. To try and realize those visions is to make them an object of will—a process which always involves pain.[5]

If the chief feature of the earlier half of life is a never-satisfied longing after happiness, the later half is characterized by the dread of misfortune. For, as we advance in years, it becomes in a greater or less degree clear that all happiness is chimerical in its nature, and that pain alone is real. Accordingly, in later years, we, or, at least, the more prudent amongst us, are more intent upon eliminating what is painful from our lives and making our position secure, than on the pursuit of positive pleasure. I may observe, by the way, that in old age, we are better able to prevent misfortunes from coming, and in youth better able to bear them when they come.

In my young days, I was always pleased to hear a ring at my door: ah! thought I, now for something pleasant. But in later life my feelings on such occasions were rather akin to dismay than to pleasure: heaven help me! thought I, what am I to do? A similar revulsion of feeling in regard to the world of men takes place in all persons of any talent or distinction. For that very reason they cannot be said properly to belong to the world; in a greater or less degree, according to the extent of their superiority, they stand alone. In their youth they have a sense of being abandoned by the world; but later on, they feel as though they had escaped it. The earlier feeling is an unpleasant one, and rests upon ignorance; the second is pleasurable—for in the meantime they have come to know what the world is.

The consequence of this is that, as compared with the earlier, the later half of life, like the second part of a musical period, has less of passionate longing and more restfulness about it. And why is this the case Simply because, in youth, a man fancies that there is a prodigious amount of happiness and pleasure to be had in the world, only that it is difficult to come by it; whereas, when he becomes old, he knows that there is nothing of the kind; he makes his mind completely at ease on the matter, enjoys the present hour as well as he can, and even takes a pleasure in trifles.

The chief result gained by experience of life is clearness of view. This is what distinguishes the man of mature age, and makes the world wear such a different aspect from that which it presented in his youth or boyhood. It is only then that he sees things quite plain, and takes them for that which they really are: while in earlier years he saw a phantom-world, put together out of the whims and crotchets of his own mind, inherited prejudice and strange delusion: the real world was hidden from him, or the vision of it distorted. The first thing that experience finds to do is to free us from the phantoms of the brain—those false notions that have been put into us in youth.

To prevent their entrance at all would, of course, be the best form of education, even though it were only negative in aim: but it would be a task full of difficulty. At first the child's horizon would have to be limited as much as possible, and yet within that limited sphere none but clear and correct notions would have to be given; only after the child had properly appreciated everything within it, might the sphere be gradually enlarged; care being always taken that nothing was left obscure, or half or wrongly understood. The consequence of this training would be that the child's notions of men and things would always be limited and simple in their character; but, on the other hand, they would be clear and correct, and only need to be extended, not to be rectified. The same line might be pursued on into the period of youth. This method of education would lay special stress upon the prohibition of novel reading; and the place of novels would be taken by suitable biographical literature—the life of Franklin, for instance, or Moritz' Anton Reiser.[6]

In our early days we fancy that the leading events in our life, and the persons who are going to play an important part in it, will make their entrance to the sound of drums and trumpets; but when, in old age, we look back, we find that they all came in quite quietly, slipped in, as it were, by the side-door, almost unnoticed.

From the point of view we have been taking up until now, life may be compared to a piece of embroidery, of which, during the first half of his time, a man gets a sight of the right side, and during the second half, of the wrong. The wrong side is not so pretty as the right, but it is more instructive; it shows the way in which the threads have been worked together.

Intellectual superiority, even if it is of the highest kind, will not secure for a man a preponderating place in conversation until after he is forty years of age. For age and experience, though they can never be a substitute for intellectual talent, may far outweigh it; and even in a person of the meanest capacity, they give a certain counterpoise to the power of an extremely intellectual man, so long as the latter is young. Of course I allude here to personal superiority, not to the place a man may gain by his works.

And on passing his fortieth year, any man of the slightest power of mind—any man, that is, who has more than the sorry share of intellect with which Nature has endowed five-sixths of mankind—will hardly fail to show some trace of misanthropy. For, as is natural, he has by that time inferred other people's character from an examination of his own; with the result that he has been gradually disappointed to find that in the qualities of the head or in those of the heart—and usually in both—he reaches a level to which they do not attain; so he gladly avoids having anything more to do with them. For it may be said, in general, that every man will love or hate solitude—in other Words, his own society—just in proportion as he is worth anything in himself. Kant has some remarks upon this kind of misanthropy in his Critique of the Faculty of Judgment.[7]

In a young man, it is a bad sign, as well from an intellectual as from a moral point of view, if he is precocious in understanding the ways of the world, and in adapting himself to its pursuits; if he at once knows how to deal with men, and enters upon life, as it were, fully prepared. It argues a vulgar nature. On the other hand, to be surprised and astonished at the way people act, and to be clumsy and cross-grained in having to do with them, indicates a character of the nobler sort.

The cheerfulness and vivacity of youth are partly due to the fact that, when we are ascending the hill of life, death is not visible: it lies down at the bottom of the other side. But once we have crossed the top of the hill, death comes in view—death—which, until then, was known to us only by hearsay. This makes our spirits droop, for at the same time we begin to feel that our vital powers are on the ebb. A grave seriousness now takes the place of that early extravagance of spirit; and the change is noticeable even in the expression of a man's face. As long as we are young, people may tell us what they please! we look upon life as endless and use our time recklessly; but the older we become, the more we practice economy. For towards the close of life, every day we live gives us the same kind of sensation as the criminal experiences at every step on his way to be tried.

From the standpoint of youth, life seems to stretch away into an endless future; from the standpoint of old age, to go back but a little way into the past; so that, at the beginning, life presents us with a picture in which the objects appear a great way off, as though we had reversed our telescope; while in the end everything seems so close. To see how short life is, a man must have grown old, that is to say, he must have lived long.

On the other hand, as the years increase, things look smaller, one and all; and Life, which had so firm and stable a base in the days of our youth, now seems nothing but a rapid flight of moments, every one of them illusory: we have come to see that the whole world is vanity!

Time itself seems to go at a much slower pace when we are young; so that not only is the first quarter of life the happiest, it is also the longest of all; it leaves more memories behind it. If a man were put to it, he could tell you more out of the first quarter of his life than out of two of the remaining periods. Nay, in the spring of life, as in the spring of the year, the days reach a length that is positively tiresome; but in the autumn, whether of the year or of life, though they are short, they are more genial and uniform.

But why is it that to an old man his past life appears so short? For this reason: his memory is short; and so he fancies that his life has been short too. He no longer remembers the insignificant parts of it, and much that was unpleasant is now forgotten; how little, then, there is left! For, in general, a man's memory is as imperfect as his intellect; and he must make a practice of reflecting upon the lessons he has learned and the events he has experienced, if he does not want them both to sink gradually into the gulf of oblivion. Now, we are unaccustomed to reflect upon matters of no importance, or, as a rule, upon things that we have found disagreeable, and yet that is necessary if the memory of them is to be preserved. But the class of things that may be called insignificant is continually receiving fresh additions: much that wears an air of importance at first, gradually becomes of no consequence at all from the fact of its frequent repetition; so that in the end we actually lose count of the number of times it happens. Hence we are better able to remember the events of our early than of our later years. The longer we live, the fewer are the things that we can call important or significant enough to deserve further consideration, and by this alone can they be fixed in the memory; in other words, they are forgotten as soon as they are past. Thus it is that time runs on, leaving always fewer traces of its passage.

Further, if disagreeable things have happened to us, we do not care to ruminate upon them, least of all when they touch our vanity, as is usually the case; for few misfortunes fall upon us for which we can be held entirely blameless. So people are very ready to forget many things that are disagreeable, as well as many that are unimportant.

It is from this double cause that our memory is so short; and a man's recollection of what has happened always becomes proportionately shorter, the more things that have occupied him in life. The things we did in years gone by, the events that happened long ago, are like those objects on the coast which, to the seafarer on his outward voyage, become smaller every minute, more unrecognizable and harder to distinguish.

Again, it sometimes happens that memory and imagination will call up some long past scene as vividly as if it had occurred only yesterday; so that the event in question seems to stand very near to the present time. The reason of this is that it is impossible to call up all the intervening period in the same vivid way, as there is no one figure pervading it which can be taken in at a glance; and besides, most of the things that happened in that period are forgotten, and all that remains of it is the general knowledge that we have lived through it—a mere notion of abstract existence, not a direct vision of some particular experience. It is this that causes some single event of long ago to appear as though it took place but yesterday: the intervening time vanishes, and the whole of life looks incredibly short. Nay, there are occasional moments in old age when we can scarcely believe that we are so advanced in years, or that the long past lying behind us has had any real existence—a feeling which is mainly due to the circumstance that the present always seems fixed and immovable as we look at it. These and similar mental phenomena are ultimately to be traced to the fact that it is not our nature in itself, but only the outward presentation of it, that lies in time, and that the present is the point of contact between the world as subject and the world as object.[8]

Again, why is it that in youth we can see no end to the years that seem to lie before us? Because we are obliged to find room for all the things we hope to attain in life. We cram the years so full of projects that if we were to try and carry them all out, death would come prematurely though we reached the age of Methuselah.

Another reason why life looks so long when we are young, is that we are apt to measure its length by the few years we have already lived. In those early years things are new to us, and so they appear important; we dwell upon them after they have happened and often call them to mind; and thus in youth life seems replete with incident, and therefore of long duration.

Sometimes we credit ourselves with a longing to be in some distant spot, whereas, in truth, we are only longing to have the time back again which we spent there—days when we were younger and fresher than we are now. In those moments Time mocks us by wearing the mask of space; and if we travel to the spot, we can see how much we have been deceived.

There are two ways of reaching a great age, both of which presuppose a sound constitution as a conditio sine qua non. They may be illustrated by two lamps, one of which burns a long time with very little oil, because it has a very thin wick; and the other just as long, though it has a very thick one, because there is plenty of oil to feed it. Here, the oil is the vital energy, and the difference in the wick is the manifold way in which the vital energy is used.

Up to our thirty-sixth year, we may be compared, in respect of the way in which we use our vital energy, to people who live on the interest of their money: what they spend to-day, they have again to-morrow. But from the age of thirty-six onwards, our position is like that of the investor who begins to entrench upon his capital. At first he hardly notices any difference at all, as the greater part of his expenses is covered by the interest of his securities; and if the deficit is but slight, he pays no attention to it. But the deficit goes on increasing, until he awakes to the fact that it is becoming more serious every day: his position becomes less and less secure, and he feels himself growing poorer and poorer, while he has no expectation of this drain upon his resources coming to an end. His fall from wealth to poverty becomes faster every moment—like the fall of a solid body in space, until at last he has absolutely nothing left. A man is truly in a woeful plight if both the terms of this comparison—his vital energy and his wealth—really begin to melt away at one and the same time. It is the dread of this calamity that makes love of possession increase with age.

On the other hand, at the beginning of life, in the years before we attain majority, and for some little time afterwards—the state of our vital energy puts us on a level with those who each year lay by a part of their interest and add it to their capital: in other words, not only does their interest come in regularly, but the capital is constantly receiving additions. This happy condition of affairs is sometimes brought about—with health as with money—under the watchful care of some honest guardian. O happy youth, and sad old age!

Nevertheless, a man should economize his strength even when he is young. Aristotle[9] observes that amongst those who were victors at Olympia only two or three gained a prize at two different periods, once in boyhood and then again when they came to be men; and the reason of this was that the premature efforts which the training involved, so completely exhausted their powers that they failed to last on into manhood. As this is true of muscular, so it is still more true of nervous energy, of which all intellectual achievements are the manifestation. Hence, those infant prodigies—ingenia praecoda—the fruit of a hot-house education, who surprise us by their cleverness as children, afterwards turn out very ordinary folk. Nay, the manner in which boys are forced into an early acquaintance with the ancient tongues may, perhaps, be to blame for the dullness and lack of judgment which distinguish so many learned persons.

I have said that almost every man's character seems to be specially suited to some one period of life, so that on reaching it the man is at his best. Some people are charming so long as they are young, and afterwards there is nothing attractive about them; others are vigorous and active in manhood, and then lose all the value they possess as they advance in years; many appear to best advantage in old age, when their character assumes a gentler tone, as becomes men who have seen the world and take life easily. This is often the case with the French.

This peculiarity must be due to the fact that the man's character has something in it akin to the qualities of youth or manhood or old age—something which accords with one or another of these periods of life, or perhaps acts as a corrective to its special failings.

The mariner observes the progress he makes only by the way in which objects on the coast fade away into the distance and apparently decrease in size. In the same way a man becomes conscious that he is advancing in years when he finds that people older than himself begin to seem young to him.

It has already been remarked that the older a man becomes, the fewer are the traces left in his mind by all that he sees, does or experiences, and the cause of this has been explained. There is thus a sense in which it may be said that it is only in youth that a man lives with a full degree of consciousness, and that he is only half alive when he is old. As the years advance, his consciousness of what goes on about him dwindles, and the things of life hurry by without making any impression upon him, just as none is made by a work of art seen for the thousandth time. A man does what his hand finds to do, and afterwards he does not know whether he has done it or not.

As life becomes more and more unconscious, the nearer it approaches the point at which all consciousness ceases, the course of time itself seems to increase in rapidity. In childhood all the things and circumstances of life are novel; and that is sufficient to awake us to the full consciousness of existence: hence, at that age, the day seems of such immense length. The same thing happens when we are traveling: one month seems longer then than four spent at home. Still, though time seems to last longer when we are young or on a journey, the sense of novelty does not prevent it from now and then in reality hanging heavily upon our hands under both these circumstances, at any rate more than is the case when we are old or staying at home. But the intellect gradually becomes so rubbed down and blunted by long habituation to such impressions that things have a constant tendency to produce less and less impression upon us as they pass by; and this makes time seem increasingly less important, and therefore shorter in duration: the hours of the boy are longer than the days of the old man. Accordingly, time goes faster and faster the longer we live, like a ball rolling down a hill. Or, to take another example: as in a revolving disc, the further a point lies from the centre, the more rapid is its rate of progression, so it is in the wheel of life; the further you stand from the beginning, the faster time moves for you. Hence it may be said that as far as concerns the immediate sensation that time makes upon our minds, the length of any given year is in direct proportion to the number of times it will divide our whole life: for instance, at the age of fifty the year appears to us only one-tenth as long as it did at the age of five.

This variation in the rate at which time appears to move, exercises a most decided influence upon the whole nature of our existence at every period of it. First of all, it causes childhood—even though it embrace only a span of fifteen years—to seem the longest period of life, and therefore the richest in reminiscences. Next, it brings it about that a man is apt to be bored just in proportion as he is young. Consider, for instance, that constant need of occupation—whether it is work or play—that is shown by children: if they come to an end of both work and play, a terrible feeling of boredom ensues. Even in youth people are by no means free from this tendency, and dread the hours when they have nothing to do. As manhood approaches, boredom disappears; and old men find the time too short when their days fly past them like arrows from a bow. Of course, I must be understood to speak of men, not of decrepit brutes. With this increased rapidity of time, boredom mostly passes away as we advance in life; and as the passions with all their attendant pain are then laid asleep, the burden of life is, on the whole, appreciably lighter in later years than in youth, provided, of course, that health remains. So it is that the period immediately preceding the weakness and troubles of old age, receives the name of a man's best years.

That may be a true appellation, in view of the comfortable feeling which those years bring; but for all that the years of youth, when our consciousness is lively and open to every sort of impression, have this privilege—that then the seeds are sown and the buds come forth; it is the springtime of the mind. Deep truths may be perceived, but can never be excogitated—that is to say, the first knowledge of them is immediate, called forth by some momentary impression. This knowledge is of such a kind as to be attainable only when the impressions are strong, lively and deep; and if we are to be acquainted with deep truths, everything depends upon a proper use of our early years. In later life, we may be better able to work upon other people,—upon the world, because our natures are then finished and rounded off, and no more a prey to fresh views; but then the world is less able to work upon us. These are the years of action and achievement; while youth is the time for forming fundamental conceptions, and laying down the ground-work of thought.

In youth it is the outward aspect of things that most engages us; while in age, thought or reflection is the predominating quality of the mind. Hence, youth is the time for poetry, and age is more inclined to philosophy. In practical affairs it is the same: a man shapes his resolutions in youth more by the impression that the out-ward world makes upon him; whereas, when he is old, it is thought that determines his actions. This is partly to be explained by the fact that it is only when a man is old that the results of outward observation are present in sufficient numbers to allow of their being classified according to the ideas they represent,—a process which in its turn causes those ideas to be more fully understood in all their bearings, and the ex-act value and amount of trust to be placed in them, fixed and determined; while at the same time he has grown accustomed to the impressions produced by the various phenomena of life, and their effects on him are no longer what they were. Contrarily, in youth, the impressions that things make, that is to say, the outward aspects of life, are so overpoweringly strong, especially in the case of people of lively and imagina-tive disposition, that they view the world like a picture; and their chief concern is the figure they cut in it, the appearance they present; nay, they are unaware of the extent to which this is the case. It is a quality of mind that shows itself—if in no other way—in that personal vanity, and that love of fine clothes, which distinguish young people.

There can be no doubt that the intellectual powers are most capable of enduring great and sustained efforts in youth, up to the age of thirty-five at latest; from which period their strength begins to decline, though very gradually. Still, the later years of life, and even old age itself, are not without their intellectual compensation. It is only then that a man can be said to be really rich in experience or in learning; he has then had time and opportunity enough to enable him to see and think over life from all its sides; he has been able to compare one thing with another, and to discover points of contact and connecting links, so that only then are the true relations of things rightly understood. Further, in old age there comes an increased depth in the knowledge that was acquired in youth; a man has now many more illustrations of any ideas he may have attained; things which he thought he knew when he was young, he now knows in reality. And besides, his range of knowledge is wider; and in whatever di-rection it extends, it is thorough, and therefore formed into a consistent and connect-ed whole; whereas in youth knowledge is always defective and fragmentary.

A complete and adequate notion of life can never be attained by any one who does not reach old age; for it is only the old man who sees life whole and knows its natural course; it is only he who is acquainted—and this is most important—not only with its entrance, like the rest of mankind, but with its exit too; so that he alone has a full sense of its utter vanity; whilst the others never cease to labor under the false notion that everything will come right in the end.

On the other hand, there is more conceptive power in youth, and at that time of life a man can make more out of the little that he knows. In age, judgment, penetration and thoroughness predominate. Youth is the time for amassing the material for a knowledge of the world that shall be distinctive and peculiar,—for an original view of life, in other words, the legacy that a man of genius leaves to his fellow-men; it is, however, only in later years that he becomes master of his material. Accordingly it will be found that, as a rule, a great writer gives his best work to the world when he is about fifty years of age. But though the tree of knowledge must reach its full height before it can bear fruit, the roots of it lie in youth.

Every generation, no matter how paltry its character, thinks itself much wiser than the one immediately preceding it, let alone those that are more remote. It is just the same with the different periods in a man's life; and yet often, in the one case no less than in the other, it is a mistaken opinion. In the years of physical growth, when our powers of mind and our stores of knowledge are receiving daily additions, it becomes a habit for to-day to look down with contempt upon yesterday. The habit strikes root, and remains even after the intellectual powers have begun to decline,— when to-day should rather look up with respect to yesterday. So it is that we often unduly depreciate the achievements as well as the judgments of our youth. This seems the place for making the general observation, that, although in its main qualities a man's intellect or head, as well as his character or heart, is innate, yet the former is by no means so unalterable in its nature as the latter. The fact is that the intellect is subject to very many transformations, which, as a rule, do not fail to make their actual appearance; and this is so, partly because the intellect has a deep foundation in the physique, and partly because the material with which it deals is given in experience. And so, from a physical point of view, we find that if a man has any peculiar power, it first gradually increases in strength until it reaches its acme, after which it enters upon a path of slow decadence, until it ends in imbecility. But, on the other hand, we must not lose sight of the fact that the material which gives employment to a man's powers and keeps them in activity,—the subject-matter of thought and knowledge, experience, intellectual attainments, the practice of seeing to the bottom of things, and so a perfect mental vision, form in themselves a mass which continues to increase in size, until the time comes when weakness shows itself, and the man's powers suddenly fail. The way in which these two distinguishable elements combine in the same nature,—the one absolutely unalterable, and the other subject to change in two directions opposed to each other—explains the variety of mental attitude and the dissimilarity of value which attach to a man at different periods of life.

The same truth may be more broadly expressed by saying that the first forty years of life furnish the text, while the remaining thirty supply the commentary; and that without the commentary we are unable to understand aright the true sense and coherence of the text, together with the moral it contains and all the subtle application of which it admits.

Towards the close of life, much the same thing happens as at the end of a bal masque—the masks are taken off. Then you can see who the people really are, with whom you have come into contact in your passage through the world. For by the end of life characters have come out in their true light, actions have borne fruit, achievements have been rightly appreciated, and all shams have fallen to pieces. For this, Time was in every case requisite.

But the most curious fact is that it is also only towards the close of life than a man really recognizes and understands his own true self,—the aims and objects he has followed in life, more especially the kind of relation in which he has stood to other people and to the world. It will often happen that as a result of this knowledge, a man

129

will have to assign himself a lower place than he formerly thought was his due. But there are exceptions to this rule; and it will occasionally be the case that he will take a higher position than he had before. This will be owing to the fact that he had no adequate notion of the baseness of the world, and that he set up a higher aim for himself than was followed by the rest of mankind.

The progress of life shows a man the stuff of which he is made.

It is customary to call youth the happy, and age the sad part of life. This would be true if it were the passions that made a man happy. Youth is swayed to and fro by them; and they give a great deal of pain and little pleasure. In age the passions cool and leave a man at rest, and then forthwith his mind takes a contemplative tone; the intellect is set free and attains the upper hand. And since, in itself, intellect is beyond the range of pain, and man feels happy just in so far as his intellect is the predominating part of him.

It need only be remembered that all pleasure is negative, and that pain is positive in its nature, in order to see that the passions can never be a source of happiness, and that age is not the less to be envied on the ground that many pleasures are denied it. For every sort of pleasure is never anything more than the quietive of some need or longing; and that pleasure should come to an end as soon as the need ceases, is no more a subject of complaint than that a man cannot go on eating after he has had his dinner, or fall asleep again after a good night's rest.

So far from youth being the happiest period of life, there is much more truth in the remark made by Plato, at the beginning of the Republic, that the prize should rather be given to old age, because then at last a man is freed from the animal passion which has hitherto never ceased to disquiet him. Nay, it may even be said that the countless and manifold humors which have their source in this passion, and the emotions that spring from it, produce a mild state of madness; and this lasts as long as the man is subject to the spell of the impulse—this evil spirit, as it were, of which there is no riddance—so that he never really becomes a reasonable being until the passion is extinguished.

There is no doubt that, in general, and apart from individual circumstances and particular dispositions, youth is marked by a certain melancholy and sadness, while genial sentiments attach to old age; and the reason for this is nothing but the fact that the young man is still under the service, nay, the forced labor, imposed by that evil spirit, which scarcely ever leaves him a moment to himself. To this source may be traced, directly or indirectly, almost all and every ill that befalls or menaces mankind. The old man is genial and cheerful because, after long lying in the bonds of passion, he can now move about in freedom.

Still, it should not be forgotten that, when this passion is extinguished, the true kernel of life is gone, and nothing remains but the hollow shell; or, from another point of view, life then becomes like a comedy, which, begun by real actors, is continued and brought to an end by automata dressed in their clothes.

However that may be, youth is the period of unrest, and age of repose; and from that very circumstance, the relative degree of pleasure belonging to each may be inferred. The child stretches out its little hands in the eager desire to seize all the pretty things that meet its sight, charmed by the world because all its senses are still so young and fresh. Much the same thing happens with the youth, and he displays greater energy in his quest. He, too, is charmed by all the pretty things and the many pleasing shapes that surround him; and forthwith his imagination conjures up pleasures which the world can never realize. So he is filled with an ardent desire for he knows not what delights—robbing him of all rest and making happiness impossible. But when old age is reached, all this is over and done with, partly because the blood runs cooler and the senses are no longer so easily allured; partly because experience has shown the true value of things and the futility of pleasure, whereby illusion has been gradually dispelled, and the strange fancies and prejudices which previously concealed or distorted a free and true view of the world, have been dissipated and put to flight; with the result that a man can now get a juster and clearer view, and see things as they are, and also in a measure attain more or less insight into the nullity of all things on this earth.

It is this that gives almost every old man, no matter how ordinary his faculties may be, a certain tincture of wisdom, which distinguishes him from the young. But the chief result of all this change is the peace of mind that ensues—a great element in happiness, and, in fact, the condition and essence of it. While the young man fancies that there is a vast amount of good things in the world, if he could only come at them, the old man is steeped in the truth of the Preacher's words, that all things are vanity—knowing that, however gilded the shell, the nut is hollow.

In these later years, and not before, a man comes to a true appreciation of Horace's maxim: Nil admirari. He is directly and sincerely convinced of the vanity of everything and that all the glories of the world are as nothing: his illusions are gone. He is no more beset with the idea that there is any particular amount of happiness anywhere, in the palace or in the cottage, any more than he himself enjoys when he is free from bodily or mental pain. The worldly distinctions of great and small, high and low, exist for him no longer; and in this blissful state of mind the old man may look down with a smile upon all false notions. He is completely undeceived, and knows that whatever may be done to adorn human life and deck it out in finery, its paltry character will soon show through the glitter of its surroundings; and that, paint and be jewel it as one may, it remains everywhere much the same,—an existence which has no true value except in freedom from pain, and is never to be estimated by the presence of pleasure, let alone, then, of display.[10]

Disillusion is the chief characteristic of old age; for by that time the fictions are gone which gave life its charm and spurred on the mind to activity; the splendors of the world have been proved null and vain; its pomp, grandeur and magnificence are faded. A man has then found out that behind most of the things he wants, and most of the pleasures he longs for, there is very little after all; and so he comes by degrees to see that our existence is all empty and void. It is only when he is seventy years old that he quite understands the first words of the Preacher; and this again explains why it is that old men are sometimes fretful and morose.

It is often said that the common lot of old age is disease and weariness of life. Disease is by no means essential to old age; especially where a really long span of years is to be attained; for as life goes on, the conditions of health and disorder tend to increase—crescente vita, crescit sanitas et morbus. And as far as weariness or boredom is concerned, I have stated above why old age is even less exposed to that form of evil than youth. Nor is boredom by any means to be taken as a necessary accompaniment of that solitude, which, for reasons that do not require to be explained, old age certainly cannot escape; it is rather the fate that awaits those who have never known any other pleasures but the gratification of the senses and the delights of society—who have left their minds unenlightened and their faculties unused. It is quite true that the intellectual faculties decline with the approach of old age; but where they were originally strong, there will always be enough left to combat the onslaught of boredom. And then again, as I have said, experience, knowledge, reflection, and skill in dealing with men, combine to give an old man an increasingly accurate insight into the ways of the world; his judgment becomes keen and he attains a coherent view of life: his mental vision embraces a wider range. Constantly finding new uses for his stores of knowledge and adding to them at every opportunity, he maintains uninterrupted that inward process of self-education, which gives employment and satisfaction to the mind, and thus forms the due reward of all its efforts.

All this serves in some measure as a compensation for decreased intellectual power. And besides, Time, as I have remarked, seems to go much more quickly when we are advanced in years; and this is in itself a preventive of boredom. There is no great harm in the fact that a man's bodily strength decreases in old age, unless, indeed, he requires it to make a living. To be poor when one is old, is a great misfortune. If a man is secure from that, and retains his health, old age may be a very passable time of life. Its chief necessity is to be comfortable and well off; and, in consequence, money is then prized more than ever, because it is a substitute for failing strength. Deserted by Venus, the old man likes to turn to Bacchus to make him merry. In the place of wanting to see things, to travel and learn, comes the desire to speak and teach. It is a piece of good fortune if the old man retains some of his love of study or of music or of the theatre,—if, in general, he is still somewhat susceptible to the things about him; as is, indeed, the case with some people to a very late age. At that time of life, what a man has in himself is of greater advantage to him that ever it was before.

There can be no doubt that most people who have never been anything but dull and stupid, become more and more of automata as they grow old. They have always thought, said and done the same things as their neighbors; and nothing that happens now can change their disposition, or make them act otherwise. To talk to old people of this kind is like writing on the sand; if you produce any impression at all, it is gone almost immediately; old age is here nothing but the caput mortuum of life—all that is essential to manhood is gone. There are cases in which nature supplies a third set of teeth in old age, thereby apparently demonstrating the fact that that period of life is a second childhood.

It is certainly a very melancholy thing that all a man's faculties tend to waste away as he grows old, and at a rate that increases in rapidity: but still, this is a necessary, nay, a beneficial arrangement, as otherwise death, for which it is a preparation, would be too hard to bear. So the greatest boon that follows the attainment of extreme old age is euthanasia,—an easy death, not ushered in by disease, and free from all pain and struggle.[11] For let a man live as long as he may, he is never conscious of any moment but the present, one and indivisible; and in those late years the mind loses more every day by sheer forgetfulness than ever it gains anew.

The main difference between youth and age will always be that youth looks forward to life, and old age to death; and that while the one has a short past and a long future before it, the case is just the opposite with the other. It is quite true that when a man is old, to die is the only thing that awaits him; while if he is young, he may expect to live; and the question arises which of the two fates is the more hazardous, and if life is not a matter which, on the whole, it is better to have behind one than before? Does not the Preacher say: the day of death [is better] than the day of one's birth.[12] It is certainly a rash thing to wish for long life;[13] for as the Spanish proverb has it, it means to see much evil,—Quien larga vida vive mucho mal vide.

In one of the Vedic Upanishads (Oupnekhat, II.) the natural length of human life is put down at one hundred years. And I believe this to be right. I have observed, as a matter of fact, that it is only people who exceed the age of ninety who attain euthanasia,—who die, that is to say, of no disease, apoplexy or convulsion, and pass away without agony of any sort; nay, who sometimes even show no pallor, but expire generally in a sitting attitude, and often after a meal,—or, I may say, simply cease to live rather than die. To come to one's end before the age of ninety, means to die of disease, in other words, prematurely.

Now the Old Testament (Psalms xc. 10) puts the limit of human life at seventy, and if it is very long, at eighty years; and what is more noticeable still, Herodotus (i. 32 and iii. 22) says the same thing. But this is wrong; and the error is due simply to a rough and superficial estimate of the results of daily experience. For if the natural length of life were from seventy to eighty years, people would die, about that time, of mere old age. Now this is certainly not the case. If they die then, they die, like younger people, of disease; and disease is something abnormal. Therefore it is not natural to die at that age. It is only when they are between ninety and a hundred that people die of old age; die, I mean, without suffering from any disease, or showing any special signs of their condition, such as a struggle, death-rattle, convulsion, pallor,—the absence of all which constitutes euthanasia. The natural length of human life is a hundred years; and in assigning that limit the Upanishads are right once more.]

A man's individual career is not, as Astrology wishes to make out, to be predicted from observation of the planets; but the course of human life in general, as far as the various periods of it are concerned, may be likened to the succession of the planets: so that we may be said to pass under the influence of each one of them in turn.

At ten, Mercury is in the ascendant; and at that age, a youth, like this planet, is characterized by extreme mobility within a narrow sphere, where trifles have a great effect upon him; but under the guidance of so crafty and eloquent a god, he easily makes great progress. Venus begins her sway during his twentieth year, and then a man is wholly given up to the love of women. At thirty, Mars comes to the front, and he is now all energy and strength,—daring, pugnacious and arrogant.

When a man reaches the age of forty, he is under the rule of the four Asteroids; that is to say, his life has gained something in extension. He is frugal; in other words, by the help of Ceres, he favors what is useful; he has his own hearth, by the influence of Vesta; Pallas has taught him that which is necessary for him to know; and his wife—his Juno—rules as the mistress of his house.

But at the age of fifty, Jupiter is the dominant influence. At that period a man has outlived most of his contemporaries, and he can feel himself superior to the generation about him. He is still in the full enjoyment of his strength, and rich in experience and knowledge; and if he has any power and position of his own, he is endowed with authority over all who stand in his immediate surroundings. He is no more inclined to receive orders from others; he wants to take command himself. The work most suitable to him now is to guide and rule within his own sphere. This is the point where Jupiter culminates, and where the man of fifty years is at his best.

Then comes Saturn, at about the age of sixty, a weight as of lead, dull and slow:—
But old folks, many feign as they were dead;
Unwieldy, slow, heavy and pale as lead.

Last of all, Uranus; or, as the saying is, a man goes to heaven.

I cannot find a place for Neptune, as this planet has been very thoughtlessly named; because I may not call it as it should be called—Eros. Otherwise I should point out how Beginning and End meet together, and how closely and intimately Eros is connected with Death: how Orcus, or Amenthes, as the Egyptians called him, is not only the receiver but the giver of all things—[Greek: lambanon kai didous]. Death is the great reservoir of Life. Everything comes from Orcus; everything that is alive now was once there. Could we but understand the great trick by which that is done, all would be clear!

Notes

1. *Translator's Note.—Schopenhauer refers to Die Welt als Wille und Vorstellung, Bk. II. c, 31, p. 451 (4th edit.), where he explains that this is due to the fact that at that period of life the brain and nervous system are much more developed than any other part of the organism.*

2. *Translator's Note.—This statement is not quite correct. The weight of the brain increases rapidly up to the seventh year, more slowly between the sixteenth and the twentieth year, still more slowly till between thirty and forty years of age, when it attains its maximum. At each decennial period after this, it is supposed to decrease in weight on the average, an ounce for every ten years.*

3. *Die Welt als Wille und Vorstellung, Bk. II. c. 31, p. 426-7 (4th Edit.), to which the reader is referred for a detailed explanation of my meaning.*

4. *Cf. loc. cit., p. 428.*

5. *Let me refer the reader, if he is interested in the subject, to the volume already cited, chapter 37.*

6. *Translator's Note.—Moritz was a miscellaneous writer of the last century (1757-93). His Anton Reiser, composed in the form of a novel, is practically an autobiography.*

7. *Kritik der Urtheilskraft, Part I, Sec.29, Note ad fin.*

8. *Translator's Note.—By this remark Schopenhauer means that will, which, as he argues, forms the inner reality underlying all the phenomena of life and nature, is not in itself affected by time; but that, on the other hand, time is necessary for the objectification of the will, for the will as presented in the passing phenomena of the world. Time is thus definable as the condition of change, and the present time as the only point of contact between reality and appearance.*

9. *Politics.*

10. *Cf. Horace, Epist. I. 12, I-4.*

11. *See Die Welt als Wille und Vorstellung, Bk. II. ch. 41, for a further description of this happy end to life.*

12. *Ecclesiastes vii. 1.*

13. *The life of man cannot, strictly speaking, be called either long or short, since it is the ultimate standard by which duration of time in regard to all other things is measured.*